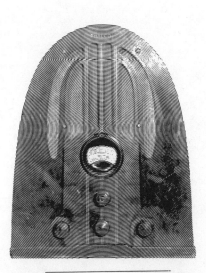

THE SMALL HOUSE
HALF-WAY UP IN
THE NEXT BLOCK

THE SMALL HOUSE HALF-WAY UP IN THE NEXT BLOCK

Paul Rhymer's <u>Vic and Sade</u>

Edited with an Introduction

by Mary Frances Rhymer

Foreword by Ray Bradbury

With drawings by Franklin McMahon and

photographs of the original radio cast

McGRAW-HILL BOOK COMPANY
New York • St. Louis • San Francisco • Düsseldorf
London • Mexico • Sydney • Toronto

Library of Congress Cataloging in
Publication Data

Rhymer, Paul. The small house half-way
up in the next block.

I. Vic and Sade. II. Title. PN1991.77.V5R5
791.44'7 72-5194 ISBN 0-07-073792-4

CONTENTS

Remembrance of Things Present
or
VIC AND SADE ARE STILL ALIVE AND WELL AND LIVING IN ORWELL-HUXLEY VISTA.
A Foreword
by Ray Bradbury

If this introduction were done out of mere Nostalgia, forget it. I would like to believe I am writing it for better reasons than that; solid and incontrovertible reasons having to do with human beings, a certain time and place, and that elusive thing called Creativity.

Paul Rhymer, like his mysterious Mr. Gumpox and his horse, passed through the alleys of our lives a long time ago. Because he worked in a field that was mostly garbage we figured that he, like Mr. Gumpox, must be a garbageman. Often, no one bothered to look in his wagon to see what it was he was gathering from the backyards of our time and living in that strange year 1932 and on up into the Forties.

In truth, Paul Rhymer was a junk collector, which is a far step up from garbage. He collected bits and pieces of mediocrity from all our commonplace occupations, all our inane conversations, all our bored afternoons and long evenings when all we could think of to do was trot down to the YMCA to watch the Fat Men Play Handball.

In my time and my town, Waukegan, Illinois, not so very far away from where Paul Rhymer was born, it was going down to the train station to watch the newer and yet newer trains roar through without stopping. Or that miraculous day when the dirigibles *Akron* or *Macon* actually flew over our lake, signifying a future we could hardly comprehend.

I was born in that little house half-way up in the next block. I am Rush Gook. My Mom and Dad were first relatives to Vic and Sade. I called my father Gov'. Which is neither here nor there, for I am writing this Introduction not because of saccharine sentiment but because of positive identification. Paul Rhymer got us dead-on in his sights but, good man that he was, didn't shoot us dead. Instead, he celebrated our incredible simplicities, our dull, long days that were made bearable through love. The things that my Mom and Dad and brother Skip threw away, he saved. String, old clocks fixed to the point of ruin, tire-swings out of trees. But, most of all, conversations more brilliant in their pointlessness, circling around nothing, than anything written since by Pinter or Beckett.

In all this, of course, Paul Rhymer and his ouija-board were helped out by his wondrous alter-ego Uncle Fletcher. We all had

an Uncle Fletcher or someone like him hidden away in the woodwork of our childhood, an aunt or grandpa, who spoke riddles and wisdom or sublime nonsense, sometimes all in one breath. And perhaps we love Uncle Fletcher above all the other live and kicking creatures in VIC AND SADE, because he glided through life, only half-hearing, half-seeing what went on around him. Amazing man, one felt he could have gone through the San Francisco earthquake and emerged with a tale of someone in East Cairo, Ill., aged 97, married a woman 101, adopted a son aged 75, later died. How can you resist a man like that? Each of us envied his half-deafness, his ability to shape Reality to *his* dream. We all felt that when death finally tapped Uncle Fletcher, mortality would be confounded and put off, too.

If I'm not careful, this Introduction will run three times longer than it should be. For suddenly, in writing it, my favorite moments come back as clear as bells ringing across a valley on a bright spring morn. I have known Bill Idelson, who enacted the role of Rush Gook, as a good warm friend for some ten years now. I never cease to love hearing him talk, for while our ages are close, his voice is still the bright young voice of Rush.

One night not so long ago, Rush, or Bill as I call him, said that one of his favorite old VIC AND SADE shows was one where Rush and Vic sang some crazy song about flowers. I stunned Bill by immediately reciting: "Would that these pale hands chrysanthemums might gather,/Would that o'er green fields these tender feet might glide." Which are, of course, the first lines from that sappy song sung more than thirty years ago by father and son on the radio show.

Now, before you accuse me of falling into the very sentiment and nostalgia I warned myself against at the start of this essay, let me make some strong points.

Middle-class America, as it existed in the 1930's was dramatized lovingly and forever by Paul Rhymer.

The reason for this book is twofold, as must be the reason for this Introduction. To say that middle-class America once *was*. But to say, just as strongly, middle-class America, with all its *virtues,* still *is.*

We have gone through a rough time of wars and depressions and technologies, but the world of Vic and Sade has *not* vanished from the world. It has changed somewhat, yes, because of the impact of television, films, radio, the computer and the jet-stream plane. But a helluva lot of America still lives in small towns, and even those who have moved into the city have brought with them, genetically or otherwise, the temperament of Vic and Sade.

The little people are still little and still making-do day by day in small ways anywhere and everywhere. You might not see them taking that fast four-hour-jet from L.A. to New York, but drive across the country, stop at any crossroads, idle through any town

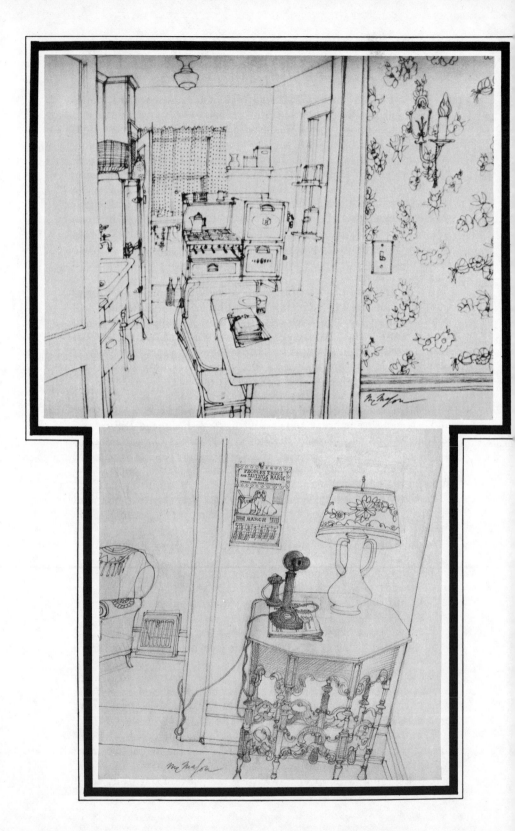

on a hot summer day, and there they are, in the breezeways, listening to baseball games, that lazy man's sport that takes forever to wind up and pitch, swatting away the flies, talking to the dogs, drinking the venerable Nehis or Orange Crushes, calling to one another across the eternal noons. Mr. Gumpox may be driving a truck these days, instead of philosophizing with his horse, but here he comes. The Thimble Club is still meeting. The Fat Men are still down at the Y swatting those handballs for the benefit of eight-year-old boys. The dime store is still a magical place for ten-year-olds to wander with free time. Alleys are still great places to find all the stuff that dumb older people are stupid enough to throw away; my own children teach me this.

In fact, of course, you don't have to go to small towns to rediscover Vic and Sade's world. It's all over Los Angeles or San Francisco or even dire and dread New York.

You want me to prove it? Easy as pie.

Think of the last weekend you spent with your family and the one before that and the one before that.

Let me describe my own, here in Los Angeles in the late spring of 1972. Big city stuff? Not on your nutmeg-scraper:

Sunday morning. Everyone slept late. Got up. Went out and brought in the Sunday papers. Read the comics first.

Just as we did in 1924 and 1929 and 1934 and 1940!

Laid around the house; just as we did in 1926 and 1933 and 1941.

Some of the kids went bicycling. Just as we did in 1922 and 1938 and 1947.

Talked to the neighbors over the backfence, just as we did in 1930 and . . .

Went to the beach for a swim, just as we used to do in 1934 . . .

Came home and read some more of the big Sunday paper. Remember 1936?

Fried some hamburgers and hot dogs, 1923.

Ate them. 1924.

Took a nap. 1925.

Went to a movie. 1926.

Came home and listened to radio. 1927. Played some records. 1928. Went over to actually sit in neighbors' living room to talk and have one, just one, beer. 1929.

I think I have ground the point into the dust.

Everything has changed but nothing has changed.

Our lives are full of Big Things. But more full of small ones. Our lives peak only on occasion. The rest of the time we are buttoning and unbuttoning and buttoning again, as my artist friend Streeter Blair once said.

It is all the little things, the so-called junky things, that Paul Rhymer has an eye and an ear for. He traps them, keeps them like

ants in a jar, and lets them out in the light later, glorified by his ability to pick just the right ants from the universal picnic. God A'Mercy, we all cry, never saw such ants before. But we have. We did see them. We were there. The picnic was ours. And it still is.

All of which adds up to this. There is no cause for nostalgia save the good and life-enhancing nostalgia for the present. That can only be good. Glancing through this book, we can take a long and loving glance not at our Past, to hell with that, but at what goes on this very splendid moment at the heart of our families Here and Now. Paul Rhymer says, in the aggregate, finally, we are Good. Not always right, no, not always happy, no, but essentially Good. Which is a nice new-fashioned message to receive in a time when we have begun to doubt our senses, sanity and any possible sane future.

Well, I've been loitering out here in the alley behind the Small House. I must finish and go to eat in that kitchen where peanut butter and plain bread and fresh cold milk are the food of the gods.

Let me make my point a final time:

Vic and Sade and Rush and Uncle Fletcher are not dead, nor gone, nor buried.

They are here. They are us.

We celebrate ourselves, as Walt Whitman *almost* said.

Thus the title of this essay: Proust had the gift of recall for the Past. Paul Rhymer's talent was: Remembrance of Things Present.

We travel way around the world, most of us, simply to find and see Green Peach, Wisconsin, clear. We travel in Time to imitate the words of the old Al Jolsen song, arrive Back In Your Own Backyard.

We can imagine that Rush Gook, grown up, did not necessarily stay on in that small town and join the kitchenware company like his Gov'. We can see him commute to the Big City. But now, late in time, an interesting thing is happening. We have noted, in a forty-year period, the pell-mell rush to Metropolis. Now we shall watch as the tide rolls back the other way. Rush Gook, finally, will retreat from jam-packed apartment high-rise Manhattan and water his roots again in Orchard Grove. He will have two children. Their names: Vic and Sade. They will grow up in that small town way out beyond the city, to which, of course, they will occasionally make visit in 1999.

But on Sunday mornings they will sleep late. They will get sick on sour cherries picked too soon and too low from the ripening tree. They will jump hopscotch. Baseball radio will laze the peach-fuzz in their corporate ears. And once a month or twice a week they may just actually walk-instead-of-ride down to the Butler House Hotel and sit in the view bay window and give grandiose, pontifical orders for simple foods.

And the world will not End after all.

So say I.

So say the inhabitants of that Small House Half-Way Up in the Next Block.

Believe us.

Turn the page.

Live in the Present.

RAY BRADBURY
Six blocks away from Palms, California.

May 20th, 1972

Introduction
by Mary Frances Rhymer

One wonders how many people today would respond to a few bars of "Chanson bohémienne" and the announcer's voice, "Well, sir, as we enter the small house half-way up in the next block, Sade looks up from her ironing as the back door opens. Let's listen." Probably many would experience a touch of remembrance because at one time millions of Americans were among the eaves-droppers on the family of three, Vic, Sade, and their young son Rush. Sade's Uncle Fletcher, in time, would move to the small Midwest town and would be a frequent caller at the house. The consummate skills of actress Bernadine Flynn as Sade, actors Arthur VanHarvey and Billy Idelson as Vic and Rush, and Clarence Hartzell as Uncle Fletcher created for the listener the illusion that he had entered the small house with the announcer. The actors read without theatrical overtones. The author, cast, and the directors had produced from practice a perfect naturalness. Fan mail, through the years, repeatedly stated, "Vic and Sade must be a real family." (Only in a real family would the wife keep her hat downstairs in one of the two cupboards of the sideboard or store old family photographs in the window seat.)

Paul Rhymer was the creator and author of the comedy series VIC AND SADE. William Ramsey, for thirty years in charge of radio programs for the Procter and Gamble Company, wrote that the ratings of the writer Paul Rhymer, and of Sandra Michael, author of the notable series AGAINST THE STORM, illustrated his contention that radio listeners instinctively and invariably chose the better programs. (Daytime radio, in the heyday of the soap opera, offered a wide range of woe ... blackmail, marital infidelity, amnesia, illegitimate babies and so on, Mr. Ramsey wrote. These were often plotted by one writer, or a team of writers, and farmed out for dialogue to still other writers. Such daytime serials, often termed "cliff-hangers," were tasteless and objectionable: parents' groups and women's clubs wrote letters of complaint to the companies which sponsored these shows.) Mr. Ramsey went on to cite Paul Rhymer, with few others, as one who had never turned in a line which he had not personally written. May I add here a credit for Mr. Ramsey's side of the ledger: the VIC AND SADE client, in the person of Mr. Ramsey for Procter and Gamble, never attempted to steer Paul nor to pressure him to change a line. The author had established his reliability: he was left alone. And the daily VIC AND SADE, sponsored by Procter and Gamble's Crisco, rode the crest of the popularity polls.

Thus, it was in the setting of morbid daytime serials that the simple, light, sometimes zany and sometimes poignant VIC AND

SADE was applauded. Each episode was complete. Each day, five days a week, Paul would roll a blank sheet of paper into his type-writer. Each show would have a beginning, a middle, and an ending. To meet a deadline each weekday with a small and complete playlet was a burdensome assignment which was approached in the most business-like fashion. Paul went directly to his typewriter early in the morning, if the idea had come along. If not, our son and I would keep out of sight and out of hearing. No questions, no nonsense, and no telephoning except behind closed doors. Only when our author had shut himself in his workroom and the typing had started was the tension off. Another day in the life of the Rhymers had gone into gear.

Several hours later that workroom door would burst open and Paul would sprint to the other end of the apartment to shave, shower, and race to the Merchandise Mart. There he would turn in the script he had just written, to be retyped and mimeographed (hectographed, probably), and dash to the studio for the rehearsal and broadcast of that day's show. And, unless the client were in town, that was the end of Paul's business day. He would then be off, with friends or family, to the races, to the farm, or to pick Parke up at nursery school for an outing. Any kind of action that involved driving his car was relaxing for him, and he had it well established with friends and family that to "talk shop" was poor manners. He was going to forget his daily deadline for VIC AND SADE until he faced it next morning.

Often people would ask Paul, in kindness, how he was able to turn out a daily show by himself. He always found the query irritating and answered that he was a writer and so it was his business to write. They probably had their own business which they tended every day? Only once did he seem to admit that all those years of writing against a deadline had been exhausting. It was when he said to me, "Do you know that I have written more words than Dickens?" (The VIC AND SADE shows total more than 3500 scripts.)

By 1938 Paul and his show were winning critics' polls and earning citations in the field of daytime radio. Indeed, newspapers and radio publications were carrying glowing notices. Paul was so genuinely pleased when The Young Men's Club of Bloomington held a Rhymer Day Rally for native son Paul and filled the Consistory Hall for an evening banquet. There was a substantial column and a half in *Time* with a picture of Paul sitting among his trophies. *Time* described the show as one in which nothing much ever happened although it had 7,000,000 listeners and was drawing thousands of fan letters a week. The interviewer quoted Paul as being unable to account for the success of the show, giving credit to the actors of whom he said. "They could read from the telephone directory and sound entertaining."

Many years later, after the demise of the VIC AND SADE show, John O'Hara wrote that he would like to see "those wonderfully indigenous radio characters, VIC AND SADE and their family and friends, revived in a musical play." He likened the characterizations to Tarkington's *Penrod* stories and Sherwood Anderson's *Winesburg, Ohio.* "And don't think there wouldn't be a message in it. The message is 'That's how it was.' " That pleased Paul . . . the assessment, "That's how it was." It annoyed him for his characters to be considered "quaint." And though he was honored by Hendrik Willem Van Loon's opinion of VIC AND SADE material as "great folk writing," he dismissed the term "folk" as meaningless when applied to writing, art, or music. He, and I, as Midwesterners, suspected that the term "folk" was a patronizing way of saying "that's how it was." Whether the story, art, or music presented was genuine would be Paul's criterion of its quality. He had an unerring eye for falseness whether in a person or in a theatrical piece.

This is borne out by one of his closest friends, Frank Walsh, who remembers that, "He had a clarity of vision, an objectivity, about people and things around him that was extraordinary. A look at his enthusiasms in literature and reading in general underlines this quality of his mind. I recall his life-long love affair with Dickens: while I wandered in the symbol-laden jungles of Joyce, Faulkner and Camus, he went surely to the realists. He insisted that the artist tell him directly what he had to say, tell him no riddles. His list of favorites would carry these names: Ring Lardner ('Shut up, he explained.'.); James Gould Cozzens (Paul, worshipful, wrote fan letters.); John O'Hara (He counted *Appointment in Samarra* one of the greatest long before the critics nominated it as a classic.); Edith Wharton, Ruth Suckow (He wore out a couple of copies of *The Folks* and turned me on to it); Anne Parrish (He could quote jewels from her endlessly.); Charles Jackson (He thought *Lost Weekend* one of the finest of modern novels.); Tarkington, of course (He could take you by the hand through scene after scene of *Seventeen* and *Alice Adams.*). And so on: Fitzgerald and Hemingway were not for him. We did agree at the summit on Tolstoy and Mann. He was a good literary playmate."

Most friends found it difficult to describe Paul's personality. Frank Walsh again: "So discreet, so all-protective was his sense of privacy that even intimates, as I, could not know him entire. He liked to keep his personal and professional lives on clearly separated bases." And he did, indeed. He was a shy man, so shy that he seemed diffident even in accepting compliments which came to him from listeners—although he took the greatest pleasure in hearing and reading good reviews of VIC AND SADE. Often we would accompany the cast to a personal appearance, or perhaps to the opening of an exposition in Chicago, for which Paul sometimes wrote a few pages of special script. At the close the author would invariably be asked to say a few words. Paul, a handsome, tallish, impeccably tailored man, would only stand in place and flash his smile. And he'd be breathing a little heavily as he sat down. In the presence of strangers he could muster no small talk, though with intimates he was an outrageous clown competing for center stage and invariably holding it.

We had first met at Illinois Wesleyan University at Bloomington; however, on the death of his father, Paul left school to go to work. It was through great good fortune (with the depression in the offing in 1929) and through the influence of a former Wesleyanite, that Paul was taken into the Continuity Department of the National Broadcasting Company. To this group of young writers in their individual glass cubicles came the routine staff assignments for copy for the broadcasts. Practically every word one heard on radio was written. Even the staff orchestra, Harry Kogan's Musical Ramblers, required copy. The writers would type out such lines for the announcer as, "And now the voices of the violins remind us 'It Was Only a Paper Moon.'" Thornton McClaughry, a fraternity brother who occupied an adjoining cubicle in the department, chuckled recently when we talked about these ridiculous circumlocutions and the running competition of the writers, at work or at parties, to top each other at this kind of nonsense. Paul would have done well in this area for he mischievously enjoyed putting incongruous words in another's mouth. He relished, for many years, the protest of a dignified actor, a retiree from the Shakespearean boards, who shook his script above his head, in mid-rehearsal, "I will *not* read this line."

Dramatic programs came as a special assignment, and one of more importance, from the network's Program Manager. During Paul's first six months he wrote a weekly series of shows set in a small-town newspaper office. NBC secretaries and page boys were drafted for the parts; script radio (as it was called) was being pioneered in Chicago, and Paul was experimenting in this coming use of the medium. Another early show he wrote was a children's Saturday morning series featuring Smokey Rogers, an actor/fireman who visited school during the week, in his clown make-up, to demonstrate to children the basics of fire prevention in the home.

The broadcasting company was rapidly going into the business of selling radio time and it was the hope of every young man in that little group of writers to create a show which would attract a sponsor. And just this happened to Paul Rhymer in 1932. The assignment for Paul, from Clarence Menser, was to prepare a family show which was to audition for the Proctor and Gamble Company which was then buying large segments of daytime radio in order to sell its home products to women. Another type of program, a comic team, I think, won that audition, but Paul's family show started on the air as a sustaining (unsponsored) feature and picked up two sponsors for short terms in the next twenty-eight months. The popularity ratings by this time, 1934, were so impressive that Procter and Gamble did buy the show after all and continued to sponsor it until the end of 1945. By this time, what with a rising scale of salary increases for cast and author, the VIC AND SADE show was a very expensive property. *And,* by this time, World War II over, that threat "television," so many years "just around the corner," had the focus of the communications industry.

On the occasion of the first sponsorship of VIC AND SADE, Paul left the staff of NBC, though its Artist's Bureau was prepared to act as his agent for standard agent's fees. Paul then became a free-lance writer, and was to remain so for the rest of his career. With this change in status he lost his office cubicle, and so a typewriter, typing table, and chair were rented and set up in our one-room apartment. Soon we could afford to move to one with a bedroom which Paul used as his workroom. (Monthly bills for the rental of the typewriter, table, and chair arrived for years. It never occurred to us, but it finally did to the typewriter service, that we had paid many times over for these properties. And the bills stopped coming.) Paul's typewriter, this typewriter, was revered in our house, and one never used it without asking permission. We lived by, and with, the sound of this old Royal, the sound of an ack-ack gun when struck with Paul's emphatic touch. When I last moved, following Paul's death in 1964, Parke inquired for his father's typewriter. When I told him it would go with me, along with the table, chair, and carbons of scripts, he said, "Good . . . never part with it."

There had been these carbons of scripts piling up in the workroom through the years although there was no conscious effort to keep a complete file. These went onto high closet shelves, into cardboard cartons stacked in the corners and into an abandoned storage trunk I had found in the basement and spilled over, eventually into another storage trunk I had bought for the purpose. Paper is heavy and slippery, especially when stapled into scripts of ten or twelve pages. Paul began forthrightly bundling thirty or forty of these scripts together with one of his old neckties into the manageable amounts for dropping onto the shelves and into the trunks. (The sheer bulk and weight of these scripts, only a fraction of the total written for VIC AND SADE, continued to present problems. When I was ready to ship the material in 1969 to the Mass Communications History Center at the State Historical Society of Wisconsin, I learned that the trunks would have to be rebuilt in our basement in order to carry the weight in transit. I was relieved when a sympathetic staff member of the Center volunteered to drive down from Madison to pick up the material. She and I placed these tie-tied bundles into small cartons which we could carry to the back of the station wagon.

The Small House Half-way Up in the Next Block

I do not remember Janice O'Connell's reaction to the bizarre wrappings, for I was busy with my own emotions as I recognized, and remembered, all those ties.)

It puzzles me that I was not the first to think of publishing some of these scripts, for I had been reading them with delight for years. It was an editor who suggested that they would make an entertaining book. The beloved voices of Vic, Sade, Rush, and Fletcher are not here, of course, but there is an amusing dimension in their absence . . . the stage directions. And when reading, rather than listening, it is possible for one to hesitate to consider a phrase, or to laugh, without missing the next line. To read allows one to observe the writer's machinations and devices as he stirs up his one medium, *sound,* and mixes it with his three characters. We can watch the writer, clinically, as he peoples the world of VIC AND SADE. By letter, by telephone, by a glimpse out of the window, by conversation at the table or in bed at night, the reader becomes acquainted with their friends and relatives, Sade's Thimble ladies, Rush's school friends, Vic's lodge brothers, the landlord, and the garbageman.

Paul was often asked by younger men how to go about breaking into the field of radio writing. He would answer, though not so bluntly, that if a writer had something to say and he said it with any merit, it would find a market. Quality would be recognized. But first, the writer had best begin by getting something on paper. He and bookish friends were always excited at the emergence of a new author as they waited for someone to write "the great American novel." The earlier listing here of Paul's literary favorites testifies to his preoccupation with the authors who pictured the American scene. This is logical when one remembers that Paul's milieu was the small house in the small town in mid-America.

The little scene which follows I found in Paul's files. Quite obviously it was not written for actors to play since it carries no indication of which character is to speak the line (nor could a *listening* audience have any way of knowing that the boy was wriggling his toes). For whatever purpose it was written, it seems to set the scene for the sudden and enforced presence of an eleven-year-old in the household of VIC AND SADE. I believe the author was experimenting with the addition of a child to his earliest scripts for a husband and a wife. At any rate, to my knowledge, Paul never resolved on the air nor referred again to the heritage of Rush, for the introduction of the boy in the casting of William Idelson, a sensitive child-actor of matchless ability, had been altogether successful.

I must admit that I am most affected each time I read this piece. It recalls so sharply the gentle and compassionate writer who cloaked his affection for his own family with just such banter and wild sorties of the imagination. For me, this vignette remains a memorable exercise of Paul's skill in blending human loving relationships with the craftsmanship of his writing.

VIC AND SADE listeners will hear a pre-echo of the homely scenes they liked through the years. Newcomers will enjoy joining us in the small house half-way up in the next block.

The Family

Two gentlemen lie in bed sleeping. The lengthier of the two sleeps with his mouth slightly agape, his respiration, more musical than otherwise, buoying his abdomen gently up and down like a ship at sea. The briefer gentleman is all but invisible. Only his hairline is to be seen. The rest of him is a compact lump under the coverlet. The six-thirty sun streams in the window, and a six-thirty breeze, fresh and fragrant, flutters the curtain. Up and down quiet Virginia avenue outside, rows of houses hold rows of sleepers. It's only six-thirty o'clock in the morning and sleepers sleep.

The smaller sleeper—he of the hairline—is awake. From under the coverlet a forehead appears, a pair of eyebrows, a nose—like Neptune emerging from the deep, a good generous mouth, and finally a chin. And there, assembled and of sleepy aspect, are the features of RUSH MEADOWS, eleven years old. Sleep still possesses those features. Their owner wrinkles his forehead, telescopes his nose, opens his mouth, winks his eyes, and is altogether unbeautiful. A hand comes from somewhere and arrives at a touseled head. Fingers scratch and peace abides. The mouth opens, widens, and collapses; a yawn, robust rather than delicate, blows away the last imp of sleep. RUSH MEADOWS is awake and ready for the business of the day. Which begins at once and in this wise: a small object with toes on it creeps out at the foot of the bed. The toes wriggle pleasantly and their owner is somewhat surprised. He tries them individually. Queer. They won't work that way. Strange business. You'd think . . .

Softly: "Rush."

"Oh, good morning."

"Are you awake?"

"Yes'm."

"Don't talk too loud. Mr. Gook don't have to get up till seven. How does it happen you're in this bed?"

"I got lonesome."

"Don't you like your own little bed?"

"Yes'm. I like it fine. Only . . . I got lonesome."

"You sleep with somebody at home? Is that it?"

"Yes'm. My brother."

"Yes. Is that a vaccination on your arm?"

"Yes'm. I got another one on my other arm. Big one. See?"

The woman bends over the bed to see. She is a pretty woman with nice eyes and a sweet face. She is sinking into her thirties, somewhat bewildered that youth is gone.

"You got hair something like my mother's."

"Have I?"

"Yes. Yours is prettier."

"No." The woman's smile is radiantly attractive.

"Yes it is. But my mother's got prettier eyes."

"I know she has. Mary always had beautiful eyes. Did you sleep well?"

"Fine. *He* snores."

The woman laughs and the boy grins. They both survey the other sleeper.

"Does he?"

"Yes."

"I hope you're going to like it here, Rush."

"Uh-huh. I like it."

"That's good. We want you to have a perfectly splendid time."

Rush looks out the bright window. His eye travels from the fluttering curtain to the ceiling, from the ceiling to the foot pendulous at the side of the bed, from the wriggling toes to the face above him.

"I gotta go home tomorrow."

There is silence for a moment. Then the woman: "Tomorrow?"

"Yes. I better go home tomorrow."

"But . . . but you've come to stay with us a long time."

"I better go home tomorrow."

"But . . . " Now the woman's eyes too are fixed upon the wriggling toes. They wriggle faster. Covertly the boy regards the sweet face above him. He senses that he is handling a delicate matter crudely. But if you're *homesick* . . . If you've never been away from your mother and your sisters and your brothers in your whole life . . . If . . . But now this kind lady is looking into his eyes again.

"I can't wriggle 'em one at a time."

"Can't you?"

"No. I wriggle the big one an' the rest of 'em just kinda *come along*."

The woman laughs briefly. "Rush, you've just got here. Your mother don't expect you back home for a long time."

Something remotely rebellious comes into the boy's eyes. He studies his toes stubbornly.

"I better go home tomorrow."

The woman sighs. She didn't expect much more really. Long ago she felt that children were to be denied her. Even other peoples'.

"Want me to get up now, Mrs. Gook?"

"You can stay in bed till Victor wakes up if you want. What would you like for breakfast?"

"I don't care."

"Pancakes?"

"Sure."

"I'll go fix them. You can call me when Victor wakes up."

"Yes'm."

The woman tiptoes from the room. The boy watches her silently. He knows she feels badly about his going home. She's real nice, too. Too bad, too, but if you're homesick you . . . *Funny* about those toes. You'd think . . .

"Good morning, Colonel."

"Good morning, Mr. Gook."

The man turns over ponderously to face his bedmate. He is a doubtful thirty-five, large and amiable of feature.

"How in Thunder does it come you're in my bed?"

The boy laughs brightly: "I got lonesome."

"Dontcha know I mighta eaten you up in my sleep?"

"Aw."

"The *last* fella that slept with me disappeared."

"Did you eat him?"

"I ain't sayin'. How'd you sleep?"

"Fine."

"That's good. You want to get plenty of sleep because you're going to need a lot of pep. You an' I are goin' fishin' tomorrow."

"Fishing!"

"Sure. I know where you can catch bass fast as you can throw in your line."

The boy's face falls. "I can't go fishing tomorrow, Mr. Gook."

"Why not?"

"I'm going home."

"Tomorrow?"

"Yes."

"Say, that's too bad. Sade and I'd like to have you stay with us a while."

"I better go home."

"Uh-huh. Well, suit yourself. Like to have you go fishin' though."

"I better go home."

The man watches the boy's face closely. The boy knows that he's being watched, and knows too the reason why. Uncomfortably he directs his gaze again to his toes. The man also turns his attention to the waving digits.

"You can wriggle your toes pretty slick."

"I can't wriggle 'em one at a time, though."

"No?"

"No."

"The King of China once gave me a pearl-handled umbrella for wrigglin' my toes."

The boy laughs in disbelief.

"That's a fact. Gave me a gold watch too."

"Aw."

"No foolin'. There it is on the table over there. See it?"

"Yes. Did he give you that for wrigglin' your toes?"

"He gave me that for bravery."

The boy leans on his elbow to contemplate the watch, which ticks soberly on the table. He studies the man's face: "What did you do to get the watch?"

"Oh"—the man pulls the coverlet under his chin, and replies with becoming modesty—"not much."

"What?"

"Oh—shot a man-eating tiger an' lassooed a half-witted prairie chicken."

Impressed: "Huh!"

"It wasn't much."

"Gosh. *I* wouldn't want to be around any man-eating tiger."

"The half-witted prairie chicken was worse. I been lots braver'n *that*."

"You have?" The boys eyes are round now and alive with interest. *This* is no ordinary bed-mate.

"Yeah, lots braver. See them pants hangin' over the chair?"

The boy surveys the pants. They hang despondently over the chair. Not very remarkable pants, either. They are an indefinite blue in the morning light, somewhat frayed at the pockets, a bit shiny in the seat.

"Those are marvelous pants." The man makes this disclosure solemnly, and with a respectful genuflection to the pants. "I wouldn't part with them pants for any money. And so—if it's all the same to you—please don't make me any offers."

"No, I won't," the boy promises, awed by the grandeur of the pants.

"Thanks. The Emperor of Greece gave me them pants for bravery an' I wouldn't want anything to happen to 'em."

"Did you kill a man-eating tiger in Greece?"

The man ponders a bit. His valorous deeds parade through his mind.

"No," he replies finally, "I had to be a lot braver than just killing a few animals to get *them* pants."

"What did you do?"

The man lifts himself to his elbow, looks about the room cautiously, and turns to his small bedmate. Then in low tones: "Can you keep a secret?"

"Yes, sir."

"You can be trusted with the secret of the pants?"

"Yes, sir."

"Well, you have an honest face. Rush, my boy, fifteen years ago the eleventh of last August I happened to be in Greece . . ."

Enrapt: "Yes, sir."

"And I got homesick. I'd been in Greece two days and I was so homesick I couldn't stand it another minute. Wanted to come home to my own bed. Well, the Emperor of Greece just laughed at me and said he heard I was a brave man but it sure didn't look like it. And I told him to bring on all the lions and tigers there was in Greece and I'd whip 'em single-handed, but I just wasn't brave enough to stick around there when I was homesick."

"Gee."

"Well, the Emperor said if I'd be brave enough to stick around for just three weeks, he'd give me the sacred pants."

"Are *them* the sacred pants?"

"Yep."

"Did you stay?"

"Sure I stayed. But it was the bravest thing I ever done. I guess there ain't one man in a million brave enough to stick around some place when they're homesick."

Noncommital: "No."

"No, *sir.*"

The boy gravely considers this wondrous tale. The man gazes at the ceiling. After a time he thrusts out a bare arm and picks up the watch from the table.

"How do you *like* this watch?"

"It's a dandy."

"Here. Take it and look 'er over."

"Thank you."

"Does it tick?"

"Yeah."

"I wish I could find some brave fella to give that watch to. The King of China told me to pass it along to the first real brave fella I come across."

"Gee."

"Are you pretty brave?"

"Sure."

"Yeah, you *look* brave. Too bad there ain't any tigers or prairie-chickens around so we could see."

"Yes. *I'd* shoot a tiger to get this watch."

"We—el, it really don't *take* much bravery to kill a tiger."

The boy luxuriates in the heavy valuable feel of the watch. Its steady heart beats close to his ear. "Gee, this is a swell watch."

"Yep. The King of China always gives good watches. Doggone, I wish I could find some brave fella that was *homesick.*"

"I'm . . . *I'm* kinda homesick."

The man is astonished. "You are?"

"Yeah. I'm homesick."

"You're just sayin' that."

"No. I'm homesick."

"That why you're going home tomorrow?"

Slowly: "Yes."

"I see. Not very brave, huh?"

"I am too brave."

"Uh—huh. Well, you're just a lad. Only about . . . how old *are* you?"

" 'leven."

"Eleven, huh. Well, you can't be expected to be very brave . . . just eleven years old. You wouldn't be brave enough to stay here three weeks."

"Yes, I . . . " The boy halts, his mind crowded with pictures of home: the faces of his mother, sisters, brothers; his own familiar bedroom; the things he's known all his life. He holds the precious watch close to his ear, and again finds comfort in his toes.

The man is talking almost to himself: "I guess I could advertise in the paper. It's awful hard to find a real brave fella these days. Give me my watch, Rush."

"I'll . . . I'll stay three weeks." A lump in the throat holds back the words.

"Promise?"

"*I* promise."

"No crying, remember."

"I won't cry." But he *is* crying. Audibly, too. But the man doesn't hear.

"What do you call my wife, Rush?" He still doesn't know the boy is sobbing.

"I call her 'Mrs. Gook.' "

"It'd be shorter to call her 'mom.' "

"Mom?"

"Yes. Mom."

"All right."

"Can you holler?"

"Yes."

"Loud?"

"Yes."

"I'd give the chain on that watch to the fella that could holler clear down to the kitchen."

"I can do it."

"Can you holler, 'Mom, I'm gonna stay three weeks.' "

"Sure."

"Let's hear you."

And the boy shouts the words, and the woman who hears them is glad, because she knows that three weeks means forever.

THE SMALL HOUSE
HALF-WAY UP IN
THE NEXT BLOCK

Left to right: VIC, UNCLE FLETCHER, played by Clarence L. Hartzell, SADE, RUSH.

Visitors in the Vic and Sade studio. Left to right seated: Art Van Harvey, VIC; Bernadine Flynn, SADE; Paul Rhymer, author; Walter Huston, actor; Edgar A. Guest, poet. Upper right, William Idelson, RUSH; upper left, producer.

Paul Rhymer

Rehearsing for the next day's program. Left to right: Arthur Van Harvey, who played VIC; Bernadine Flynn, who played SADE; Paul Rhymer, who wrote Vic and Sade; and William Idelson, who played RUSH.

RUSH, SADE, and VIC.

VIC and SADE at the microphone.

MR. DEMPSEY
AND MR. TUNNEY
MEET IN
A CIGAR STORE

[*Rush wails from his bedroom*]

SADE: [*Waking up*] Vic! Vic!

[*Shakes him*]

VIC: [*Wakes up*] What is it, Sade!

SADE: I heard something.

VIC: What?

SADE: I don't know what. A noise.

VIC: Aw, you been dreamin' prob'ly. G'wan back to sleep.

SADE: Oh, I never can go back to sleep once I wake up in the middle of the night.

VIC: Well, I can.

SADE: I know I heard something.

VIC: Your imagination. Wonder what time it is.

SADE: I don't know.

[*Clock strikes once*]

VIC: One o'clock.

SADE: Or half-past something. I wish I knew.

VIC: Why?

SADE: Well, if it's only one o'clock I know I can go back to sleep because it's so early. But if it's later I'll get the idea there's no use *trying* to go back to sleep it's so late and . . .

VIC: Aw, I never heard such nonsense. Now if you'll excuse me I think I'll just sneak on back to dreamland. I . . .

SADE: Please see what time it is first, won't you, Vic?

VIC: Aw, why don't ya just figure it's one o'clock and go back to sleep? Gosh, I . . .

SADE: Oh, lean on your elbow and look at your wrist watch on the little table.

VIC: Aw, thunder . . . [*Raises himself*] . . . it's . . . it's three-thirty.

SADE: Oh, now I know I'll never go back to sleep. Wish you hadn't told me what time it was.

VIC: Well, you asked. Sade, I'd like to talk all this over with you a little later . . . say about daylight. Right now I'm bein' paged in the land of dreams and . . . [*Rush wails*] Now what?

SADE: *That's* what I heard. It's Rush.

VIC: Yellin' in his sleep. Maybe we oughta gag him.

SADE: Maybe he's sick.

VIC: Aw, if he was we'd know it quick enough.

SADE: Better go see, Vic.

VIC: Aw, Sade . . . what's the sense in traipsin' around in the middle of the night. For Gosh sakes, I . . .

9

[*Rush again*]

SADE: Go see, Vic.

VIC: [*Getting up and out*] Oh, all right. Golly, I wonder if there's any other poor dub in the world got a family like mine [*Rush again*] [*Calling to Rush*] S'matter, son?

SADE: [*Calling after him*] If he's just talking in his sleep, Vic, don't wake him up.

VIC: [*Softly*] Oh, Rush son. . . . awake?

RUSH: Yeah, gov.

VIC: What's the matter?

RUSH: I got a stomach ache.

VIC: Stomach ache, huh?

RUSH: Yeah . . . hurts awful.

VIC: Wanta go to the . . .

RUSH: No.

[*Moans a little*]

VIC: Well, why don't you try to go to sleep, Rush?

RUSH: I don't want to go to sleep.

VIC: Why not?

RUSH: My sick stomach makes me have awful bad dreams. *Scary* ones. Gee, gov, I was dreamin' that there was a great big snake on my neck and some lions with false teeth in my lap and . . .

SADE: [*Calling*] What is it, Vic?

VIC: Stomach ache.

[*Calls*]

RUSH: Don't tell mom I got a stomach ache, gov.

VIC: Why not?

RUSH: 'Cause I ate a whole lot of strawberries, and she *said* I'd get a stomach ache, and I said I wouldn't, and . . .

SADE: Want *me?*

[*Calls*]

VIC: No, Sade. We'll be all right [*To Rush*] I won't tell her, son. You better try goin' back to sleep, boy. You'll be right as a rivet by mornin'.

RUSH: I'm afraid to go back to sleep, gov.

VIC: 'Fraid of bad dreams, huh?

RUSH: Yeah. [*Moans a little*] Gee, my stomach hurts, gov. Gov.

VIC: Yeah, son.

RUSH: Can I come in bed with you'n mom?

VIC: What for?

RUSH: I think I could go to sleep and not dream bad dreams if

I was sleepin' with you'n mom.

VIC: Three in a bed's altogether too many, Rush. Besides you kick.

RUSH: I won't kick, gov. I'll be still as anything. C'mon, let me. My stomach hurts so.

VIC: Well . . . don't want you in here suffering alone, Rush. We'll see what mom says.

RUSH: I wish you would, gov. I won't even *stir* if you let me.

VIC: [Calls] Sade, Rush wants to come in our bed.

SADE: In our bed? Why?

VIC: Oh, he isn't feeling so hot. Has bad dreams. Wants company.

SADE: Oh, lands. Well, bring him.

VIC: C'mon, Rush . . . get on my back.

RUSH: Gee, you're a sport, gov.

VIC: [*As they go*] You won't think I'm such a sport if you go to kickin' me in bed. I'll break you in little pieces.

SADE: What's the matter, Rush?

RUSH: I ain't feelin' very well, mom. My . . . my elbow . . .

SADE: Elbow nothing! That box of strawberries . . . well, guess there's no use rubbing it in about that box of strawberries. If you're sick you've learned your lesson.

VIC: Move over, Sade. I'll dump this bag of uselessness in the middle.

SADE: Now you gotta lie quiet, Rush. Gov and mom've got to go to sleep.

RUSH: I will, mom.

SADE: Ooh, your feet are cold, Rush. Get 'em over.

RUSH: Wanta get 'em warm, mom.

SADE: Well, wait till gov comes back and use *his* feet for a stove. [*Calling*] Oh, Vic, while you're in the bathroom, get those pills . . .

RUSH: Aw, mom.

SADE: Get those pills on the top shelf and a glass of water. D'ya hear, Vic?

VIC: [*From bathroom*] Yeah. The pink pills?

SADE: Yes. Two.

VIC: O.K.

RUSH: Aw, mom I don't want no pills. It's my elbow . . .

SADE: Elbow nothing. Listen child, you just be quiet about that sick elbow and I'll not say a single word about that box of strawberries.

RUSH: Gosh, mom, my stomach.

[*Moans*]

SADE: Well, as soon as you've taken your pills you go to sleep.

[*Vic comes in*]

VIC: Here y'are, son. Two snappy delicious pink pills. Just the thing for the stomach ache.

RUSH: Aw, I . . .

SADE: Take 'em, Rush, or back to your own bed you go. Take 'em.

VIC: And don't spill any water on my side of the bed.

RUSH: Aw . . . [*Takes pills*] Nasty! Gimme the water.

VIC: Here it is. Be careful now. [*Rush drinks*] Gimme back the glass.

SADE: You'll feel lots better in the morning.

RUSH: *Gee,* them pills are awful. Rather have the stomach ache a darn sight.

VIC: Now mooch over. There's another party got a reservation in this bed. And that party's *me.*

RUSH: Can *you* move over a little, mom?

SADE: No, I can't.

VIC: [*Crawling in*] Rush, get your feet over.

RUSH: Mom, get *your* feet over.

VIC: Well, here we are. And I gotta get some sleep. Of course it's a great pleasure to be in bed with so many dear old friends, but I'm in favor of cutting out jolly conversation and settlin' down to some good old shut-eye.

SADE: Me too. Rush, stop wiggling.

RUSH: [*Moans a little*] My stomach hurts.

VIC: Rush, you said you'd be quiet if we let you come in bed with us.

SADE: He can't help it if he's suffering, can he?

VIC: No, I s'pose not. Try to lie still, Rush, will ya?

RUSH: Yeah, gov. I'm going right to sleep.

[*Little pause*]

VIC: [*Grunts suddenly*] Aw, I knew you'd begin to *kick*. Listen, I'm gonna go sleep in the little bed.

RUSH: It's too short for you, gov. Your feet'll stick out the end.

VIC: Anything's better'n this.

RUSH: Aw, don't go, gov.

VIC: But I got to get some sleep, Rush. Work in the morning.

SADE: That's right, Rush. You better let gov go sleep in your bed.

RUSH: Gov, if you'd tell me a little story—just a little one—I'd go to sleep and never *budge* till tomorrow.

VIC: I should be telling stories at pretty near four o'clock in the morning.

RUSH: Please, gov.

SADE: Go on, Vic. Maybe it would put me to sleep too.

VIC: Well, what'll I tell about?

RUSH: Tell about one of your funny dreams.

VIC: I'd like to be *having* a funny dream . . . 'stead of entertainin' my family in the middle of the night.

SADE: Go on, Vic.

VIC: Well. Lemme see. Well, the other night I was dreamin' that I was going to a party and I wore Mis' Fisher's night-shirt only it had wheels on it, and I took a bobsled and hitched it onto Mr. Bucksaddle and we got to going so fast Mr. Bucksaddle couldn't stop and . . .

RUSH: You oughta of put a *brake* on the bobsled, gov.

SADE: Or one on Mr. Bucksaddle.

VIC: Listen, who's telling about this dream? You two go to sleep instead of buttin' in? Well, when we got to the party I found out the party wasn't a party at all but a funeral. Well sir, they wanted to have the funeral but they didn't have any corpse handy so I volunteered.

RUSH: Why didn't you use Mr. Bucksaddle? He'd make a nice corpse.

SADE: [*Giggling*] Aw, Rush.

VIC: Listen, I quit. I'm going to sleep.

SADE: Go on with the story, Vic. We'll be still.

RUSH: Yeah, gov. While you were telling about your dream I forgot all about my stomach. Didn't hurt a bit. Hurts *now,* though.

    [*Moans a little*]

VIC: Nope. I'm through story-tellin'. I'm going to sleep. Let mom tell you a story.

RUSH: Will ya, mom?

SADE: Will you promise to go to sleep if I do?

RUSH: Yes.

SADE: All right, then. But first, get your foot away.

VIC: Has he got a foot stabbin' you too? Rush, get your feet in the middle of the bed.

RUSH: All right, gov. Tell me the story, mom.

SADE: Well, one time there were three bears: a big bear, a middle-sized bear, and . . .

RUSH: I know that story.

SADE: Well, let's see. How's this. Once upon a time there was a beautiful princess and she . . .

RUSH: Is this the one where she went to sleep and didn't wake up for fifty years?

SADE: Yes. Gee you've heard all my stories.

VIC: I wish to thunder *I* was a beautiful princess and could go to sleep for fifty years. Let's cut out the story-tellin' and be quiet. You can go to sleep if you try, Rush.

RUSH: No, I can't.

SADE: Try, Rush.

RUSH: I did try. Hey, I bet I know how I could go to sleep.

VIC: How! . . . for goodness sake!

RUSH: Well, both of you tell a story at the same time. Gov, you can be somebody, and mom, *you* can be somebody. And talk back and forth.

VIC: No soap, son. Mom and me ain't puttin' on no three-act plays at this time of night.

RUSH: Aw, please. I know who you could be.

SADE: Who, Rush?

RUSH: Well, Mom, you could be Jack Dempsey.

SADE: Jack Dempsey, huh?

RUSH: Yes. And gov can be Gene Tunney.

VIC: Want us to put on a six-round battle right here in bed, huh? Nonsense. Go to sleep and no more foolishness.

RUSH: Aw, please. Listen . . . mom, you're Jack Dempsey, see. And you meet Gene Tunney—that's gov—in a cigar store. And he accidentally steps on your foot, and . . .

VIC: Have a heart, son. I got to go to work in the morning.

SADE: Let's do it, Vic. We might as well do that as lie here bawling each other out. C'mon. I'm Jack Dempsey and you're Gene Tunney.

RUSH: And ya just met in a cigar store and Gene Tunney accidently steps on Jack Dempsey's foot.

VIC: Aw, criminy. Who'm I?

SADE: You're Gene Tunney. And you accidentally step on my foot. We're in a cigar store.

[*Chuckles*]

VIC: All right. 'Morning, Mr. Dempsey.

SADE: Good morning, Mr. Tunney. Get off my foot.

[*Giggles*]

[*Rush laughs*]

VIC: I ain't on your foot, Mr. Dempsey.

14

SADE: You are too. Look, Mr. Tunney.

VIC: Well, gosh, Mr. Dempsey, I'm awful sorry. I . . .

RUSH: Aw, gov. Gene Tunney's an awful tough fella. He wouldn't apologize for stepping on somebody's foot.

VIC: Well, what if I *am* on your foot, Dempsey. Don't ya like it?

SADE: No, I don't like it. I think I'll give you a hit in the face.

RUSH: Aw, mom, Jack Dempsey wouldn't say that. He'd say 'a sock on the beazer'.

SADE: No, I don't like it. I think I'll give you a sock on the beazer.

VIC: Oh, yeah. Well, looka here, Dempsey, I got half a notion to lay one up side your jaw.

SADE: You just try it, Gene Tunney, and I'll give you a biff on the snoot.

RUSH: [*Laughs*] That's it, mom, That's it!

VIC: Now, is this putting you to sleep or isn't it?

RUSH: Sure, sure. I'm almost asleep.

VIC: You were never wider awake in your life. I'm quittin' this stuff. You'll just have to round yourself up another Gene Tunney.

SADE: You're *not* going to sleep, Rush.

RUSH: Aw, please be Jack Dempsey and Gene Tunney a little while longer. I'll go to sleep in no time.

VIC: Listen, Rush, if you'll promise not to open your trap till the clock strikes four . . . not say a single word . . . we'll go on with this. Do you promise?

RUSH: Yes, gov.

VIC: All right, then . . . not another word. Aw . . . Mr. Dempsey.

SADE: Yes, Mr. Tunney.

VIC: I think I'll smash you in the jaw.

SADE: You just try it and see what you get, Mr. Tunney.

VIC: Aw, what'll I get, ya flat-head.

SADE: You'll get a smack in the coco. that's what you'll get.

VIC: [*Lowering his voice somnolently*] Say, Mr. Dempsey.

SADE: I don't want none of your lip, Mr. Tunney.

VIC: Mr. Dempsey, I was down by the stock-yards the other day and I saw some sheep.

SADE: Is that so, Mr. Tunney?

VIC: Yes, Mr. Dempsey. They were coming out of a barn one at a time. First I saw *one* sheep.

SADE: [*Giggling*] Uh-huh, Mr. Tunney. And then I bet you saw *two* sheep.

VIC: Uh-huh. And three sheep.

[*Softly and slowly*]

SADE: And four sheep.

VIC: And five sheep.

SADE: And six sheep.

VIC: And seven sheep.

SADE: And eight sheep.

VIC: And nine sheep.

SADE: And ten sheep.

VIC: And eleven . . . [*Rush sighs sleepily*] And eleven sheep.

SADE: And twelve sheep.

VIC: And thirteen sheep.

SADE: And fourteen sheep.

VIC: And fifteen . . . sh.

[*Giggles*]

SADE: [*Whispering*] Is he asleep?

VIC: Dead to the world.

SADE: Goodnight, Mr. Tunney.

VIC: Night, Mr. Dempsey.

[*Clock strikes four times*]

1932

SADE KEEPS
A SECRET
UNDER HER HAT

RUSH: [*Coming in*] Hi, Mom.

SADE: Hello, Rush. You look warm. Been playin' hard?

RUSH: Gee, yes. Been playin' ball over in Seymour's vacant lot.

SADE: Football?

RUSH: No, baseball.

SADE: Is it time for baseball already?

RSH: We-el, not quite. Warm enough *today* for baseball, though.

SADE: Yes. *Was* warm.

RUSH: We had a swell game. I made two home-runs.

SADE: *Did* you? Let's see 'em.

RUSH: See what, mom?

SADE: The home runs you made.

RUSH: [*Laughs*] Guess you don't know what home runs are, mom.

SADE: No, I guess I don't. What are they?

RUSH: That's when you hit the old apple and get around the bags before they get the pill back in the diamond.

SADE: [*Altogether in the dark*] Why, yes . . . uh-huh . . . the old pill. Uh-huh.

RUSH: I socked one clean over in Mr. Bucksaddle's potato patch. Coulda gone around the bases twice while they were gettin' the ball.

SADE: Did you do it?

RUSH: What?

SADE: Go around the bases twice in Mr. Bucksaddle's potato . . .
[*Interrupted by Rush's laughter*]

RUSH: Aw, mom, you don't know *nothin'* about baseball. Hey, goin' somewhere?

SADE: Why, son?

RUSH: Got your hat on.

SADE: [*Giggling in confusion*] No, I'm not going anywhere.

RUSH: *Been* somewhere, huh?

SADE: [*Giggling*] Now aren't *you* curious?

RUSH: Just wondered, mom. Whatcha got your hat on for?

SADE: Now, wouldn't you like to know?

RUSH: Is it a secret, Mom?

SADE: No, son. Not a secret.

RUSH: [*Mystified*] Oh.

SADE: C'mere, Rush and take it off.

RUSH: Take off your hat?

SADE: Yes.

RUSH: What for, mom?

19

The Small House Half-way Up in the Next Block

SADE: Just do it and see what you see.

RUSH: All right. I . . .

SADE: Wait a minute. Count three before you do it.

RUSH: O.K. One—two—*three*. Why, *mom!*

SADE: [*Giggling*] Do you like it?

RUSH: Mom, it's swell. Just swell!

SADE: I'm glad you like it, Rush.

RUSH: I never *saw* you so pretty, mom. Gee!

SADE: You're sweet to say so, Rush.

RUSH: How'd you happen to do it, mom?

SADE: It was real funny how it happened. I been over to Ruthie's this afternoon—Mis' Stembottom, you know . . .

RUSH: Yeah.

SADE: . . . and we got to talkin' about bobbed hair. Ruthie's is bobbed and looks real cute. And Ruthie says, 'Sade, why don't you bob yours?' But I just laughed and told her I'd look like a peeled onion with my hair bobbed, and . . .

RUSH: Gee, you don't at all, mom.

SADE: [*Giggling*] Well, she just kept after me and kept after me, and I kept telling her no and kidding back and forth, and finally she got out her shears and things and just wouldn't listen to me any more.

RUSH: Mis' Stembottom cut hair, mom?

SADE: Land, yes . . . been doing it for years for all the neighbor ladies. Does a real nice job, too.

RUSH: I'll say she does. Gosh, mom, you look like a movie star.

SADE: [*Giggles*] Aw, g'wan, I don't.

RUSH: Yes, you do, mom.

SADE: Well, I was real surprised when I saw myself in the glass. Ruthie wouldn't let me look till she'd finished with me. It looks so much better than I thought. My face is kinda fat and . . .

RUSH: It is not, mom. It's a pretty face.

SADE: [*Giggles*] You're an old flatterer, that's what you are.

RUSH: No, I'm not, mom. Hey, c'mon over to Seymour's lot with me, will ya?

SADE: Whatever for, child?

RUSH: So's I can show you off to the kids.

SADE: Aw, they wouldn't want to see me.

RUSH: Yes, they would, mom. C'mon.

SADE: No, Rush. They'll see me some time or another. Anyway, I don't care what *they* think just so long as my little boy likes me. And . . . gov.

RUSH: Oh, wait'll *gov* sees you. Will *he* be proud!

SADE: I *hope* so. He's always been kinda against bobbed hair. Thinks it cheapens married ladies. I said to Ruthie, I said, 'Gee, Vic'll just kill me!' and she said, 'No, Sade, he'll *kiss* you' . . . but I don't know. I'm worried as can be he won't like it.

RUSH: Oh, *he'll* like it. Mom, you look just like a little girl . . . so pretty.

SADE: [*Giggles*] Aw! Anyway, I bet Mis' Fisher disapproves. She never did favor bobbed hair.

RUSH: What do you care what Mis' Fisher thinks, mom. So long as gov and *me* like it.

SADE: Well, all I hope is gov *does* like it. If he doesn't . . . well, I'll just go and hide my head. Oh, I should have *asked* him.

RUSH: Wait'll you see his face when he sees you, mom. I bet he just grins and *grins*.

SADE: [*Happily*] Well, Rush, if I really look as nice as you say I do, I guess it'll be all right.

RUSH: Mom, you look perfectly swell. Guess I'll give you a kiss.

SADE: Make it two. [*Kisses—two*] There!

RUSH: I could use another.

SADE: [*Giggling*] Here!

 [*Two kisses*]

RUSH: What'd Mis' Stembottom do with all the hair she cut off?

SADE: I have it upstairs, Rush, Say, Rush . . .

RUSH: Yes, mom.

SADE: Listen: When gov comes home I wish you'd . . . I wish you'd tell him you think I look nice so he'll . . .

RUSH: I *do* think you look nice, mom. I think you look beautiful.

SADE: Yes, but tell gov that. I'm just a little bit worried . . .

RUSH: Aw, mom. Wait'll you see his face when . . .

SADE: [*Happily*] Oh, all right, son. Gee, I'm real happy now. I never knew there was such a thrill in getting your hair cut. Guess I'll call up Ruthie and tell her . . . [*Click*] . . . 2572-X please. Yes. Rush, if it happens that gov *doesn't* like my . . . oh, hello, Ruthie . . . Sade . . . yes . . . say, Ruthie, I guess you musta done an awful good job on my hair . . . [*Giggles*] . . . Rush thinks it's marvelous [*Rush shouts into the phone:*] Made her look just like Miss America, Mis' Stembottom. [*Sade giggles and says:*] That's Rush, Ruthie. Says you made me look just like Miss America. [*Giggles*] Uh-huh. Now if only my husband feels that way, I . . .

RUSH: [*Excitedly*] Hey, mom, gov's comin' up the walk.

SADE: [*Excitedly*] Guess I better hang up, Ruthie. Vic's comin' in.

Wanta surprise him. Yes. I'll tell you how he likes it. Yes. 'By, Ruthie.

[*Hangs up*]

RUSH: Gov stopped to talk with Mr. Donahue out in front, mom.

SADE: Did he? S'pose I better go out on the front porch and . . .

RUSH: No. No. Put your hat back on. S'prise him like you s'prised me.

SADE: [*Excitedly*] All right. All right.

RUSH: Here's your hat, mom. Tuck in the edges of your hair.

SADE: All right. How's this?

RUSH: O.K. Now don't let on, mom.

SADE: I won't.

RUSH: Here comes gov. Sit down, mom.

SADE [*Excitedly*] Yes, yes. All right.

[*Gov enters*]

RUSH: Hi, Gov.

VIC: How do, son. 'Lo, Sade.

SADE: How are you, Vic?

VIC: O.K. Had a beastly day at the office.

SADE: That's too bad. Anything happen?

VIC: Enough. Old Ruebush bawled the pants off me.

RUSH: What for, gov?

VIC: Aw, the plant inspector let a shipment of eggbeaters without handles get out.

SADE: The men forget to put on the handles, Vic?

VIC: Yeah . . . *somethin'* happened down in the packing department.

SADE: Well, it wasn't your fault, was it?

VIC: No, but the plant inspector is in my department. He went to sleep on the job and I'm the guy that suffers. Old Ruebush was in my office for a half hour this afternoon yellin' at me.

SADE: That's too bad, Vic.

VIC: Oh, well, ya gotta take 'em like they come, I guess. Paper come yet?

RUSH: Here it is, gov.

VIC: Thanks.

[*Rustles paper*]

[*Little pause*]

RUSH: Gov, mom's got her hat on.

VIC: Huh?

RUSH: Mom's got her hat on.

VIC: Has she? Well. What's the idea, Sade?

SADE: [*Giggling*] Oh, nothing particularly. I just thought . . .

VIC: Says here them flyers that started from New York only got to Pittsburgh. I don't wonder. So many guys are flyin' around in airplanes ya wonder how there's enough room in the sky for 'em all to make any headway. Shucks, I . . .

RUSH: Hey, gov, mom's got her hat on.

VIC: Huh? Oh. Why don't you take it off, Sade? Goin' somewhere?

SADE: [*Giggles*] Oh, no. I just thought I'd . . .

VIC: [*Reads*] 'Peoria Man's Stomach Lots Better'. What a headline? Now, what the heck do *I* care if . . .

RUSH: Gov, mom's *hat* . . .

VIC: [*Irritably*] Why don't you go out and play until supper time?

RUSH: Look, gov, I'm gonna pull mom's hat off. Look!

VIC: Look at what?

RUSH: I . . . I pulled mom's hat off.

VIC: I see ya did. And now that you've pulled mom's hat off let's forget about mom's hat for a while. Peoria Man's *stomach* lots bett . . . gosh! . . . if I . . .

RUSH: Gov, I . . .

VIC: Son, for gosh sakes' what do you want?

SADE: Never mind, Rush.

VIC: What's eatin' ya, son? Ya been interruptin' everything I say and actin' foolish ever since I got home.

RUSH: I was just gonna ask, gov . . . which way do you like mom best? With her hat *on* or with her hat *off*?

VIC: Well, if *that* ain't a bright question. Son, why don't you go out and play and quit botherin' around?

RUSH: All right, gov, I'll go.

VIC: Well, go on then.

RUSH: But gov, which way *do* you like best?

VIC: Which way what?

RUSH: Which way do ya like mom best . . . with her hat *on* or with it *off?*

VIC: Well, what difference does it . . .

SADE: Never mind, Rush.

VIC: Rush, are you going to stop asking dumb questions and go out and play or not?

RUSH: I'm going, gov . . . right now. Before I go, though, gov, can I ask you something else?

VIC: What?

RUSH: I'd like to ask about mom's *nose*.

VIC: First it's mom's hat and now it's mom's nose. What *about* mom's nose?

RUSH: Gov, look at mom's *nose*.

VIC: What's the matter with it?

RUSH: Well, look at it.

VIC: I *am* looking at it. Anything the matter with your nose, Sade?

SADE: [*On the point of tears*] Why, no-o. Nothing the matter with my nose, I guess.

VIC: Let's not have any more tomfoolery, Rush. I'm not in a mood for it. Old man Ruebush took all the ginger outa me.

RUSH: But, gov . . .

SADE: [*Still on the edge*] Never mind, Rush.

> [*Little pause*]
> [*All of a sudden, Sade jumps up, crying unrestrainedly, and dashes out*]

VIC: [*Startled and a little frightened*] What in the . . . Hey, Sade, Rush . . .

RUSH: Don't be scared, gov. [*Almost crying himself*] It's all right.

VIC: What's the matter with her?

RUSH: [*Tears*] Nothin'.

VIC: What's the matter with you?

RUSH: Nothin'

VIC: Where'd mom go?

RUSH: Upstairs.

VIC: What'd she go upstairs for?

RUSH: To cry, I guess.

VIC: Cry? What for?

RUSH: You didn't notice her hair.

VIC: S'matter with her hair?

RUSH: It's bobbed.

VIC: Bobbed? Mom's hair bobbed?

RUSH: Yes . . . and it's just as pretty as it can be.

VIC: Well, I'll be darned! Gosh, I *did* think I noticed something different . . . was gonna say somethin' about it, too. But my mind's so cluttered up with office stuff that I hardly know whether I'm going or coming. When'd she have it done?

RUSH: S'afternoon. Mis' Stembottom done it.

VIC: Well, I'll be . . . Now I *am* in it. Did *you* notice it, Rush?

RUSH: Sure . . . the minute I saw it. It looks swell, gov. I never seen mom so pretty.

VIC: Jiminy! Gosh, this is *awful*. I musta been asleep *right. Now* what am I gonna do?

RUSH: I'd go upstairs if I was you, gov?

VIC: What'll I do when I get there? Apologize?

RUSH: I wouldn't do that, gov.

VIC: What would you do?

RUSH: I'd go up to mom and say you *saw* she had her hair cut when she first took her hat off but you got so darn *mad* you wouldn't say anything about it.

VIC: That wouldn't be the truth, Rush.

RUSH: I know it wouldn't, gov . . . but I'd tell her that just the same. Gov, I been thinkin' over lies and things a whole lot the last couple days . . .

VIC: Ya have, huh?

RUSH: Yes . . . an' I allowed myself three lies for the rest of my life.

VIC: Three lies, huh?

RUSH: Yes, just three . . . because I figure maybe there'll be three times in my life when a lie'll be better'n the truth.

VIC: Zat so?

RUSH: Yes . . . an' *this* is one time when a lie's better.

VIC: Well, go on. What'll I say to mom?

RUSH: Tell her you saw she had her hair cut but it made you mad . . . but she looks so awful *pretty* with it cut that you just couldn't *stay* mad.

VIC: I see, colonel. I'll do just as you say.

RUSH: An' *kiss* her, gov.

VIC: I'll do that all right. Anything else?

RUSH: Well, tell her she looks pretty *lots* of times . . . every few minutes all evening tell her how nice her hair is. Because it *does* look swell, gov. I bet when you get a good look at mom you'll say she's the prettiest girl you ever saw.

VIC: O.K. Here—catch.

RUSH: A quarter!

VIC: I'd have to pay a lawyer that much and prob'ly not get near such good advice. Go on to the movies.

RUSH: Gee! Thanks, gov.

VIC: That's O.K. Run along. [*Calls*] Sade. Oh, Sade . . .

[*Into theme*]

1933

RUSH'S TONSILS,
SQUEAKY SHOES,
AND MIXED NUMBERS

THEME

COMMERCIAL CREDIT

INTRODUCTION: Our scene is a peaceful one as we join the little family on Virginia Avenue now. It is early in the evening; the floor lamp is casting its red glow about the tidy living-room; and Vic and Sade are comfortably settled for a few pleasant hours before it's time for bed. Sade, who is industriously bending over her sewing-basket, looks up from her work as Vic, speaking from behind his newspaper, says . . .

VIC: See the hospital notes, Sade?

SADE: I just glanced at 'em.

VIC: See about Mis' R. T. Legthorne?

SADE: No. Paper state somethin' about her?

VIC: Yeah, she had an operation.

SADE: No.

VIC: That's what the paper says. [*reads*] Mrs. R. T. Legthorne's condition is satisfoctory after an appendectomy operation Tuesday.

SADE: Tuesday, huh? Well, what do you know?

VIC: *That'll* set Ralph back somethin'.

SADE: The paper don't state who delivered the operation, does it?

VIC: Uh-uh.

SADE: Let's see.

VIC: I read you all there was.

SADE: Let me see anyway.

VIC: Shucks, Sade, if it said anything more I'd a . . .

SADE: Gimme the paper.

VIC: [*Giving it to her*] You'd think I was a half-wit.

SADE: [*Interested in the paper*] Yes. Now, let's see: [*Reads*] Mrs. R. T. Legthorne's condition is satisfactory after an appendectomy operation on Tuesday. [*To herself*] Uh-huh.

VIC: That's what *I* read.

SADE: Uh-huh. Let's see [*Reads on*] Mr. Carl Trigger of Minier returned home yesterday. He underwent a mastoid operat . . . [*To Vic*] No, I guess it don't say who delivered Mis' Legthorne's operation.

VIC: I *told* ya it didn't.

SADE: [*Paying him no attention*] I just wonder if Doctor Whipfang delivered the operation. He's Mis' Legthorne's brother-in-law. That is he *used* to be. He was her first husband's brother. If *he* did it, I don't suppose he'd charge so much.

VIC: Gimme my paper back.

SADE: Vic.

VIC: Gimme my paper.

SADE: Would he be Mis' Legthorne's brother-in-law?

VIC: Who?

SADE: Doctor Whipfang.

VIC: How do I know?

SADE: Well, ya know Mis' Legthorne was Mis' Homer Whipfang before she married Ralph.

VIC: Uh-huh.

SADE: An' Homer Whipfang is Doctor Whipfang's brother.

VIC: Uh-huh, gimme my paper back.

SADE: So, of course, when Mis' Legthorne was Mis' Whipfang, she was Doctor Whipfang's sister-in-law.

VIC: Sure. Gimme my paper.

SADE: Well, what *I* want to know is, is she *still* Doctor Whipfang's sister-in-law? Bein' Ralph Legthorne's wife an' all.

VIC: I'm sure I don't know.

SADE: If she is, Doctor Whipfang would prob'ly deliver the operation for next to nothing. Blood's thicker'n water. The way operations cost nowadays, a person . . .

VIC: Will you give me back my paper?

SADE: What?

VIC: Will you gimme back my paper. I was readin' it an' you . . .

SADE: Oh, sure. Here it . . . Wait a minute.

[*Sees something interesting*]

VIC: [*Little irritated groan*]

SADE: Did you see this?

VIC: [*Mad*] About the prairie chicken?

SADE: [*Puzzled*] Prairie chicken? It don't say nothin' about a prairie chicken.

VIC: Don't it?

SADE: No. What *about* a prairie chicken?

VIC: Well, thunder, you take my paper away from me an' then say, 'did you see this?' How *can* I see that? You got the paper. *I* don't know what you're talking about. I only . . .

SADE: *I'm* gonna tell you about it. Lands. Paper states: 'Harold and William McVeigh, young sons of Mr. and Mrs. Eustance McVeigh of 910 North Mason street, underwent tonsil operations early this morning. The boys are doing nicely.'

VIC: Gimme my paper.

SADE: Oh, *here*.

VIC: [*Grunt*]

SADE: Vic, when we gonna have Rush's . . .

30

VIC: Huh?

SADE: Put down your paper a minute an' talk to me.

VIC: Aw, shucks, a fella no more gets settled comfortable than . . .

SADE: Stop talkin' to me like that.

VIC: [*Tough*] I would *prefer* to . . .

SADE: Do you want to be tickled? Old bear.

VIC: [*Tough*] Aw, doggone it, Sade, why can't I ever be . . .

SADE: I *told* you to stop bein' mean to me. Take *this*.

    [*Tickles him*]

VIC: [*Goes through the hysteria attendant to being tickled*]

SADE: [*Laughing*] You gonna stop being mean?

VIC: [*Trying to recapture his dignity*] Sade, if you don't . . .

SADE: If I don't *what?*

    [*Tickles him again*]

VIC: [*Completely undone, gives himself up to wild laughing*]

SADE: Gonna stop?

VIC: Yeah. Now quit.

SADE: You *better* be good.

VIC: Get off my lap.

SADE: No.

VIC: You've had your fun. Get off my lap.

SADE: No.

VIC: I'll dump you on the floor.

SADE: I'll tickle you again.

VIC: [*Terror-stricken*] No.

SADE: Do I get to stay on your lap?

VIC: Yes, but for gosh sakes get over on my other knee a little. Criminy.

SADE: [*Shifting*] That better?

VIC: Yeah. Now whatcha want?

SADE: It's about Rush's tonsils.

VIC: What about 'em?

SADE: They oughta come out. He gets sore throat after sore throat. No sense in lettin' 'em go year after year.

VIC: [*In paper*] Uh-huh.

SADE: Don't get interested in your paper. Talk to me.

VIC: I can hear you.

SADE: *I'll* take that paper

    [*Takes it*]

VIC: Hey, you gimme back that . . .

31

SADE: Here comes a tickle.

VIC: [*Starts to go insane again*] Now, doggone it, Sade, I ain't gonna . . . [*Hysteria over*] Shucks.

SADE: Gonna talk to me?

VIC: Whatcha want me to say?

SADE: I want you to . . .

RUSH: [*Comes in*] Hi.

SADE: Hello there.

VIC: How do, Roosevelt.

RUSH: [*Laughing*] Where'd ya get that fat lady on your knee, gov?

SADE: Don't you call *me* a fat lady. You through studyin' already?

RUSH: I still got my arithmetic to do.

SADE: You better go do it. We don't want any more report cards like *last* time.

RUSH: I'm *gonna* do it. I wanta ask a favor first.

SADE: [*On the defense*] Yes?

RUSH: Is it all right if I walk around the house?

SADE: Walk around the house?

RUSH: Yeah.

SADE: What for?

RUSH: I just wanta walk around the house.

SADE: It don't sound like a very bright thing to do.

RUSH: I can do it though, huh?

SADE: I s'pose. Put on your coat, though. It's chilly out.

RUSH: Oh, I ain't goin' *outside,* mom.

SADE: Thought you wanted to walk around the house.

RUSH: I want to walk around the house *inside.* Just walk around, ya know . . . in the dining-room an' upstairs an' down to the basement an' around.

SADE: What notion ya got in your head now?

RUSH: It's kind of a secret.

SADE: You an' your secrets. Lands.

RUSH: It's all *right,* though, huh, mom, if I . . .

VIC: Hey, whatcha doin'?

RUSH: Thought I'd sit on your other knee.

VIC: No.

RUSH: *Mom's* sittin' on your knee.

VIC: Sittin' on my knee is a privilege granted only to a select few. You keep off.

RUSH: I guess you only allow ladies to sit on your knee, huh?

VIC: That's all.

RUSH: Well, I guess I'll start in on my walkin'.

SADE: How you gonna get your arithmetic done?

RUSH: I can do it while I'm walkin'.

SADE: *How,* for goodness sakes?

RUSH: We haven't got any problems for tomorrow. Just definitions. I can be learnin' 'em while I walk.

VIC: Where you gonna walk first, son?

RUSH: Upstairs.

VIC: I've seen *brighter* boys.

RUSH: [*A little way off*] Huh?

VIC: Nothin'. Have a pleasant stroll.

RUSH: It ain't exactly a stroll, gov.

VIC: What is it?

RUSH: It's a secret.

VIC: Have a pleasant secret, then.

RUSH: [*Off*] Yeah.

VIC: Shift over on my other knee, Sade. You're killin' me.

SADE: I s'pose I'm a fat lady, huh?

VIC: Sure, you're a . . .

SADE: *Tickle.*

VIC: [*Starts to go insane*] No. No, you're not a fat lady.

SADE: All right then. [*Getting serious*] Really, Vic, he oughta have his tonsils out.

VIC: Let's take 'em out then.

SADE: He'd never let us get him to the hospital. Never.

VIC: Are we the boss or is he?

SADE: I know, but . . .

VIC: But what?

SADE: You know how he is with the dentist. Gets scared out of his wits just *thinkin'* about the dentist.

VIC: That's foolishness.

SADE: I notice *you're* afraid of the dentist.

VIC: Who said so?

SADE: It's like pullin' teeth to get you to go to the dentist.

VIC: [*Laughs*] It *is* pullin' teeth.

SADE: An' *I'm* worse scared than anybody else when it . . .

RUSH: [*Walking near*] A mixed number is a whole number an' a fraction combined. A mixed number is a whole . . .

VIC: Hey.

RUSH: Yeah?

VIC: Whatcha doin'?

RUSH: Walkin' around.

VIC: What for?

RUSH: That's the secret.

VIC: What's all that you're sayin'?

RUSH: That's my arithmetic. I'm learnin' definitions.

VIC: Go walk somewhere else an' learn your definitions.

RUSH: [*Walking away*] Sure. A mixed number is a whole number an' a fraction combined. A mixed number . . . [*Etc.*]

VIC: [*To Sade*] When we're havin' his tonsils taken out, we better have the doc take a look at his head too. Wouldn't be surprised to learn there was something radically wrong. Bone pressin' on the brain or somethin'.

SADE: How we *ever* gonna get him to the hospital?

VIC: Just use the steel hand in the iron glove. That kid's got to do like we say. We give him too much free rein as it is. We let him run over us.

SADE: Oh, not so much, Vic. *Rush* is a good boy. But he'll just raise an *awful* storm if we mention goin' to the hospital.

VIC: Let him. He's got to learn that what we say goes.

SADE: Yes, I know, but . . . Take the other day now. I wanted Rush to take castor oil. He just fussed an' *yelled*. An' finally he saw I meant business, an' he took the spoon, an' was about to take it . . . an' ya know what *I* done?

VIC: What?

SADE: I cried. Couldn't help it. Couldn't *bear* to make him do something I'd rather die than do myself.

VIC: Did he take the castor oil?

SADE: No. [*Giggles*] An' we was both so relieved.

VIC: You coddle him, Sade.

SADE: Oh, not so much. It's just that . . . Well *I* don't know. He's got to have his tonsils out. We wouldn't be fair to *him* if we didn't have it done. But lands, when I think of the way he'll carry on, I can't bring myself to . . .

VIC: *I'll* tell him.

SADE: You won't scare him?

VIC: I don't know about *that,* but I'll see that his tonsils get taken out.

SADE: Vic.

VIC: Yeah?

SADE: *I'll* tell him. I'll just kinda break it gentle to him an' . . .

VIC: That's what's the matter. Breakin' things gentle to him. The way to do is . . .

RUSH: [*Returning*] A mixed number is a whole number an' a fraction combined. A mixed number is a whole number an' . . .

SADE: Son.

RUSH: Yeah?

SADE: Come here a minute, will ya?

RUSH: Sure.

SADE: Ya know your definitions?

RUSH: Know *one* of 'em. A mixed number is a whole number an' a fraction combined.

SADE: Through walkin' now?

RUSH: No. I gotta walk about ten miles.

SADE: What for?

RUSH: It's a . . . Well, I guess I can tell ya.

SADE: Don't need to if it's a secret.

RUSH: I'd just as soon tell. Know what I got in my shoes?

VIC: Feet?

RUSH: [*Laughs*] Bum joke, gov.

SADE: Whatcha got in your shoes, son?

RUSH: I got some of Skinny Martin's magic powder. Know what it does?

SADE: What?

RUSH: Makes your shoes squeak.

SADE: It does?

RUSH: Sure. After I've walked about twelve miles my shoes'll squeak like the dickens. You can hear me for half a block. Y'oughta hear Skinny Martin's shoes. Make more noise.

VIC: Whatcha want your shoes to squeak for?

RUSH: Oh—attract attention.

SADE: Lands.

RUSH: You want some powder for your shoes, mom?

SADE: I don't think so.

RUSH: It'll make 'em squeak.

SADE: I don't believe I want my shoes to squeak.

RUSH: Dontcha want to attract attention?

SADE: I guess not.

RUSH: I *like* to attract attention. What I want for Christmas is gonna attract a lot of attention.

SADE: What's that? What do you want for Christmas?

RUSH: I'm not gonna tell yet.

SADE: Well, what is it?

RUSH: I better wait before I tell. You'd say no.

SADE: Maybe not.

RUSH: I better wait.

SADE: Listen, son, if you'd do something for me an' gov, we might give you whatever you wanted for Christmas. Whatever you wanted.

RUSH: I bet you won't give me what *I* want for Christmas.

SADE: Well, what is it you want?

RUSH: I better not tell.

SADE: Go on an' tell.

RUSH. I better not.

SADE: Is it very expensive?

RUSH: Yes.

SADE: Well, tell us. There's somethin' gov an' me want you to do awful bad, an' if you'll do it . . . well, I ain't sayin' for sure but . . . but we'd give an awful nice Christmas present to the little boy that does what we want him to. Wouldn't we, Vic?

VIC: Sure.

RUSH: What is it you want me to do?

SADE: Tell us what you want for Christmas first.

RUSH: You'd say no.

SADE: Don't be too sure. What is it you want?

RUSH: If I tell ya, will you promise not to say 'no' first thing?

SADE: Yes. What is it?

RUSH: [*Warningly*] It costs a lot of money.

SADE: What is it?

RUSH: I . . . I . . .

SADE: Yes.

RUSH: I . . . I wanta have my tonsils cut out.

VIC & SADE: Your tonsils cut out!

RUSH: Yes. Ya see, I'm the only kid in my room that ain't had their tonsils cut out, an' when ya have your tonsils cut out ya get to go to the hospital an' take ether an' lay in bed an' everybody comes to see you, an' all the kids write letters an' . . .

   [*Fade*]

END OF SCRIPT

ANNOUNCER: The human mind operates in queer, queer ways, and great is the mystery thereof. Have a merry, merry Christmas at the hospital, Rush.

1933

MR. POWERS' BICYCLE
AND THE SHED

ANNOUNCER: Once again we present your friends Vic and Sade —at whose small house half-way up in the next block you are invited to spend a little while at this time. [*Pause*]
COMMERCIAL CREDIT
ANNOUNCER: It is late afternoon as our scene opens now, and here in the living-room we discover a man and his young son matching wits in a game of rummy. The card-players are Vic and Rush . . . and since a hotly-contested hand has just been concluded, it might be a good time for us to step up close . . . and listen.

RUSH: I win, gov.

VIC: So you do.

RUSH: You lose.

VIC: A natural sequence—since you win.

RUSH: You know what the loser *is,* don'tcha?

VIC: It escapes me for the moment.

RUSH: An ol' dirty banana peel with all the insides scooped out.

VIC: Ah, yes.

RUSH: How's it feel to be an ol' dirty banana peel with all the insides scooped out?

VIC: Feels O.K. Care to play another game?

RUSH: Sure. I'll beat ya worse than ever.

VIC: You're welcome to try. Whose deal?

RUSH: Yours.

VIC: Toss me over the rest of the cards.

RUSH: What's the loser hafta be *this* time?

VIC: *You* name it.

RUSH: How about: a bashed-in cook-stove some ol' tramp threw out in the alley?

VIC: Excellent.

RUSH: Hey, *I'll* tell ya: let's let the *winner* be somethin' *too.*

VIC: All right.

RUSH: What can he be?

VIC: A dead horse that's been mean to his grand'ma an' . . . ?

RUSH: Naw, the winner's got to be somethin' *good.*

VIC: Apple pie?

RUSH: How about fire-chief of the world with his pockets full of diamonds?

VIC: Just right: Ready for your tickets?

RUSH: Yeah.

VIC: Here they come.

RUSH: [*Chuckles*] That's pretty darn good.

VIC: What is?

RUSH: When we get through with this game, one of us'll be a bashed-in cook-stove some ol' tramp threw out in the alley, an' the other'll be fire-chief of the world with his pockets fulla diamonds.

VIC: Uh-huh.

RUSH: If *you* win an' get to be fire-chief of the world with your pockets fulla diamonds, you'll *still* be an ol' dirty banana peel with all your insides scooped out.

VIC: I'll be quite a sight.

RUSH: An' if you *lose,* you'll be . . .

VIC: C'mon: your first play.

RUSH: A couple guys can have a lotta fun playin' rummy when they make up stuff to . . .

SADE: [*Entering*] Vic.

VIC: Uh-huh.

SADE: I just this minute had another set-to with Mr. Powers.

VIC: Fight?

SADE: We didn't *fight,* but we had a few little words. He was very snippy to me. *Very* snippy.

VIC: [*Mildly*] Doggone him.

SADE: Ya know what I've decided to do?

VIC: No. [*To Rush*] Hey, ya want that jack or *don't* ya?

RUSH: I *want* it, but I . . .

SADE: [*Who is somewhat exercised*] Be quiet a minute, son. Vic, I'm gonna tell Mr. Powers I hafta have my shed.

VIC: Make him take his bicycle out, ya mean?

SADE: Wouldn't *you?* When a person rents out their shed for a man to keep his bicycle in, they expect common courtesy.

VIC: What's Brother Powers been *doin'*?

SADE: Well, I was out on the porch just now an' . . . stop playin' cards while I tell you this.

VIC: O.K.

SADE: . . . an' he come ridin' his bicycle across the back yard big as you please. I've *told* him about that, ya know. Told him three or four times. Just day before yesterday he did it an' I said, 'Mr. Powers, I'd *prefer* that you drive your bicycle up the *alley* instead of across the lawn.'

VIC: Yeah. [*To Rush*] Hey, Stevenson, quit lookin' underneath to see what's been discarded. The rules of the game . . .

SADE: Vic, *listen* to me.

VIC: *I'm* listenin'.

SADE: An' just now it was the same thing over again. I was standin' on the porch an' here he come along on his bicycle . . . ridin' right by Mis' Fisher's fence without an 'aye', 'yes', or 'no'.

VIC: Um.

SADE: *I* walked *out* there.

VIC. Um.

SADE: Walked right out to the shed. Mr. Powers was puttin' the lock on his bicycle. When he saw me he said, 'Oh, good afternoon, Mis' Gook.' I said, 'Mr. Powers, I've asked you several times not to drive your bicycle across my yard.' He looked at me funny an' said, 'It's *winter* time. Don't see how I can be hurtin' any *grass*.' 'Nothing was *mentioned* about grass, Mr. Powers,' I said. 'But the ground is soft an' your bicycle wheels make deep ruts. Just step outside an' see for yourself.' But he didn't move. Just stood there an' looked at me impudent for a minute. Then he said, 'I guess I won't bother. I got an idea what ruts look like.' Just as *snippy*.

VIC: He's a *fiend,* that guy.

SADE: Wouldn't *you* ask him to give up the shed?

VIC: You made the deal, Sade. He's your tenant. Do as you think best.

SADE: No reason in the world why a person should hafta put up with a thing like that, is there?

VIC: None that *I* can see.

SADE: *Another* thing he does is sit in there *evenings*.

VIC: He sits in the *shed* evenings?

SADE: Yes—to smoke his pipe. Mis' Harris don't allow her roomers to smoke pipes in the house, so Mr. Powers does *his* smokin' in the shed.

VIC: What a heck of a place to spend your evenings.

SADE: That's *dangerous,* him doin' that. Might start a fire.

VIC: Yeah.

SADE: Anyway I rented him that shed to keep his *bicycle* in—not to *live* in.

VIC: The right's all on your side, Sade.

SADE: You'd throw him out then?

VIC: Don't know but what I would.

SADE: [*Going*] Think I'll call him up this very evening. When a person rents out their own property, they don't hafta stand for . . .

[*Fades*]

VIC: [*To Rush*] Did ya decide to keep that jack?

RUSH: Yeah.

VIC: All right, discard somethin' else.

RUSH: I'll discard the deuce of spades.

VIC: Looks like Mr. Powers' bicycle's gonna lose its *home*.

RUSH: Yeah.

VIC: Seems a shame in a way there should be all this trouble an' heartbreak, but Mr. Powers brought it on *himself*.

RUSH: Uh-huh—mom won't let anybody get smart with *her*.

VIC: This little drama goes to show that life is made up of tears an' . . .

SADE: [*Returning*] Vic.

VIC: Yeah?

SADE: Another thing about Mr. Powers, he's 'way behind in his rent.

VIC: Is he?

SADE: Moved his bicycle in the shed the first of August, paid me for one month, an' never come across with one red cent *since*.

VIC: As I remember it, the rental on our shed is very low too.

SADE: Fifteen cents is all.

VIC: Fifteen cents a month?

SADE: Yes.

VIC: [*Laughs*]

SADE: What's the matter?

VIC: That *is* low rent.

SADE: 'Course it is. It's about *right* though. A person can rent a garage for their *auto* for three *dollars* a month. Fifteen cents for a bicycle in a shed makes it just about *fair*.

VIC: [*Chuckles*] Uh-huh. An' Mr. Powers has only paid you for one month?

SADE: Just one little fifteen cents. Paid him up through August. He owes for all of September, all of October, an' half of November. How much does that make?

VIC: Makes . . . a . . . thirty-seven an' a half cents.

SADE: Call it thirty-seven.

VIC: O.K.

SADE: He's thirty-seven cents behind in his rent, he drives his bicycle over my yard, he's snippy with me, an' he uses the shed to *sit* in evenings. Don't *you* think I'm justified in throwin' him out?

VIC: [*Judicially*] Yes, I believe I do.

SADE: I'll call him up right after supper. What'd I better say: 'Mr. Powers, I must ask you for the wood-shed'?

VIC: Uh-huh.

SADE: Or shall I say, 'Mr. Powers, under the *circumstances,* I must ask you for the wood-shed.'?

VIC: Either one sounds O.K.

SADE: Ya don't s'pose he'll get mad an' fly into a tantrum?

VIC: Naw. Guys get thrown outa places every day in the week. Anyway he richly *deserves* harsh treatment.

SADE: I don't care if he *does* get mad. I'll say, 'Mr. Powers, you haven't been at all satisfactory in my shed. You've driven your bicycle across my yard after I asked you not to, an' you haven't talked to me the way I'm *used* to being talked to.'

VIC: Yeah.

SADE: When had I better tell him to vacate . . . first of December?

VIC: Be a good time.

SADE: See this is the sixteenth of November. Can't hardly make him get out in the middle of the month.

VIC: No.

SADE: First of December'll give him two weeks to remove his bicycle.

RUSH: [*Laughs*]

SADE: [*Sharply*] What's the matter with *you?*

RUSH: Sounded kinda *funny* what you said. It don't take a guy two weeks to move a little bicycle out of . . .

SADE: That'll be enough, son. I'll *tell* him that then, huh, Vic? I'll say, 'Mr. Powers, I must ask you for the wood-shed on the first of December.'

VIC: Yeah.

SADE: [*Her soft heart asserting itself*] You . . . you don't think I'm doing *wrong*, do you?

VIC: Not at all.

SADE: Well, I don't like to have *trouble* with people.

VIC: You're doin' exactly the right thing.

SADE: [*Going*] I'll call him up after while then. A person can't let themselves be run over by *other* people when . . .

   [*Fades*]

VIC: [*To Rush*] Whose move?

RUSH: Yours.

VIC: I'll snag onto this Queen.

RUSH: Remember what the loser an' winner's gonna be?

VIC: To be absolutely *certain* I oughta have my memory refreshed.

RUSH: Loser's gonna be a bashed-in cook-stove some ol' tramp threw out in the alley. Winner's gonna be fire-chief of the world with his pockets full of diamonds.

VIC: To be sure.

RUSH: Wonder where Mr. Powers is gonna keep his bicycle *now*.

VIC: Let's not think about the *sad* aspects of this tragic business, Pete. Mr. Powers is a wicked man who . . .

SADE: [*Returning*] Vic, would you say anything about the thirty-seven cents?

VIC: Huh?

SADE: When I call up Mr. Powers had a I better mention the back rent?

VIC: He *owes* it to ya.

SADE: Yes, but I hate to . . . I don't wanta be *too* hard on him all at a clatter.

VIC: *I'd* dun him for it.

SADE: Would, huh?

VIC: Sure I would.

SADE: Well, maybe I could . . . kinda give him a discount. Maybe only ask thirty-*five* cents. Or *twenty*-five.

VIC: Whatever you think best.

SADE: Vic, *another* thing I thought of was Mr. Powers was in *jail* one time.

VIC: Yeah?

SADE: He got in a fight an' smashed a fella in the nose, an' the fella had him put behind bars.

VIC: When was all that?

SADE: Oh, a long time ago. But it *does* make kind of a bad reputation.

VIC: Uh-huh.

SADE: [*Building up a case against Mr. Powers*] Person oughta be good an' careful who they have around their property, don'tcha think?

VIC: Darn right. No use rentin' out your wood-shed to a *jail*-bird.

SADE: You . . . you really think I oughta throw him out, huh?

VIC: Sure.

SADE: After all it's not like throwin' *him* out on the street *personally*. Just his bicycle.

VIC: That's right.

SADE: Well, I . . . I think I'll call him up right *now*. Get it over with.

VIC: Go ahead.

SADE: Gracious, but I hate unpleasant things like this.

VIC: A human being's got to take the bitter with the sweet.

SADE: [*Off a little*] I'll say, 'Mr. Powers, I must ask you for the wood-shed on December first,' huh?

VIC: Yeah.

SADE: [*To phone*] 2379-J, please. Yes. [*To Vic*] Hope this don't spoil his *evening* or anything.

VIC: You're too soft-hearted, kiddo. [*Chuckles*] Heck, *I* been kicked outa . . .

SADE: [*To phone*] Hello, Mis' Harris? This is Mis' Gook. Yes. Say, is Mr. Powers there? Well, may I speak to him, please? Thank you. [*To Vic*] She's gonna call him.

VIC: He little knows the fate that awaits him.

SADE: Poor fella.

VIC: Why poor fella?

SADE: Mr. Powers is really not a *bad* man. Just one of those harum-scarum sorta . . . [*To phone*] Hello, Mr. Powers? This is Mis' Gook, Mr. Powers. Yes. Say, Mr. Powers, I'm . . . I'm very sorry, but I'm afraid I'll hafta ask you to give up the bicycle . . . I mean the wood-shed on December . . . What? Talk louder? [*Louder*] I say I'm very very sorry but I'm afraid I'll hafta ask you to . . . What? Well, I don't see *why* you can't hear me. I'm *talking* loud. I say, Mr. Pow-ers, I'd like to have my wood-shed on December first. Yes. Well . . . because of . . . of *circumstances*. Yes. I don't think you've acted just the way . . . What? (to the others) Know what he's doin'?

VIC AND RUSH: What?

SADE: Pretending to *cry*.

VIC AND RUSH: Cry?

SADE: Just boo-hooin' away. [*To phone*] There's no call for any foolishness like that, Mr. Powers. If you feel that . . . What? What'll become of your poor little bicycle now? I'm *serious* about this. I'd appreciate it very much if you'd vacate the first of . . . What? You will? Thank you very much, Mr. Powers. I'm sorry things didn't turn out . . . What? All right then. All right then, Mr. Powers. Good-by.

[*Hangs up*]

VIC: Did he say he'd get out?

SADE: Yes.

VIC: Did he sound very sad?

SADE: No. Such a smart-aleck he is. Said he'd get out December first like I asked, but he'd rather not talk about it any more now. His heart was too full.

RUSH: Shucks.

SADE: You really think I done the right thing, Vic?

VIC: Sure.

SADE: It oughta be easy for him to find another place for his bicycle.

VIC: Of course.

45

SADE: [*Going*] Well, I'm glad it's over. I can't abide trouble an' hard feelings with people. I like to have everything smooth an' . . .
  [*Fade*]

VIC: [*To Rush*] Whose play?

RUSH: Yours.

VIC: I'll take this king of hearts. An' *with* this king of hearts I expect to . . . Whatcha laughin' at?

RUSH: What *you* laughin' at?

VIC: Oh, this an' that.

RUSH: I'm laughin' at this and' that *too*.

VIC: Well, let's not hold up the game. *I've* played. It's your turn. Shoot.

END OF SCRIPT

ANNOUNCER: Vic, Sade, and young Rush invite you to tune in for them every time they're on the air. They'd like to think of you as regular members of their family circle.

1934

MILDRED TISDEL'S
MEMORY BOOK

ANNOUNCER: Opening announcement and credits.

[*Pause*]

INTRODUCTION: It is early evening as our scene opens now, and here in the living-room we find Vic and Sade comfortably established with newspaper and sewing basket. Vic, who has apparently come across an interesting item, looks up and says to his wife . . .

VIC: Much colder tonight.

SADE: That what the weather man says?

VIC: Yeah.

SADE: Better bank the fire good before you go to bed, an' leave the damper half-way open.

VIC: Another blanket or two might not be amiss either.

SADE: Oh, we'll be warm enough.

VIC: I don't wanta go prowlin' around *lookin'* for blankets in the middle of the night.

SADE: Did you *ever? I'm* always the fall guy when it comes to . . . [*Phone*] I'll get it.

VIC: Prob'ly doctor Rush wantin' to know if he can't stay over to Heinie's house an hour or so longer.

SADE: [*To phone*] Hello? Yes. Oh, hello, Mr. Kneesuffer. Rush? No, he's not. I think he's over at Call's house playin' with Heinie. Yes. Is there anything I can . . . Oh. Oh, I see. Well, I imagine . . . Uh-huh. Yes. How are *you,* Mr. Kneesuffer? *That's* good. Oh, we're all just hunky-dory. Yes. All right, Mr. Kneesuffer. Good-by.

[*Hangs up*]

VIC: What's bitin' *him?*

SADE: He sent Rush down town after some cigars forty-five minutes ago an' he hasn't showed up yet.

VIC: Doesn't sound like our young son has been faithful to his sacred trust.

SADE: Oh, Mr. Kneesuffer ain't *mad.* Just thought maybe Rush had forgot or somethin'.

VIC: Probably dropped in for a quiet chat with his pal Julius down at the shoe-shining parlor.

SADE: Lands, I hope it don't turn *too* cold. I'd like to see it wait till *December* before . . . Listen.

VIC: A door opens in the distance?

SADE: Uh-huh. Rush. I was gonna say I hope it don't turn *too* cold. A person gets enough winter in the months of December an' January clear up to April. I saw Mis' Freeston in the grocery store today an' she said her sister in Omaha, Nebraska . . . (raises voice) Hello there.

RUSH: Hi, mom. Gov.

VIC: Hi.

SADE: Say, Mr. Kneesuffer's lookin' for you. He just called up an' wanted to know . . .

RUSH: Yeah—about the cigars. Gonna run over with 'em in just a minute. Hey, look what I got.

SADE: Book?

RUSH: Yeah. Betcha can't guess what kind.

SADE: No, I can't. Vic, like I started to say, I saw Mis' Freeston in the grocery store this morning an' . . .

RUSH: Ah—excuse me, mom.

SADE: Whatcha want?

RUSH: Are you an' gov very busy?

SADE: We're just sittin' here.

RUSH: Would you like to help me a little while?

SADE: What doin'?

RUSH: Show ya soon as I get this book unwrapped.

SADE: What's in the other package—Mr. Kneesuffer's cigars?

RUSH: Yeah.

SADE: Long as he called *up* about 'em, he prob'ly *wants* 'em.

RUSH: *I* don't think he's in any hurry. He was smokin' a great big long cigar when I left his house. Anyway I gotta get somethin' *else* outa the way first. Somethin' important.

SADE: Well, you know Mr. Kneesuffer's *temper*. Tickle him on the wrong side an' . . . (sees an attractive object) Oh, what's that?

RUSH: Memory book. Ain't it pretty?

SADE: Yes. Let's see.

VIC: Going in for memory books now, Oscar?

RUSH: No, this is Mildred's.

VIC: I was gonna *say:* when a son of mine almost ready for long pants brings home darling little . . .

SADE: See, Vic. Ain't it cute?

VIC: Sweet.

SADE: Says on the front 'Fragrant Memories'. All in little gold letters. Mildred's, you say, son?

RUSH: Yeah. You an' gov wanta help me fill it up with junk?

SADE: Fill it up with junk?

RUSH: Write different stuff in it an' sign peoples' names?

SADE: How ya mean?

RUSH: Well, here's how it is: I promised Mildred I'd take her memory book home an' doctor it up so it'd look like she had a lot of high class friends. Catch on?

SADE: No.

RUSH: Babe Ruth an' Mary Pickford an' Henry Ford an' different guys?

SADE: Don't know what you're talkin' about, son.

RUSH: I'll explain it to ya. All the girls in Mildred's Sunday school class got memory books like this. They go around an' get people to write poetry an' dope inside, ya know.

SADE: Yes.

RUSH: An' sign their names underneath?

SADE: Yes. Usta have a memory book myself when I was little.

RUSH: Uh-huh. Well, Mildred had one just like everybody else but come to find out Bernice Miller's memory book laid hers all in the shade.

SADE: Laid it in the shade?

RUSH: Bernice got her dad to get *important* guys to write in her memory book—the mayor, an' the fire-chief, an' Mr. Mackalhany down at the bank, ya know?

SADE: Yes?

RUSH: An' all *Mildred's* got is names of *neighbors* an' *school*-teachers an' relations.

SADE: Oh.

RUSH: An' when Bernice got to rubbin' it in about how much better her memory book was than Mildred's, Mildred bought *this* one an' asked me to fix it up so it'd make *Bernice's* look like thirty cents.

SADE: Well . . . a . . . how ya gonna do it?

RUSH: Have you an' gov write stuff in here an' sign some names.

SADE: [*Who has a feeling there's dishonesty involved*] But that wouldn't be quite . . . I mean Mildred'd be . . .

RUSH: Oh, it's *cheatin'* in a way. But that Bernice Miller's got it *comin'*. Will ya do it? I told Mildred I'd have her memory book all doctored up an' over to her house by ten o'clock.

SADE: Vic, you been listenin' to this?

VIC: With half an ear.

RUSH: You understand what I *want,* don'tcha gov?

VIC: You'd like to have your mother an' myself indite some tender thoughts in yonder memory book an' then forge a few signatures.

RUSH: Yeah. Babe Ruth an' Mary Pickford an' Henry Ford an' different guys.

VIC: It's a penitentiary offense.

51

RUSH: Naw. It's perfectly O.K. Mildred just *wants* it so she can get a toe-hold on Bernice Miller. She ain't gonna show it to anybody else. Whatcha say?

VIC: *I'll* help out a friend. Would *you* like to involve yourself in a little low treachery, Sade?

SADE: I don't want to ruin this pretty *book* with foolishness.

RUSH: *You* won't ruin it, mom. Look: we'll figure out what we're gonna put inside on some scratch paper, an' then write it in the memory book real neat *afterwards*. Gov, is that scratch paper *you* got there?

VIC: Uh-huh, an' I already got a sentiment ready.

RUSH: What is it?

VIC: 'Am having a fine time in the White House. Wish you were here. Franklin D. Roosevelt.'

RUSH: Naw.

VIC: What's the matter with that?

RUSH: Bernice'd catch *on* it was a fake. Make up one with somebody else.

VIC: 'All day through I think of you'?

RUSH: Who?

VIC: Yoo-hoo?

RUSH: I mean what name ya gonna sign?

VIC: John D. Rockefeller?

RUSH: Ye-ah . . . but . . . but I think ya better not put that in about 'all day through I think of you'. Sounds kinda fishy, John D. Rockefeller writin' that to Mildred Tisdel.

VIC: Maybe it does. I'll try again.

RUSH: *You* wanta help, mom?

SADE: I don't think this is bein' very *honest,* son.

RUSH: *It's* honest enough . . . Mildred just gettin' back at Bernice. C'mon—think up some junk.

SADE: Why don't you just let gov an' me write our *own* names in the book?

RUSH: [*Hesitantly*] We-el, I . . . I don't hardly think . . . a . . .

SADE: Guess we're not *important* enough.

RUSH: You're important enough to *me,* y'understand, mom, but . . . a . . . but *Mildred* wants . . .

SADE: [*Giggles*] *I* catch on.

RUSH: Shall I get you some scratch paper an' a pencil?

SADE: If I think of anything, I'll tell gov an' *he* can write it down.

RUSH: O.K. How ya comin', gov?

VIC: Fine. 'I hope you enjoyed the box of fudge I sent you. Henry Ford.' How's that?

SADE: [*Laughs*] Oh, gracious.

VIC: Whatcha think of it, Pete?

RUSH: It's O.K. but . . . but wouldn't it be better to make it somethin' else besides fudge? Fudge sounds like maybe Henry Ford *made* it.

VIC: All the better.

RUSH: Henry Ford prob'ly don't make much fudge to send people.

VIC: *Chocolates* then.

RUSH: Yeah—chocolates. An' listen: let's make it so Mildred sent *him* the chocolates. Sound more like the straight dope.

VIC: O.K. 'I certainly enjoyed the box of chocolates you sent. Henry Ford.'

RUSH: Swell. *You* got any, mom?

SADE: [*Laughs*] No, I haven't.

RUSH: Wish you'd *try*. I hafta get five or six, an' I promised Mildred I'd have her memory book *back* by ten o'clock.

SADE: Five or six names won't even make a *dent* in this big memory book.

RUSH: Oh, there's gonna be lots more. Later on in the evening, Mildred's *father's* gonna help out.

SADE: Oh, he is?

RUSH: Sure. Ya see it'd look like a *hoax* if all the names were in the same *handwriting*. [*Lifts voice*] Gov.

VIC: Uh-huh.

RUSH: Remember that.

VIC: Remember what?

RUSH: When ya start writin' the junk in the *book,* make all the handwriting *different*.

VIC: Science tells us it's *impossible* to disguise our . . .

RUSH: Bernice'll never know the difference. Just make some of the names plain an' some with curlicues.

VIC: O.K.

RUSH: Got any more?

VIC: A few.

RUSH: What are they?

VIC: 'I shall never forget that afternoon we spent together in New York. Mary Pickford.'

RUSH: Mildred's never *been* to New York.

VIC: Chicago?

RUSH: Never been there either.

VIC: Funk's Grove?

RUSH: Let's not *make* it a town. Let's make it some place like the *park,* or the . . . Oh, *I* know,—the *depot.* The Illinois Central Depot.

VIC: 'I shall never forget the afternoon we spent together in the Illinois Central Depot. Mary Pickford.'

RUSH: Dandy. Gives the impression maybe Mildred met her at the train.

VIC: Uh-huh.

RUSH: Got any more?

VIC: 'My wife an' I hope to see you for a few minutes at Christmas time. Charles A. Lindbergh.'

RUSH: No-o, I don't believe Bernice would believe . . .

VIC: Governor Horner?

RUSH: No-o.

VIC: S. P. Henderson?

RUSH: Who's he?

VIC: County Clerk down at the court-house.

RUSH: Mildred could prob'ly get *his* name anyway. Let's try an' think up some guy that . . .

[*Phone*]

SADE: There's Mr. Kneesuffer again. *I'll* bet twenty-five cents. Answer it, son.

RUSH: Yeah. Gov, how about Mickey Cochrane, manager of the Detroit Tigers?

VIC: He oughta do.

RUSH: Write him down. [*To phone*] Hello? Yes, speaking. Oh, hello, Mr. Kneesuffer. Ya see, I was delayed because I hadda do something that . . . Yeah. All right Mr. Kneesuffer. Yes, sir. Goodby.

[*Hangs up*]

SADE: Was he crabby?

RUSH: Yeah. Gov, I thought of somebody *else* that . . .

SADE: Rush, does he want his cigars?

RUSH: Yeah.

SADE: Why dontcha take 'em *over* then?

RUSH: I wanta get these names first an' call up Mildred an' tell her we're gettin' along O.K.

SADE: I bet he just bites your head off.

RUSH: Oh, no. Heck, he just *likes* to be crabby. He's *smokin'* a cigar a yard long. What'd ya write down, gov?

VIC: 'My wife an' I hope to see you for a few minutes at Christmas time. Mickey Cochrane.'

RUSH: Better put down 'Manager of Detroit Tigers'. Bernice might not get the connection.

VIC: All right.

RUSH: Who all we got now?

VIC: Ah—Mickey Cochrane, Mary Pickford, Henry Ford, an' John D. Rockefeller.

RUSH: What'd ya have *him* say?

VIC: Rockefeller? 'I shall never forget the afternoon we spent together in the Chicago an' Alton depot.'

RUSH: That's what ya had Mary *Pickford* say.

VIC: In *her* case, we used Illinois *Central* depot.

RUSH: They're too much alike, gov. Gives the impression Mildred's always hangin' around the railroad tracks.

VIC: I'll dope out something else.

RUSH: We got four now. If you can fix up two more, we'll have six an' that'll be enough.

VIC: I'll turn the gray matter loose.

RUSH: *You* thought of any, mom?

SADE: No. But I've thought of *this:* why don't you hike on over to Mr. Kneesuffer's?

RUSH: *I* will in half a second. Just wanta get this off my mind.

SADE: Looks to me like you're just gonna out-an'-out *spoil* this pretty book.

RUSH: Naw. *Gov'll* write the names in neat an' nice. Maybe *you'd* like to copy some?

SADE: Don't believe I wanta have anything to do with it.

RUSH: It'd help make the *handwriting* look different.

SADE: Sounds like an awful *tricky* business to *me.*

RUSH: Not at *all,* mom. Mildred's got a *right* to get back at Bernice for all the . . .

VIC: O.K., Charley.

RUSH: Got the rest of 'em?

VIC: Yeah. I'll let you pass judgment.

RUSH: All right.

VIC: 'Thank you very much for your last letter. We were very much pleased to hear you are all well. John D. Rockefeller.'

RUSH: Fine.

VIC: 'I shall never forget the afternoon we spent together in the Chicago, Burlington, an' Quincy . . .

RUSH: Aw. ▬

VIC: [*Chuckles*] Take it back. 'I shall never forget the pleasant little chat we had last August. Ethel Barrymore.'

RUSH: Swell.

VIC: 'Sincerely hope the lilies-of-the-valley I sent you arrived in good condition. Strangler Lewis.'

RUSH: Dandy.

SADE: Gracious!

RUSH: *That* makes six, don't it?

VIC: Yeah.

RUSH: Will ya start copyin' 'em in the memory book now?

VIC: Sure.

RUSH: O.K. An' mom I wish *you'd* help . . .

    [*Phone*]

SADE: Go see what Mr. Kneesuffer's got to say *now,* Rush.

RUSH: Shucks, just because a guy don't break his neck bringin' over a few . . . [*To phone*] Hello? Oh, hello, Mildred. Yeah. Got six of 'em. Peachy ones too. We're just about to copy 'em in the memory book an' . . . [*Door-bell in the distance*] [*To his folks*] Door-bell.

SADE: *We* heard it. Go see, Vic.

VIC: [*Going*] Pretty late for callers.

RUSH: [*To phone*] Mildred? I said we're just about to copy the junk in the memory book. Yeah. Wanta hear some of 'em? O.K. 'Thank you very much for your last letter. We were very much pleased to hear you are all well. John D. Rockefeller.' How ya like that? Uh-huh, *I* thought it was fine. Here's another—"Sincerely hope the lillies-of-the-valley I sent you arrived in good . . .

VIC: Rush.

RUSH: [*To phone*] Just a second, Mildred.[*To Vic*] Yeah, Gov?

VIC: There's a gentleman at the door to see you.

RUSH: Who?

VIC: Mr. Kneesuffer.

RUSH: Oh—well, I put his cigars there on the . . .

VIC: He's *got* his cigars. I just gave 'em to him. But he says if it's convenient he'd like to speak to you *personally.*

END OF SCRIPT

ANNOUNCER: We'll withdraw now, Rush, so as not to embarrass you during your interview with Mr. Kneesuffer. And we're a little afraid it *is* going to be an embarrassing interview.

1934

CASTING THE PAGEANT "SHINING WATERS FLOWING TO THE SEA"

THEME

ANNOUNCER: Once again we'd like to ask you to come with us to the house half-way up in the next block—where Vic and Sade live. [*Pause*] It is late afternoon as our scene opens now, and here in the living room is young Rush. He's been home from school only a short while, and surprisingly enough he's at the library table *studying* . . . instead of playing baseball over in Seymour's vacant lot. And here's a newcomer. The newcomer is Vic . . . who says . . .

VIC: Well-a-day.

RUSH: Hi, gov.

VIC: You're not studyin'?

RUSH: Yeah.

VIC: The world is full of wonderful things.

RUSH: I'm studyin' *now* so I can go to the movies *tonight*.

VIC: I knew there must be *some* ulterior motive.

RUSH: Thanks.

VIC: Are you in a frame of mind for some news?

RUSH: Sure.

VIC: Well, sir, your old man has been signally honored this day.

RUSH: Yeah?

VIC: I suppose you've heard of Mrs. L. J. Driscoll of the East Side?

RUSH: The rich people?

VIC: Right. This afternoon that same Mrs. Driscoll phoned me up with a request that I appear at her *house* tonight.

RUSH: The great big house on Chester Avenue?

VIC: The great big house on Chester Avenue. Where's mom?

RUSH: I dunno. I just got home myself.

VIC: Won't *she* fall over when she hears the news?

RUSH: What's Mrs. Driscoll want ya for?

VIC: I have nothing to conceal; I'll *tell* ya.

RUSH: [*Chuckles*] She *stuck* on ya?

VIC: She didn't say. However, I'll disclose what I know of the matter. Mrs. Driscoll is putting on a pageant an' your pop has been asked to take one of the principal parts in it.

RUSH: You're gonna be in a play, huh?

VIC: Right. Tonight promptly at seven I appear at the Driscoll mansion for the first rehearsal.

RUSH: Whatcha gonna *be* in the play?

VIC: The Voice of the Congo.

RUSH: [*Chuckles*] What?

VIC: There's nothing humorous about this, Ralph.

59

RUSH: The Congo is a *river*.

VIC: Mrs. Driscoll is aware of that.

RUSH: She's gonna give a play about a river, huh?

VIC: A play about *many* rivers. It's called "Shining Waters Flowing to the Sea." The idea is that the whole world is a network of streams. *Somewhere* all these streams join one another. That kinda makes us all cousins, see?

RUSH: No.

VIC: Well, it does. Reflect.

RUSH: Huh?

VIC: Think about it. Ya know the Mackinaw River, don'tcha?

RUSH: Sure.

VIC: Well, the Mackinaw flows into the Illinois: the Illinois flows into the Mississippi; the Mississippi flows into the Gulf of Mexico; the Gulf of Mexico also receives the turbid waters of the Snake, the Rio Grande, an' the White. All these flow into the Pacific Ocean an' join, through devious routes, the Nile, the Niger, the Amazon, an' the Elbe. Follow me?

RUSH: No.

VIC: It matters little. Nevertheless, by means of all these shining ribbons of water, every man on earth is joined by strong bonds to every *other* man on earth.

RUSH: [*Neg.*] Uh-uh.

VIC: They are *too,* I tell ya.

RUSH: I mean I don't understand it.

VIC: It isn't important that you do. The point *is* that your old man has been selected to take the part of the "Voice of the Congo."

RUSH: I . . . I guess that's pretty good.

VIC: I hope to snort. Wait'll your *mother* hears about me goin' over to brush elbows with the folks on Chester Avenue.

RUSH: Do what?

VIC: Hob-nob. You may have occasion to *remember* this day, son. It marks the time when the doors to high society were laid open to admit your father, a humble toiler in the vineyard, a simple soul, whose only ambition was to . . .

RUSH: Here comes mom.

VIC: Huh?

RUSH: Mom's comin' in the back door.

VIC: Oh. Well, listen, let *me* break the news. You just don't say nothin', see?

RUSH: About Mrs. Driscoll, ya mean?

VIC: Yeah.

60

RUSH: Is the Voice of the Congo s'pose to . . .

VIC: Sh. [*Raises voice*] Sade?

SADE: [*Answers*] Yes. It's me.

VIC: [*To Rush*] *I'll* do the tellin', Albert.

RUSH: *I* wasn't gonna . . .

SADE: [*Entering*] You home *too,* son?

RUSH: Yeah. Thought I'd study now so I could go to the movies with Fat tonight.

SADE: Oh, uh-huh. Say, Vic, I got somethin' to tell ya.

VIC: [*Supercilious laugh*]

SADE: What's the matter?

VIC: Nothin'.

SADE: What'd ya laugh for?

VIC: I got a little somethin' to tell, myself.

SADE: What?

VIC: It can wait. [*Lofty chuckle*] It can wait.

SADE: Well, what is it?

VIC: Not a word, son.

RUSH: *I* wasn't gonna say nothin'.

SADE: Vic.

VIC: Uh-huh.

SADE: How would you like to take in a roomer?

VIC: Roomer?

SADE: Yes. [*Hurriedly*] Listen, now, an' don't be mad. I was over to Mis' Call's just now, an' I got a chance to take in a roomer . . . Mis' Call's brother.

VIC: What do we want with a roomer?

SADE: I could use the money, an' that front room upstairs is just goin' to waste. We could have a roomer in there just as well as not. I could clean up after three just as easy as after *two.* An' he's a *real* nice young man.

VIC: *We* don't want any roomer.

SADE: Why not? Just for the summer. Listen: he's just gonna be here a few months. He's gonna teach the chemistry at high school.

RUSH: The what, mom?

SADE: The chemistry. Whatcha say, Vic?

VIC: Roomers are more trouble than they're worth.

SADE: I don't see why. Think of the extra dollars.

VIC: Roomers are always around under foot.

SADE: *No.* You'd never even *see* him. He could use the back door.

VIC: You wouldn't make any money.

SADE: I would too.

VIC: Got to give him soap an' towels—heat—electricity.

SADE: I'll get a pencil an' figure up.

VIC: *We* don't want any roomer.

SADE: I bet you'd *like* him. *Elton* his name is. Elton Wheeney. He's comin' over this evening.

VIC: He is?

SADE: Don't be mad. He's just gonna drop in a minute on his way home from the chemistry. I told him I'd talk it over with you. Gimme your pencil.

VIC: What for?

SADE: Wanta figure out the money I'll make.

VIC: Listen, kiddo, I won't be *home* this evening.

SADE: You won't? Oh, that's *right*—you an' the junkman are gonna get that load of dirt for the back yard.

VIC: Nope—we're not. I hafta call up the junkman an' tell him the date's *off*. I'm goin' somewhere else.

SADE: Where?

VIC: Your *head'll* fall off when you hear.

SADE: Where you goin'?

VIC: At seven o'clock tonight I make a social call on Mrs. A. J. Driscoll.

SADE: On Chester Avenue?

VIC: On Chester Avenue.

SADE: What for?

VIC: [*Lofty chuckle*]

SADE: What for?

RUSH: He's gonna be the Voice of the . . .

VIC: [*Coming out of his laugh*] *I'll* tell this, Rush. Sade, tonight I consort with the blue-bloods. Mrs. A. J. Driscoll has personally selected me to take a prominent part in a high society pageant soon to be given at her residence.

SADE: Really?

VIC: Fact. Received the telephone call this afternoon.

SADE: Well, what do you know!

VIC: I shall in all probability brush elbows with the elect.

SADE: What kind of a thing is it?

VIC: The pageant, you mean?

SADE: Yes.

VIC: I expect it'll be a royal affair. I expect . . .

RUSH: Gov's gonna be the Voice of the Congo.

VIC: *I'll* tell this, if you please.

SADE: Whatcha gonna be?

VIC: I'm going to take the part of the Voice of the Congo in a pageant called "Shining Waters Flowing to the Sea."

SADE: A sort of a *show,* huh?

VIC: You might call it that, yes.

SADE: What kind of a show is it?

VIC: I'll tell ya: the world is covered with rivers. Ain't it?

SADE: Why?

VIC: Don't say why.

SADE: I don't know what you're talkin' about.

RUSH: [*Chuckling*] Neither did *I.* Gov started to tell *me* about . . .

VIC: Son.

RUSH: Yes.

VIC: Silence. *Now,* Sade:—all the rivers in the world have a common meeting place, haven't they?

SADE: Honest, I don't know what . . .

VIC: Let me *finish,* why don'tcha?

SADE: Well, you ask me silly questions about . . .

VIC: I'm tryin' to *tell* you somethin'.

SADE: Well, go *on.* Goodness.

VIC: I'll make it simple for ya. You know the Mackinaw River?

SADE: No.

VIC: Aw, ya do too.

SADE: I know where it *is,* yes.

VIC: Very good. Where does it flow?

RUSH: It flows . . .

VIC: Let *mom* tell this. Where does it flow, Sade?

SADE: Somewhere between here an' Peoria, don't it?

VIC: I mean into what body of water does it empty?

SADE: I didn't know it *emptied* into any . . .

VIC: Forget it. You can figure it out when you see the show.

SADE: Did Mrs. Driscoll call you up herself?

VIC: Personally.

SADE: Think of that! An' they're gonna put on the thing at her house?

VIC: So I was given to understand.

SADE: What time you s'posed to be there, did ya say?

VIC: Rehearsal starts prompt at seven.

SADE: Gracious!

VIC: Whatcha think of the old man *now?*

SADE: I got half a notion to call up Ruthie an' tell her.

VIC: Don't bother. She'll prob'ly see my name in the society notes. I s'pose she *reads* the society notes.

SADE: Oh, sure.

VIC: [*Patronizing*] Uh-huh.

SADE: When do you *give* your thing?

VIC: Early in May.

SADE: Well . . . a . . . That is . . . I s'pose Rush an' *me* can come?

VIC: I see no objection.

SADE: [*Giggles*] Mrs. Driscoll will prob'ly make *us* stay out on the lawn, hey, son?

RUSH: I was *in* the basement once. Hoddy Miller's dad is second gardener.

VIC: *I'll* see that my family is taken care of.

SADE: You want to dress up nice tonight, Vic.

VIC: I shall.

SADE: Wear the shirt with the little stripe an' the tie you got from Aunt Bess.

VIC: We'll see.

SADE: Think of that: callin' on Mrs. Driscoll on Chester Avenue.

VIC: [*Lofty laugh*]

SADE: Ya know, I think I'll call up Ruthie. She'll just fall through the floor.

VIC: [*Lofty laugh*]

SADE: Wish you'd tell me more about what kind of a thing it is, so if she *asks.*

VIC: Just tell her it's a pageant called "Shining Waters Flowing to the Sea."

SADE: An' you're what?

VIC: The Voice of the Congo.

SADE: Is that . . . is that a pretty important part?

VIC: I judge it is. The Congo is one of our principal rivers.

RUSH: It's one of *Africa's* principal rivers, gov.

VIC: Listen, Sam, when I want . . .

SADE: Oh, say, don't forget to call up the junkman. You got a date with him, ya know.

VIC: [*Lofty laugh*] Life's irony. I hafta break a date with the junk man to fill an engagement with Mrs. A. J. Driscoll.

SADE: Well, I hafta hand it to ya . . . gettin' invited to that place. Why, there's people in this town'd give their right ear.

64

VIC: [*Laughs*] *I* know. *I* know. Well, I must call up the junk man. I must . . .

SADE: Wait a minute before you do that. What we gonna do about Mr. Wheeney?

VIC: Who?

SADE: The young man that's comin' here this evening.

VIC: Dismiss him.

SADE: Vic, I think we oughta *take* him. It'd just be for the summer. I could *use* them extra dollars.

VIC: We want no roomers.

SADE: I don't see why we *don't*.

VIC: Roomers are constantly under foot.

SADE: How do you know? We never had roomers before. Why, I bet I could . . . give me your pencil.

VIC: I haven't got any on me.

RUSH: Here's one, mom.

SADE: Thanks. Now look, Vic.

VIC: You'll excuse me? I must call up the junk man.

SADE: I wanta show you somethin'.

VIC: Really, kiddo, I'm quite busy. I hafta call up the junk man an' then get myself ready to go over on Chester Avenue.

SADE: This won't take but a minute.

VIC: Have you *forgotten* that I have a date over on Chester Avenue?

SADE: Seems to me you're pretty stuck up about it.

VIC: [*Lofty laugh*] Maybe so. Maybe so.

SADE: Well, I hafta tell Mr. Wheeney *somethin'* when he comes.

VIC: Tell him we want no roomers.

SADE: I can't tell him that. Wish *you* were gonna be here. Bet if you *met* him, you'd *want* him for a roomer.

VIC: Tell him I'm over on Chester Avenue. Callin' on the Driscolls.

SADE: Guess all we're gonna hear from now on is Chester Avenue.

VIC: [*Lofty laugh*]

SADE: Shall I tell him . . . [*Phone*] Answer it, son.

VIC: I'm goin' upstairs, Sade; if it's Mrs. Driscoll on the phone, just . . .

SADE: If you'll wait a minute, you can *see* who it is.

RUSH: [*At phone*] Hello. Yes. Yes, this is Rush Gook speaking. Oh—uh-huh. Why, yes. Sure. Uh-huh. Seven o'clock? All right. Certainly. Yes, Ma'am. Thank you. Good-by. [*Hangs up*]

VIC AND SADE: Who was it?

The Small House Half-way Up in the Next Block

RUSH: Mrs. Driscoll over on Chester Avenue.
VIC AND SADE: No.
RUSH: Yeah.
VIC AND SADE: What'd she want?
RUSH: Wants me in her show.
VIC: Not kiddin' us?
RUSH: *No.* I'm the Mississippi River an' her tributaries.
SADE: *Really,* son?
RUSH: Sure. I'm s'posed to be there seven o'clock. Gov.
VIC: Huh?
RUSH: I can walk over with *you.*
VIC: [*Disturbed*] Yeah.
SADE: Well, lands, Vic, guess you're not the *only* fish in the sea.
VIC: No.
RUSH: An' I'm the *Mississippi* river. That's *lots* bigger'n the *Congo.*
SADE: [*Giggling*] That's right, Vic.
VIC: What's so funny?
SADE: You been blowin' about how Mis' Driscoll invited you to . . .
VIC: Heck, don't you see through that?
SADE: See through what?
VIC: Rush gettin' to go along.
SADE: I s'pose they need somebody to be the Mississippi River.
VIC: Sure. Well, the reason Mrs. Driscoll invited *Rush* is because he's my little boy.
SADE: Oh, is that it?
VIC: Why of course. Plain as day. *Evidently* she's tryin' to get in good with me.
SADE: Looks like it all right. If she wasn't a grandmother I'd be jealous.
VIC: You *oughta* be *proud.* Your husband an' young son received as old friends on Chester Avenue.
SADE: I *am* proud.
VIC: Guess I'll go upstairs now an' start gettin' ready to . . .
SADE: Wait a minute. What we gonna do about Mr. Wheeney?
VIC: *Forget* Mr. Wheeney.
SADE: He's *comin'* this evening an' he'll wanta *know.*
VIC: Tell him we want no roomers.
SADE: But, Vic, *I* think . . . [*Phone*]
RUSH: I'll get it.

66

VIC: [*To Sade*] Tell Mr. Wheeney to call around when your husband's home. Tell him I'm absent tonight filling an engagement on Chester Avenue.

RUSH: [*To phone*] Hello. Yes. Just a second. [*To Sade*] Mom.

SADE: Who is it?

RUSH: Some man.

SADE: All right.

RUSH: Hey, gov.

VIC: Yeah?

RUSH: The Mississippi's a heck of a lot bigger'n the Congo.

VIC: Don't brag. The thing for *you* to do is take a bath an' be shining bright for this evening. You want to make a good impression.

SADE: [*To phone*] Yes? Oh, yes. Uh-huh. Oh, I see. Certainly. Perfectly all right. Of course. Surely. Uh-huh. You bet. Good-by. [*Hangs up*] [*To Vic*] Well, we don't hafta worry about Mr. Wheeney.

VIC: Ain't he comin'?

SADE: No. He's busy this evening.

VIC: Spares us bother and embarrassment.

SADE: Know where he's *going* this evening?

VIC: No.

SADE: He's going over to Mrs. Driscoll's on Chester Avenue.

VIC: The heck he is.

SADE: Yes. He's gonna be in some sort of a show. Takes the part of the Breath of the Euphrates.

VIC: You're foolin'.

SADE: No.

VIC: Whatcha know about that?

SADE: [*Devilishly*] Must be a real high-society doin's. Mr. Wheeney just got to *town* this afternoon. Already he's been asked to take the part of the breath of the Euphrates.

RUSH: The Mississippi's a heck of a lot bigger'n the Euphrates. The Mississippi . . .

VIC: Quiet, Rush. Listen, Sade, who *is* this Wheeney guy?

SADE: Just a young man from the country that's gonna teach the chemistry.

VIC: Yeah, I *know,* but . . . but he must be *somebody.*

SADE: He's just Mis' Call's young brother.

VIC: Just the same . . . Listen, you know what I bet?

SADE: What?

VIC: What time were you *talkin'* to him?

SADE: I dunno. Came right home from there.

67

VIC: I just wonder if . . . Ya don't s'pose he's noised it around town he's gonna live here an' Mrs. Driscoll's *heard* about it, do ya?

SADE: Don't see how *that* could be.

VIC: I just betcha it got out he's gonna room here, an' Mrs. Driscoll got wind of it an' . . . whatcha laughin' at?

SADE: You an' your high society.

VIC: Listen, sister, you may or may not know that . . . [*Phone*] Answer that.

RUSH: Yeah.

SADE: [*Giggling*] That oughta be pretty nice.

VIC: What?

SADE: If Mr. Wheeney comes to room with us we'll have the Voice of the Congo an' the Mississippi an' her tributaries an' the Breath of the Euphrates all under one roof.

VIC: Yeah, well . . .

SADE: Sh.

RUSH: [*At phone*] Yes. Yes, sir. Uh-huh. O.K. Oh. Uh-huh. Uh-huh. Yeah, I'll tell him. Yes, sir.

[*Hangs up*]

VIC: Who was that?

RUSH: The junk man.

VIC: What'd he want?

RUSH: He can't have the date with you tonight.

VIC: No?

RUSH: No. He's going over to Mrs. Driscoll's on Chester Avenue.

VIC: [*Hollowly*] Yeah?

RUSH: Yeah. He's gonna be Moonlight on the Ganges.

END OF SCRIPT

ANNOUNCER: And so we conclude our brief interlude with Vic, Sade, and young Rush.

Undated

RUSH BRINGS IN
ROOSTER'S PANTS
FOR MENDING

THEME
ANNOUNCER: OPENING AND COMMERCIAL CREDITS
INTRODUCTION: It's a few minutes after ten o'clock in the morning as our scene opens now, and here in the kitchen we find the lady of the house busy at her ironing board. The *man* of the house is present too—doing a little office work at home. And at this particular moment he's saying to his wife . . .

VIC: Take a look out the window.

SADE: I just did. Some blizzard.

VIC: I'll say.

SADE: If this keeps up we'll have our white Christmas all right.

VIC: If this keeps up we'll have a white Fourth of *July*. Never *seen* so much snow.

SADE: Soon as it lets up you better get out your shovel an' scoop off the walks.

VIC: Yeah.

SADE: [*Giggles*] Saw the mail-man go by a while ago. His face was so red from the cold an' his mustache so white from the snow he looked like . . . Somebody stompin' their feet on the back porch.

VIC: Gas-meter guy, I expect.

SADE: Uh-huh. Now why don't he go down the *cellar* door? Traipsin' through a person's kitchen with feet all over . . . [*Door opens*] *Well*.

RUSH: Hi, mom. Gov.

VIC: Hello.

RUSH: [*Giggles*] Talk about your *winter*-time.

SADE: What *you* doin' home at ten o'clock?

RUSH: It's recess. Rooster Davis an' me ran through the blizzard to see if you'd sew up his pants. He tore 'em. Will ya?

SADE: Where *are* his pants?

RUSH: Got 'em here under my overcoat.

SADE: Where's *he?*

RUSH: Out in the shed.

SADE: Without any pants on?

RUSH: Yeah. He's kinda bashful, see. Didn't like to come in the house. *Here's* the pants. See the terrible rip?

SADE: How'd he do that?

RUSH: Leaned up against a telephone pole that had a nail in it. Will ya fix the pants?

SADE: Oh, I s'pose. Listen, though, *you* boys won't have time to get back to school before recess is over, will ya?

RUSH: No, but that's O.K. Under circumstances like these, Mis' Kinney'll excuse us.

SADE: Is Rooster sittin' out there in his bare legs?

RUSH: Sure.

SADE: Run out an' tell him to come in the house. He'll freeze.

RUSH: He don't *wanta* come in. He's *bashful* without his pants on.

SADE: Is he wearin' long underwear?

RUSH: No. Short.

SADE: Go down cellar an' take him out some overalls or somethin'. Tell him he can sit upstairs till I've fixed his pants.

RUSH: O.K. Guess he'll agree to *that*. [*Moving off*] Can ya sew up the rip all right?

SADE: I can baste it with coarse thread so it'll hold till his mother can sew it on the machine.

RUSH: [*Off*] I'll tell him.

SADE: [*Raises voice*] If ya go out the cellar door, be sure an' close it again good an' tight.

RUSH: [*Off*] Yeah.

SADE: [*To Vic, giggling*] How'd *you* like to sit out in that shed without any pants on?

VIC: Don't believe I'd care for it.

SADE: Such notions kids get. Vic, will ya open the drawer an' hand me the needle an' thread that's there?

VIC: Uh-huh.

SADE: Did ya *see* this rip?

VIC: No.

SADE: Look.

VIC: Gosh.

SADE: Mighta killed himself on that nail.

VIC: Are they good pants?

SADE: Just corduroy. Old ones at that.

VIC: This what you want?

SADE: Uh-huh. Thimble there too?

VIC: Yeah.

SADE: It's a wonder children ever grow *up* they expose themselves to so many dangers. *Girls* is the *safest*.

VIC: Um.

SADE: An' still *they* do crazy things *too*. You know Mis' Hemstreet's Lois May, don'tcha?

VIC: I guess so.

72

SADE: She's the one in between Geraldine an' Grace. With the brace on her teeth?

VIC: Uh-huh.

SADE: She's as bad as any boy that ever lived. Guess what her mother caught her doin' the other night.

VIC: Couldn't imagine.

SADE: Caught her hoppin' street cars.

VIC: Yeah?

SADE: True as I'm standin' here. They live on the Market Street car line, ya know, an' when the car'd slow down to make that turn, Lois May'd run out an' jump on the back end of . . . [*door opens*] Didn't hear that boy wipe his feet . . . Why *Rush Gook!*

RUSH: I couldn't find any *clean* overalls, mom, so I . . .

SADE: Where are your pants?

RUSH: I give 'em to Rooster.

SADE: Did you come up from the shed to the house like that?

RUSH: Yeah. Nobody was *lookin'*. An' . . .

SADE: An' you a big man goin' on thirteen years old.

RUSH: Well, heck, I couldn't find any clean overalls down cellar an' Rooster . . .

SADE: Why didn't Rooster come inside?

RUSH: Said he'd just as soon stay out there.

SADE: Gracious.

VIC: Don't know which one is the most half-witted, Ralph. You or your pal.

RUSH: Not *my* fault if he wants to sit out in the cold.

SADE: Did he put your pants on?

RUSH: Yeah. *He's* gonna be O.K. Said he was very comfortable. Gettin' the rip sewed up, mom?

SADE: As well as I can. Listen, ya s'pose Rooster'd mind if we emptied out his pockets?

RUSH: Not at all.

SADE: Be lots easier to *work* with.

RUSH: Give 'em to me. *I'll* take the junk out.

SADE: Won't be necessary for a minute yet. I'm sewin' up the bottom here. Tell ya what ya *can* do: run up an' get yourself some pants.

RUSH: *I* don't need any.

SADE: Oh, yes you do.

RUSH: I'm warm as toast.

73

SADE: Do like I say.

RUSH: I am warm as toast, mom. My legs . . .

VIC: Mind your mother, Pete. The fact that you're warm as toast is beside the point. It's a matter of decency. When a lady requests a gentleman to wear pants in her presence . . .

SADE: Somethin' fell out here, Rush. Pick it up.

RUSH: Where'd it go?

SADE: By my feet somewhere. Look.

RUSH: Rooster's a guy that can carry more junk around in his pocket than a *horse*. He'll pick up a piece of iron off the street an' carry it around till . . . Well, by gosh!

SADE: What was it?

RUSH: Piece of green chalk. Why that dirty crook. Mom, remember the other day when I come home with writin' on the back of my leather jacket?

SADE: Yes.

RUSH: Said "Rush is crazier than his uncle's grandmother"?

SADE: Yes.

RUSH: It was *green* writing, wasn't it?

SADE: Don't remember.

RUSH: *You* remember, gov?

VIC: No.

RUSH: Well, it *was* green writin'. An' here's the green chalk that wrote it. An' that doggone Rooster tried to lay it on Heinie Call.

SADE: Rush, will you go get somethin' to cover up them bare legs?

RUSH: Why can't I wear your *apron?* You'll be *done* there in a *minute,* won't you?

SADE: Take it off of me then.

RUSH: Talk about your low-down *crooks*. Wish I hadn't given Rooster my pants. Serve him right to sit out there in the shed all *day.*

SADE: Here—wanta empty these pockets?

RUSH: Yeah.

SADE: My needle's danglin'. Careful you don't stick yourself. How's the blizzard look, Vic?

VIC: Looks like it's gonna keep right on going.

SADE: Is Rooster peekin' out the window of the shed?

VIC: Don't see him.

SADE: [*Giggles*] All them holes an' *chinks* in the wall, I bet the snow's just *flurryin'* around his ears.

VIC: Rooster's a reflective young man. He prob'ly loves the peace an' quiet of . . .

RUSH: Hey!

VIC: What aileth *you*?

RUSH: Look here what I found in that guy's pocket.

VIC: What?

RUSH: My *ink*-eraser. Rooster claimed he never set eyes on it.

SADE: Hurry up there, son. I got *other* things to do, ya know?

RUSH: Why, that *skunk*. Had my ink-eraser all the doggone time.

VIC: How do you imagine it come in his possession?

RUSH: Plain as day. Yesterday when the teacher wasn't lookin', I hauled off an' hit Rooster in the back of the *head* with this ink-eraser. An' when I went over after school to hunt for it, I couldn't find it. Asked Rooster about it an' he said he didn't know a thing. Here it was in his pocket.

VIC: I don't know how a court of *law* would act in the case, but if somebody hit *me* in the back of the head with something valuable, I'd feel perfectly justified in *keeping* . . .

RUSH: By gosh, he's got *money*. Look here: eleven cents.

VIC: The same eleven cents you put in his drinking water, I suppose.

RUSH: Well, whatcha know about *that:* got eleven cents cash an' been stallin' me off about the three cents he's owed me for six weeks.

SADE: Rush, if you want me to fix those pants, give 'em here.

RUSH: Ain't got all the stuff outa the pockets yet.

SADE: Bet poor Rooster's turned into an icicle out there.

VIC: Sade.

SADE: Yes?

VIC: What do you think of this man's costume?

SADE: [*Giggles*] My apron?

VIC: Have you observed the view from behind?

SADE: No.

VIC: Well worth your while. An apron, though ideal for covering the *anterior* part of the body, is utterly inadequate when it comes to covering up the *posterior* . . .

RUSH: Why that darn rattlesnake!

VIC: What'd ya find *now*?

RUSH: Note he wrote to my girl . . . to Mildred Tisdel. [*reads*] Mildred: are you walking home after school?

VIC: A false friend if there ever was one.

RUSH: Anyway he got turned down. Says on the other side: "I am walking home with Elizabeth Miller an' Gracie Klemm." Well, watcha know about that! I bet I make Rooster Davis . . .

SADE: Rush, give me those pants.

RUSH: Here. Gov, wouldn't you jump down that guy's throat?

VIC: Don't know but what I would.

RUSH: Here I was doin' a *favor:* lettin' him sit in my own woodshed while my own mother sewed up his darn ol' pants. An' all the time he had this *evidence* in his pockets: piece of green chalk he wrote on my back with an' said he didn't: eleven cents in cash when he's owed me three cents for six weeks: ink-eraser he *copped* offa me; an' a note to Mildred Tisdel when he knows *I'm* the guy she walks home with when she don't walk home with the girls.

VIC: A black unbelievable story.

RUSH: Just wait'll I get *him.*

VIC: Did you find anything incriminating in those other articles there?

RUSH: No.

VIC: What *are* those other articles?

RUSH: Just junk Rooster carries in his pocket: little book about how to fix your cook-stove: comb with all the teeth out; busted fountain pen: hinge off a screen door; heel-plate; lady's shoe button; huntin' license good in Ohio in 1914; horse-shoe nail . . . just different stuff.

SADE: Here's the pants, son—all fixed.

RUSH: Thank you very much, mom.

SADE: Tell Rooster to look *out* for nails in telephone poles after this.

RUSH: Yeah. Say, guess I'll put these pants *on.* Trade with Rooster out in the shed.

SADE: Shed's a pretty cold place for changin' pants.

RUSH: That's O.K. Here's your apron back, mom.

SADE: Don't forget to put these things back in the pockets.

RUSH: I'll put *some* of 'em back. Gonna *keep* my ink-eraser an' my three cents.

SADE: Will Miss Kinney want a *written* excuse to let you boys back in class?

RUSH: *Naw. We'll* explain it to her. We'll just say . . .

SADE: Here's somethin' you dropped.

RUSH: Yeah—thing to cut your fingernails with. Rooster's carried that around in his pocket for *years. Never* cuts his fingernails with it. Well, I'll go on out now. Don't be scared if ya hear a lot of hollerin'.

SADE: Hollerin'?

RUSH: I'm gonna take a good *poke* at Rooster. *I'll teach* him.

SADE: Better take a good poke at your school-books. Teach *yourself.*

RUSH: [*Off*] Thanks again for fixin' the pants, mom.

76

SADE: Perfectly all right.

RUSH: [*Off*] See you at dinner time. So long, gov.

VIC: So long. [*Door opens and closes*]

SADE: [*To Vic*] Look out an' see how the blizzard is now.

VIC: Comin' along fine.

SADE: I like snow around Christmas-time all right but . . . Oh, he forgot his overcoat.

VIC: *He'll* be back in to get it.

SADE: Hope *Rooster's* got a good warm overcoat. [*Giggles*] Sittin' out in that ol' shed.

VIC: [*Chuckles*] He'll prob'ly get warmed up when Rush takes that poke at him.

SADE: I don't think he'll take any poke at *Rooster*. Tried it twice before an' come out the dirty end of the stick. [*Giggles*] *Was* kinda funny them things in the pants pocket.

VIC: Uh-huh. Wonder what *I'd* find if *I* went through *my* best friend's clothes.

SADE: It's kinda like that business about eavesdroppers seldom hear good of themselves.

VIC: Uh-huh. After all, the contents of a man's pants pocket are . . . [*Door opens*]

RUSH: [*Entering*] I forgot my overcoat.

SADE: Yes. There on the chair.

VIC: Changed pants yet?

RUSH: No. We decided to wear each *other's* pants the rest of the morning. *Awful* cold out in that shed. Rooster says thanks, mom.

SADE: Tell him glad to help.

RUSH: [*Moving off*] Well—see ya at dinner time.

VIC: Oh, son, did you take that poke at Rooster?

RUSH: No, I didn't. We . . . we kinda fixed things up.

VIC: How so?

RUSH: Well . . . a . . . ya see, he had my pants on just now?

VIC: Uh-huh.

RUSH: An' he got to monkeyin' around an' found some stuff in *my* pockets.

VIC: What'd he find?

RUSH: Oh—just a few different articles.

VIC: What were they?

RUSH: A buffalo nickel with a hole in it I swiped off him, an' a little tube of mucilage that gave it away I was the guy that stuck his arithmetic book to his geography book, an' a piece of wire just like the piece of wire somebody tied his overshoes together with, an' a bottle of red sand like the red sand he found in his hat at school the other day.

VIC: Oh.

RUSH: So we . . . we kinda fixed it up.

VIC: Uh-huh.

RUSH: I agreed to overlook what I found in *his* pockets, an' he agreed to overlook what he found in *my* pockets.

VIC: I see.

RUSH: Well, I'll get on to school now. [*Moves off*] So long, gov.

VIC: So long.

RUSH: So long, mom.

SADE: So long.

RUSH: [*Opens door*] See you at dinner time.

SADE: Uh-huh.

RUSH: Good-by. [*Closes door*]

END OF SCRIPT

ANNOUNCER: Which concludes a tale of torn pants, revealing pockets, storm, threats, heart-break, and the final reconciliation of two friends.

1934

NEW YEAR'S DAY:
RUSH HAS THREE JOBS

INTRODUCTION: The holiday dinner has been over just a little while as our scene opens now, and here in the living-room we find Victor Gook, lolling loosely in his big chair, and looking just about as sluggish and drowsy as we'd *expect* a man to look who has gotten away with half a roast chicken and two pieces of pumpkin pie. And here's Sade coming in from the kitchen. She surveys her somewhat uninspiring husband a moment, giggles, and says . . .

SADE: *Knew* you were eatin' too much.

VIC: 1935 comes only once a year, ya know.

SADE: Bet *you* feel like layin' down an' takin' a nap.

VIC: Oh, no. *I* shall carry on.

SADE: If ya don't *feel* like goin' to the movie, just say so.

VIC: *I'll* go to the movie all right but don't expect me to stay awake.

SADE: I'm not quite sure how *I* feel *yet*. Never put so much in my stomach before at one clatter in my life. Is Rush upstairs?

VIC: No. I sent him to the drug store for some cigars.

SADE: *He's* got a chance to make thirty-five cents this afternoon.

VIC: How come?

SADE: Talked to Mis' Harris just now when I took out my garbage. They're playin' Five Hundred over there an' little Gerald is so cranky an' bothersome, Mis' Harris wondered if Rush wouldn't take him for a walk to the park or somewhere.

VIC: Uh-huh.

SADE: Rush has done that before, ya know, an' William always gives him thirty-five cents. I told Mis' Harris I'd ask Rush if he wanted to.

VIC: Um.

SADE: Well, watcha think: shall we go to the movie?

VIC: Up to you, kiddo.

SADE: *I'd* kinda enjoy it, I think. Donna Dreamerson's on.

VIC: Aw, shucks. I wouldn't walk across the street to see that half-wit.

SADE: I imagine she's real good in *this* picture. The name of it is . . . What'd ya do with the paper?

VIC: Behind my chair here.

SADE: [*Leaning over to get it*] Person oughta fold *up* their news-papers after they get through . . . See T. R. Loomis's picture on the front page?

VIC: Yeah.

SADE: He musta shaved off his mustache.

VIC: No, I think that was taken before he *grew* the mustache. In fact, I'm *sure* . . .

SADE: Sort of a cute little piece here in the middle section about New Year's. Read it?

VIC: Don't believe so.

SADE: Tells about good resolutions an' turnin' over a new leaf an' love thy neighbor an' judge not that ye be not . . . *Here*—[Reads] Donna Dreamerson in "True Hearts an' Red Balloons."

VIC: Heck.

SADE: . . . the soul-stirring saga of a girl who yearned for something besides the quiet simplicity of her small-town home . . . a girl who wanted lights—love—glamor—and most of all the tender sympathy of some fine man who . . .

VIC: [*Disgusted*] Bunk.

SADE: *Does* sound like the same ol' business. But I *do* enjoy lookin' at Donna Dreamerson's *clothes*. They say the gowns she wears in this picture cost . . .

RUSH: [*Approaching from the kitchen*] Mom.

SADE: [*Calls*] I'm in here.

SADE: [*To Vic*] It might not be so bad, Vic. Let's see: who else is in it. [*Reads*] Conway Clayton. [*Aside*] Remember him?

VIC: No.

SADE: Dark hair all plastered down? Burn-sides? Generally wears a dress suit an' smokes cigarettes in a long . . .

RUSH: [*Closer*] Mom, I won't be goin' to the show with ya. I got a job for this afternoon.

SADE: Oh, ya talk to Mis' Harris?

RUSH: Mis' Harris? Uh-uh.

[*Neg.*]

SADE: She wants to know if you'd like to take little Gerald for a walk.

RUSH: Oh, heck, an' that's a thirty-five cent job too.

SADE: Gonna be doin' somethin' else?

RUSH: *Yeah.* I just fixed it up with Gran'pa Snyder to wheel him around in his wheel-chair. He wants the doggone *air*.

SADE: Well, you better run over an' tell Mis' Harris then. I think she's sort of expectin' ya.

RUSH: Shucks, I hate to turn down a thirty-five cent job for a two-*bit* one.

SADE: Cantcha take Gran'pa out in his wheel-chair later on in the afternoon?

RUSH: He wants to go *now*. Well—my tough luck, I guess. Here's your cigars, gov. Couldn't *get* Arc De Triomphe de Cuba. Hadda get Cleopatra Del Vesuvio Del Colombia.

VIC: Same price?

RUSH: Yeah. Gee, mom, I wish there was some way of ditchin' the Gran'pa job an' takin' the little Gerald job.

SADE: Gran'pa Snyder's been awful good to *you,* son. See to it that you're good to *him.*

RUSH: Oh, *I'll* give him a square deal. I sure could use that extra dime though. Well, guess I might as well be gettin' over there. You an' gov goin' to the movie?

SADE: We're not sure yet.

RUSH: They ain't *got* nothin' but that dumb ol' Donna Dreamerson struttin' around with no back on her underwear.

VIC: That just about sizes her *up*. Of all the doggone half-witted . . .
   [*Phone*]

SADE: I'll answer it.

RUSH: Gov, I don't know but what the Gran'pa job is the best job at *that*. I have a *terrible* time with little Gerald. He wants to walk in water an' climb over . . .

SADE: Just a second, son. [*To phone*] Hello? Yes. Oh, hello, Mis' Crane. How are you? That's fine. Oh, we're all well. Uh-huh—hope you're havin' a Happy New Year too. Rush? Yes. Just a moment. [*Aside*] It's Mis' Crane over on Elm street wants to talk to ya.

RUSH: She say why?

SADE: No.

RUSH: [*To phone*] Hello. Yes. Just fine, thank you. Yes. I see. Uh-huh. Why . . . a . . . *yes*. Yes. Be glad to, Mis' Crane. Uh-huh. Certainly. In about five minutes. Yes, ma'am. Good-by.

   [*Hangs up*]

SADE: She want you to do somethin'?

RUSH: Yeah. Take her dog out to the park an' back.

VIC: You're pretty much in demand, ain't ya, Fido?

RUSH: *Looks* like it. [*Thoughtfully*] Now what'd I better do?

SADE: Why?

RUSH: I'll hafta make up some excuse to ditch Gran'pa.

SADE: Can'tcha take Gran'pa an' the dog out all at the same time?

RUSH: [*Neg.*] Uh-uh. Crane's dog is on a *leash*. An' if I take the Gran'pa job, I'll need both hands for the wheel-chair.

SADE: Tie the leash *to* the wheel-chair.

RUSH: Gran'pa won't stand for it. Ya see, I *did* that once. With *Evans'* dog. He got the leash tangled up in the wheels an' almost dumped Gran'pa out in the *mud*.

SADE: If that's the way it is, why did you *take* the dog job?

RUSH: The dog job pays fifty cents. I'm not gonna turn down any fifty *cent* jobs.

SADE: Nice way to treat *Gran'pa*.

RUSH: Not *my* fault, mom. He can't *expect* my services for less money than *competitors* are willing to pay.

SADE: Oh, 'competitors.' You better go to the phone, call up Mis' Crane, an' say you're sorry but . . .

RUSH: Uh-*uh*. That'd be just throwin' a whole *quarter* away. I'll figure out some way to take care of Gran'pa.

SADE: Get some other little boy maybe?

RUSH: [*Hesitantly*] Ye-ah. That'd be *one* way. But I kinda hate to . . . [*Halts*]

SADE: Hate to what?

RUSH: Hate to let some other guy clean up that two-bits.

SADE: Don't be *selfish* on New Year's day.

RUSH: [*Moves off*] Well, guess I might as well get goin'.

SADE: You'll fix things with Gran'pa *some* way, won't ya?

RUSH: [*Off*] Sure.

SADE: [*Raises voice*] Don't forget to stop by Mis' Harris's house.

RUSH: I won't.

VIC: [*Calls*] Hey, son.

RUSH: Yeah?

VIC: Didn't I promise you a nickel for gettin' me my cigars?

RUSH: I already collected, gov. Cleopatra Del Vesuvio Del Colombia cigars are *cheaper* than Arc De Triomphe De Cuba.

VIC: They are, huh?

RUSH: Yeah. I collected a dime on the deal.

VIC: [*More to himself*] Um.

RUSH: [*Off*] So long, mom. Gov.

VIC AND SADE: [*Calls*] So long.

VIC: [*With some irony*] Smart guy, ain't he?

SADE: [*Giggles*] Anyway it looks like plenty of people wanta *hire* him.

VIC: *I'll* hire him one on the reverse side of his stomach if he tries any more high finance stuff on *me*. Cleopatra Del Vesuvio Del Colombia *indeed*.

SADE: That was kinda hard luck gettin' offered three jobs all at once an' the lowest-pay one callin' up first an' terra firma.

VIC: Vice Versa.

SADE: What?

VIC: You don't mean terra firma; you mean vice versa.

SADE: Six of one; half dozen of the other. Well, whatcha say: shall we go to the show?

VIC: Donna Dreamerson don't strike me as any alluring prospect, kiddo.

SADE: Let's see what else they got. Maybe they'll have . . . Where's the paper?

VIC: Behind my chair.

SADE: Person oughta fold *up* their newspaper after they get through readin' . . .

VIC: *You* were lookin' at that paper last.

SADE: [*Giggles*] Oh, that's right. Joke on *me*. Kinda like that old saying, "Give a dog a bad name an' he'll hang himself."

VIC: I don't recognize *that* old saying, but there *is* an old saying . . .

SADE: *Here.* [*Reads*] Added attractions: Fatty Frisco an' Dimples Duffy in "Look Out Below." Two volcanic reels of tempestuous nonsense crammed with chuckles an' choked with laughter. [*Aside*] That's the comedy.

VIC: Uh-huh.

SADE: I imagine it's one of them businesses where they throw pies at each other—policemen runnin' around an' all that, don'tcha s'pose?

VIC: Yeah.

SADE: *I* never laugh at such goings-on. They don't tickle me the least bit. [*Laughs*] I always feel kinda sorry for the fella that gets hit with the pie.

VIC: Uh-huh. What else they got?

SADE: [*Reads*] A special New Year's presentation by the Management, showing pictures of local points of interest, together with short talks by various leading citizens.

VIC: [*Interested*] Oh, uh-huh. Believe Mr. *Ruebush* is in that crowd.

SADE: *That* oughta be interesting.

VIC: Sure.

SADE: An' besides that there's . . . [*Reads*] . . . A Colorful Travelogue Depicting the Lovely Scenes in the vicinity of Mount Blanc, with running comments by Doctor Benton J. Blatz, noted lecturer an' explorer.

VIC: Uh-huh.

SADE: [*Reads*] This gala Holiday Program being concluded with News Events an' short snaps of coming attractions.

VIC: Yeah.

SADE: Shall we go?

VIC: *I'd* just as soon.

SADE: I'll hafta run upstairs an' slip on my other dress.

VIC: O.K.

SADE: Think you better change to your good suit?

VIC: Naw.

SADE: Can't tell who we might bump into.

VIC: *This* suit'll do.

SADE: New Year's Day, ya know. Person's s'posed to be kinda dressed up.

VIC: *I'm* dressed up enough.

SADE: [*Moves off*] Well, I'll go on upstairs then. Don't you fall asleep there so I hafta fight to wake ya up.

VIC: No.

SADE: [*Returning*] Here—fold the paper, will ya, an' lay it nice on . . . *Say*—here's somethin' about Mabel Coomer.

VIC: Yeah? What?

SADE: [*Reads*] Mabel Coomer heard in recital. [*Aside*] *Well*—she musta finished up all her singing lessons there in Chicago.

VIC: Read the piece.

SADE: I hope her singing lessons did her some *good*. Remember how she used to screech there in church?

VIC: Yeah. Read the piece.

SADE: [*Reads*] Mr. an' Mrs. Arthur Coomer, 1102 North Main street, were hosts Christmas Eve to a small group of friends gathered to hear a short recital by Miss Mable Coomer, who until recently was a student of the Commonwealth-Proctor Music Academy in Chicago. Miss Coomer obliged with "Red Bird Dying," "Why is Life so Short and Sweet," "Into the Gloomy Grave Gladly Shall I Go," an' "Heaven, Thou Art Very Near to Me."

VIC: Must of been a real jolly party.

SADE: Such dismal songs to sing on Christmas Eve. Goes on to say —[*Reads*] "The guests applauded for several encores, which were graciously given." [*Aside*] I'll just *bet*. That girl'd sing all night, give her half a chance. [*Reads*] "Mr. Clinton Morris played Miss Coomer's accompaniment capably on the piano, an' delicious refreshments were served by the hostess later in the evening."

VIC: Uh-huh.

SADE: Here—fold up the paper nice. I'll run an' slip on my . . . say, what's across the street?

VIC: I don't *know* what's across the street.

SADE: [*Moving off*] It's Rush. C'mere.

VIC: [*Getting up*] Anything remarkable to see?

SADE: [*Off*] Uh-huh. Come here to the window.

VIC: Is Mr. Rush busy with his business?

SADE: *I'll* say he's busy with his business.

VIC: What job did he take?

SADE: Look an' *see* what job he took.

VIC: [*Looking*] Well, I'll be darned.

SADE: Gran'pa Snyder's in the *wheel*-chair.

VIC: Little Gerald is in Gran'pa's *lap*.

SADE: An' the dog is in *Gerald*'s lap.

VIC: He took all *three* jobs.

SADE: Fifty cents plus thirty-five cents plus *twenty*-five cents.

VIC: A dollar an' ten cents.

SADE: Pretty good New Year's Day.

VIC: Pretty smart boy.

END OF SCRIPT

ANNOUNCER: And so—with father and mother looking out the window . . . and their son, a prince of high finance, parading down the street . . . we tiptoe away from the small house half-way up in the next block.

1934

**RUSH CHARTS
HIS FUTURE TO THE
YEAR 2000**

ANNOUNCER: OPENING AND COMMERCIAL CREDITS
INTRODUCTION: A bright noon-day sun is beaming down on the small house half-way up in the next block as our scene opens now, and here in the swing on the front porch we discover Mr. and Mrs. Victor Gook enjoying a beautiful May day and awaiting that moment when the meat on the kitchen stove shall have finished cooking. And the wife is saying to the husband . . .

SADE: Ain't that a summer sun for ya though?

VIC: That's a summer sun for me because this is a summer *day*.

SADE: Yes, but I never think of it's bein' really summer till *June* comes an' it's *always* warm. You take it in the middle of May an' some mornings a person could even stand a *fire* in the furnace.

VIC: Uh-huh.

SADE: Ya know somethin' we could do when summer actually gets here?

VIC: No.

SADE: Run a hedge out by the front side-walk.

VIC: That's up to the land-lord.

SADE: *He* wouldn't do anything like that. Hedges are expensive.

VIC: Well, why should *we* pay out money to decorate somebody *else's* house?

SADE: We're the fellas that's got to *live* here.

VIC: *I* can live here without a hedge runnin' along the front side-walk.

SADE: Guess we *would* be foolish to stand an expense like that ourselves. But you know that *land*-lord: it was like pullin' *teeth* to get him to paper the big bed-room last year.

VIC: Uh-huh.

SADE: He hangs onto his nickels like Grant took Richmond.

VIC: Well, he's smart at that. If *I* was rentin' a house I think *I'd* be about as stingy as . . .

SADE: *Here* comes a fella.

VIC: What fella is that?

SADE: Fella named Rush. Comin' around the corner from Kelsey.

VIC: Ah, yes—my man-child.

SADE: What a monster he's gettin' to be. I never *realize* how he's growin' till I see him off at a distance an' catch sight of him all of a *sudden*. Person's kids get enormous right under your nose.

VIC: Certainly do. Pretty soon he'll be so big I'll be scared to thrash him within an inch of his *life* like I do every Saturday.

SADE: [*Giggles*] Don't believe you ever *did* give him a downright *lickin'*, did ya?

VIC: *I* believe the young man's memory is dotted with memories of considerable pain as inflicted by the sturdy arm of his pop.

SADE: You never hit him with anything bigger'n a little *switch*.

VIC: I've always found the flat of my *hand* brought results.

SADE: You got a good tough hand. [*Giggles*] *I* tried that one time an' almost killed myself it hurt so bad.

VIC: He have somethin' in his pocket?

SADE: No. He had corduroy pants on an' my poor hand just *burned*. Never hurt Rush the least bit. Finally I quit an' we *both* hadda laugh.

[*Laughs*]

VIC: [*Chuckles*]

SADE: About that hedge though, they *are* so pretty in the summer time. If we got one like Mis' Harris's got we wouldn't even need to bother much *trimmin'* it. Hers come from a place in Chicago an' it's s'posed to . . . [*Calls*] All right, mister, use the sidewalk.

RUSH: [*Off*] I can *always* fool you with that fake lunge, mom.

SADE: [*To Rush, knowingly*] Uh-huh. [*To Vic*] Fake lunge nothin'. *He'd* cut across the grass.

VIC: Um.

SADE: Say, there's *another* reason to have a hedge. Keeps kids from trompin' on . . .

RUSH: [*Closer*] Not talkin' about *me*, I hope.

VIC: [*Raises voice*] Who'd waste time on a subject like *that*.

RUSH: [*Closer*] Bet two berries I can tell ya just what mom was sayin'.

SADE: What was I sayin'?

RUSH: [*Up*] You were sayin', "*This* summer it's gonna be *different*. That boy is altogether too big to be trompin' down grass like a three-year old baby." That correct?

SADE: I wasn't sayin' anything of the kind, smarty.

RUSH: All right then, *here's* what you were sayin'. You were sayin' . . .

SADE: Sit down an' rest your bones.

RUSH: Dinner not ready, huh?

SADE: No.

RUSH: Move over, gov.

VIC: [*Moving over*] Um.

SADE: [*Moving over*] You get any bigger, son, an' your mother get any fatter, there won't be *room* for all of us in this porch swing.

RUSH: [*Chuckles*] Yeah.

VIC: Plannin' on a little studyin' this noon, Quick-Lime?

RUSH: No, I just brought home my geography book to keep my *chart* in. Wanta keep it clean. Gonna frame it.

VIC: What chart is that?

RUSH: Just a chart us eighth-grade kids hadda make out this morning. Another one of Superintendent Chinbunny's ideas.

VIC: Superintendent Chinbunny come on deck again today?

RUSH: No, but teacher's meetin' was last Friday at the high school an' he made a speech to 'em. Miss Kinney told us this morning what he *said* in the speech.

VIC: Anything interesting?

RUSH: *Lotsa* things interesting. Here's the scheme he doped out. He figures every kid just entering high school should plan their . . .

SADE: Excuse me, son. Vic, ya know what we'd hafta do if we *did* run a hedge out front?

VIC: Water it?

SADE: No, ya don't water hedges. Here's what I was gonna say: we'd hafta run it clear around to the side of the house. It looks *unfinished* to see a hedge just *end*.

VIC: Expect it does.

SADE: Mis' Kilgore over on Elder street's got a hedge that ends like that. Always makes *me* think of a little dinky fence.

VIC: Um.

RUSH: Boy, this certainly is a swell day.

SADE: *Summer* day.

RUSH: Yeah.

VIC: What was that scheme of Chinbunny's, wet-wash?

RUSH: It's a scheme he wants to see go in actual practice in every grade school in the city.

SADE: Mr. Chinbunny's *always* got schemes in his noodle, ain't he?

RUSH: Yeah.

SADE: Ruthie told me Mis' Johnson's daughter Harriet that works in the Board of Education office told *her* Mr. Chinbunny was a real up-an'-comer. Got some stunt cookin' in the fryin' pan twenty-one hours outa the day.

RUSH: He's generally on the *go* all right, Superintendent Chinbunny.

SADE: Well, I'm glad they *give* it to a younger man. That ol' Mr. Robertson poked around an' never done *nothin'*. Harriet told Ruthie half the time he never knew . . . There goes Mis' *Frost*. I didn't see her. [*Calls*] Hello, Mis' Frost. [*Aside*] Oh, she don't hear good, *does* she.

RUSH: No.

SADE: Why didn't one of you fellas *say* she was walkin' by? *I* was lookin' at the yard where I'd like to put my hedge.

RUSH: She didn't *go* by, mom. She come out of *Call's* house.

SADE: Oh, she did? Wonder what on earth she was doin' in *there*.

RUSH: [*Who wouldn't know*] Um.

VIC: What's Uncle Chinbunny's latest mental creation, Ike? You didn't get around to that.

RUSH: Well, he's got the idea every kid—girl or boy—when they reach the age of thirteen years should start workin' on a plan for their future life.

SADE: [*Approvingly*] Uh-huh. That sounds like him.

VIC: What kind of a plan, Arthur?

RUSH: *Just* an ordinary plan. A *chart,* get the angle, so ya don't waste time foolin' around. Figure out how you're gonna put in your time an' then put *in* your time that way.

VIC: Oh. You kids make yourselves charts like that this morning?

RUSH: *Some* of us did. Ya see Miss Kinney said anybody that had any *ideas* about their future life could work on a chart an' not go to geography recitation.

VIC: *I* see.

RUSH: Care to look at *my* chart? I got it all done.

VIC: Yeah. Whip it out.

RUSH: [*Getting it out of his book*] It looks kinda scribbly because I wrote it in pencil. Think maybe I'll ask Lawrence Kirby's sister to typewrite it for me. Here it is.

VIC: Uh-huh.

RUSH: Want me to read you some of it?

VIC: Go ahead.

RUSH: I'm gonna read about what I got doped out for my future life, mom.

SADE: All right.

RUSH: [*Reads*] Future Life Chart of Rush Gook. Edwards School. Nineteen-thirty-five.

VIC AND SADE: Uh-huh.

RUSH: Here's where it starts now. [*Reads*] 1935 to 1939—attend high school.

SADE: [*Giggles*] Four years all at a clatter, huh?

RUSH: That's the way it's *s'posed* to be. As I go along I can put *sub*-heads in my chart for weeks an' months, appreciate the slant?

SADE: Yes.

RUSH: All right. [*Reads*] 1935 to 1939—attend high school. 1939 to 1943—attend college.

SADE: Nineteen-forty-three—sounds like a million years off.

RUSH: *That's* only eight years from now. See, I got the different *ages* I'll be written down too. In 1943 I'll be twenty-one.

SADE: Goodness, *I'll* be . . . Oh, my, hate to think of it.

RUSH: Well, anyway, [*Reads*] 1935 to 1939—attend high school. 1939 to 1943—attend college. 1943 to 1947—attend medical school.

VIC AND SADE: Medical school?

RUSH: Yeah. I decided to be a doctor.

VIC AND SADE: When?

RUSH: This *morning*. A guy's got to be *somethin'*. I might as well be a doctor. What the heck.

VIC: Have you *thought* about bein' a doctor much?

RUSH: No, it just happened to occur to me this morning.

SADE: Oh, goodness, son, little boys can't tell what they're gonna be all in a *minute*.

RUSH: Don't see why *not*. Is it agreeable with *you* folks if I be a doctor?

SADE: Sure, but *lands*.

RUSH: It's all settled then; I'll be a doctor. O.K.—[*Reads*] 1943 to 1947—attend medical school. 1947 to 1949—be interne in hospital. [*Aside*] Gotta do that before ya get your license an' hot water bottle an' knife an' pills an' chloroform an' junk, see?

VIC AND SADE: Uh-huh.

RUSH: Let's see here: when I'm all graduated an' a doctor an' everything in 1949, I'll be twenty-seven years old.

SADE: Think of that, Vic, he'll be twenty-seven years old.

VIC: Uh-huh. Our son can come around to the ol' folks home an' give us a free shot of castor oil.

RUSH: Sure thing.

VIC: What's next after internin' in the hospital?

RUSH: [*Reads*] 1949 to 1950—trip to Europe.

VIC: Hey, hey.

RUSH: I'll be *tired,* grasp the point? Here I been to *school* ever since I was *six*. Now I'm twenty-seven. Twenty-one years I been to school. Almost a quarter of a century. I *deserve* a trip to Europe.

SADE: [*Giggles*] Guess ya do at that, son.

RUSH: Darn right.

VIC: Who's gonna buy your *ticket* to Europe?

RUSH: Maybe *you* will, huh?

VIC: O.K.

RUSH: Thanks.

VIC: Forget it. When ya get back from Europe, what?

RUSH: [*Reads*] . . . Ah . . . 1950 to 1955—run doctor's office.

SADE: Nineteen-fifty-five—*gracious*.

RUSH: Yeah, nineteen-fifty-five. I'll be thirty-three years old.

SADE: Where ya gonna *put* your doctor's office?

RUSH: Oh, I don't care. Where'd be a good place?

SADE: I don't know, I'm sure.

RUSH: I can think about that later on. No rush.

VIC: No rush *particularly*. You got twenty *years* to pick a spot.

RUSH: Uh-huh. Well . . . [*Reads*] 1950 to 1955—mmm run doctor's office. 1955 to 1956—get married.

SADE: Get *married?*

RUSH: Sure. I'll be thirty-three years *old*.

SADE: Who ya gonna marry?

RUSH: *I'll* dig up a lady somewhere. Oughta be *plenty* of ladies around willin' to marry a rich *doctor*.

SADE: My gracious.

VIC: How ya know you'll be *rich?*

RUSH: I been runnin' my doctor's office for five *years*, ain't I?

VIC: *That's* right.

RUSH: O.K.—[*Reads*] 1955 to 1956—get married. 1956 to 1957— get married. Oh, I'm *already* married. Mistake here. Hafta fix that.

VIC: I'll say.

RUSH: 1956 to 1957—trip to Europe.

VIC: Another mistake. You *been* to Europe.

RUSH: My *wife* ain't. *She* oughta have a little vacation.

VIC: *Sure* she ought to, poor kid.

RUSH: Well—1957 to 1967—run doctor's office. 1967—to 1968— trip to Europe.

VIC: Oughta be a *lot* of ya *this* time?

RUSH: Uh-huh, I'll be forty-five years old. [*Reads*] 1968 to 1978— run doctor's office. 1978 to 1988—enter politics.

VIC: Gettin' in kinda *late,* ain't ya?

RUSH: I'll be sixty-five years old.

VIC: Uh-huh.

RUSH: Nice age to get elected *governor* or somebody.

VIC: *Peach* of an age.

RUSH: [*Reads*] 1988 to 1998—hold office an' fool around makin' public speeches. 1998 to 2000—retire an' take trip to Europe.

SADE: Gracious—the year twenty hundred.

RUSH: Uh-huh. Gov. don'tcha think I got another trip to Europe *comin'* in 1998? I'll be seventy-five years old.

VIC: *You* got it comin' all right.

RUSH: [*Reads*] Twenty-hundred to twenty-hundred an' ten—loaf around an' see all the ball-games. [*Aside*] I'll be *retired,* appreciate the slant? . . . have *plenty* of time for baseball.

VIC: Yeah.

RUSH: [*Reads*] Twenty-hundred an' twelve—die.

SADE: *Die.*

RUSH: *Sure.* I'll be eighty-seven years old. Prob'ly die in around there *some*where.

SADE: [*Disturbed*] Gracious, gracious me!

RUSH: [*Reads*] Twenty-hundred an' twelve—die, an' have a great big monument with electric lights on it.

SADE: [*A little faint*] Oh.

RUSH: Ain't that a snappy life-time, gov?

VIC: It sure is, sport.

RUSH: Ain't that a snappy life-time, mom?

SADE: Yes.

RUSH: Boy, that's what I call a high-class life-time. [*Laughs at what a high class life-time it is . . . and fades laughing*]

END OF SCRIPT

ANNOUNCER: During the past fifteen minutes we have had the pleasure to looking into the future and examining a high-class life-time as lived by Mister Rush Gook of Virginia Avenue.

1935

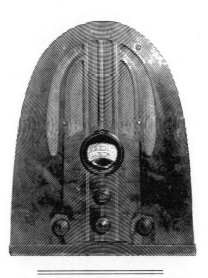

RUSH'S FIRST DAY
AT HIGH SCHOOL

THEME
ANNOUNCER: OPENING AND COMMERCIAL CREDITS
INTRODUCTION: It's a few minutes past twelve o'clock as our scene opens now, and here in the kitchen of the small house half-way up in the next block we find the noon-day meal in progress, with all members of the family present. Yesterday, you'll remember, young Rush Gook embarked on his high school career. He found that opening day consisted only of one short session during which the students straightened out kinks in their schedules, met their teachers, and were told what text-books to purchase. Today, however, school began in earnest . . . and no one is more earnest about it than young Rush himself. He's giving his parents a few high-lights this very moment. Listen to him.

RUSH: By gosh there's as much difference between high school an' grade school as there is between day an' night. In grade school when ya move into a new room, they assign you a seat an' ya sit there day after day an' week after week an' month after month until the end of the semester. Ya sit there minute after minute an' hour after too except for recess. In high school, by George, ya have *seven* different rooms an' *seven* different seats. An' in every room there's a different bunch of kids.

SADE: You have seven different teachers too, don't ya?

RUSH: *Yeah.* Seven different teachers. Feature that? An' the Study Hall teachers change around a lot so it makes *more* than seven over the course of a week. I never realized . . .

VIC: Will ya pass the beans please?

RUSH: Huh?

VIC: Will ya pass the beans please?

RUSH: Oh—thought you asked a question about school.

VIC: No, I just asked a question about the beans.

SADE: Hand me your plate. I'll give you some.

RUSH: I never *realized* what a change high school'd be from Edwards. 'Course I knew everything'd be different but I never paused to reflect *how* . . . Whatcha say, gov?

VIC: Nothin'.

RUSH: You waved.

VIC: I was wavin' at your mother. Indicatin' that she had put sufficient beans on my plate. I didn't wanta cut in on your flow of remarks.

RUSH: Oh. Well, I started to say I knew everything in high school'd be different but I didn't pause to reflect how *much* different. In Edwards we'd kinda slide down in our desk at nine o'clock, sing a song or two, go to the blackboard an' work arithmetic problems,

101

listen to the other class recite, go out to recess, come back in again, have geography . . . just sorta do things lazy an' comfortable, ya know. But in high school ya dash into whatever classroom you're due at, chew the rag a minute, the bell rings, ya shut up, ya recite an' listen to the teacher for forty minutes or so, the bell rings again, ya bounce outa there like a fire engine, an' go whippin' down the corridor to wherever your *next* classroom is. Oh, it's the *life*.

SADE: Like it, huh?

RUSH: [*Who does*] I sure do, kiddo. Mom, you just oughta come *around* those halls some day between classes. You never saw so many people sloshin' back an' forth in your life. Teachers an' students an' janitors an' librarians an' office girls an' I don't know *who* all. Looks like *thousands* of 'em. An' in three minutes—as quick as the bell rings—there's not a soul in sight. The whole place is as empty as if it'd been cleaned out by magic.

SADE: [*Mildly*] My. My.

RUSH: [*Somewhat breathless*] Oh, I wanta *tell* ya.

VIC: Spear me a slab of bread, will ya, Sade?

SADE: Oh, Vic, say "please *pass* the bread." You said "Spear me the bread" the other night at Ruthie's in front of that cousin from Colfax an' I could of sunk through the floor!

VIC: That cousin from Colfax looked like a *hay*-seed to *me*. I sized him up as a . . .

RUSH: [*Off again*] An' *hey,* I got gymnasium class fourth hour an' the guys . . . Oh, excuse me for buttin' in, gov.

VIC: Perfectly O.K.

RUSH: I got all this stuff on my mind, see, an' I can't hardly wait to let you an' mom in on it.

VIC: Uh-huh. Kick the bread up the trolley before ya start in.

SADE: Vic, *please* don't. You get in the habit of sayin' things like that an' then they bust out in front of company.

VIC: Will *nobody* bounce the bread off the bank-board?

RUSH: Here y'are, gov. Mom, I started to tell ya about my fourth hour gym class. I'm in Physical Geography third hour under Miss Shade, an' ya know what the guys do that have got fourth hour gym?

SADE: What do they do?

RUSH: They get half undressed durin' third hour so they can scoot down as soon as the bell rings an' be in their gym suits ahead of everybody else. I noticed a kid this morning. He's a sophomore that graduated from Emerson school last year. By gosh, he took off his socks, put 'em in his pocket, put his shoes back on an' left 'em untied; put his *necktie* in his pocket, an' unbuttoned his shirt. Then he got clear on the edge of his seat so when the bell rang he could get a flyin' start. When it *did* ring, you'd of thought a fire-cracker'd gone off under him.

SADE: Do the teachers put *up* with such didoes in high school?

RUSH: Teacher couldn't *see* him. In the first place he sits in a back seat an' in the second place he ducked behind the guy in front of him.

SADE: Don't sound to me like a very smart thing for *big* boys to be doin'.

RUSH: Oh, it's a case of dog eat dog in high school, mom. It's really the life.

SADE: How about your subjects? Don't *they* get any attention?

RUSH: Plenty of it. Plenty of it. By the way I haven't *told* you my complete schedule yet, have I?

SADE: You said you were takin' Algebra an' Latin an' English an' . . .

RUSH: Let me describe the whole works to ya.

SADE: All right.

RUSH: Well, when I get to school a little before nine in the morning, I go to my locker, hang up my hat, an' grab whatever books I want. Then I loaf around the halls till the first bell rings an' chat with friends. When I hear the bell I go to my algebra class, which is room 209 on the second floor, teacher Miss Lorah Monroe. Algebra is my first-hour class. When the bell rings for *second*-hour classes, I have three minutes to get to Study Hall, which is room 215. We got three Study Halls altogether—rooms 215, 115 an' 205. Third hour I have Physical Geography under Miss Shade. Fourth hour I have gym. On Fridays we have *Assembly* between third an' fourth hours. That's when everybody in school gets together in the auditorium. Assembly between third an' fourth hours is mighty convenient for me because I can take a short cut down to the gymnasium. That's all of the morning. In the afternoon there's fifth hour, sixth hour, seventh hour, an' eighth hour. Eighth hour is for the kids that hafta stay after school. Fifth hour I have Study Hall 205; sixth hour I have English under Miss Tyson; an' seventh hour I have Latin under Miss Kinney. There's my day in a nut-shell.

VIC: Seems to make quite a day.

RUSH: Oh, it's the *life,* boy. I sure feel sorry for Harry Chatam an' Wally Wilson an' them guys that quit school to take *jobs.* They can *have* their ol' salary.

SADE: Maybe you'd like to go to high school the rest of your life.

RUSH: *I'd* just as soon.

VIC: All this'll be stale in a week or two, Hank.

RUSH: Stale *nothin'.* No, *sir.*

VIC: Could you spare a fella another dab of beans, Sade?

SADE: We got all these to finish up.

VIC: Spit me over a throat-load, will ya?

SADE: Vic, I wish you wouldn't. S'pose you were havin' dinner with Mis' *Brighton* an' come out with somethin' like that.

VIC: I'd expect Mis' Brighton to . . .

RUSH: Mom, let me tell you somethin' *funny* that . . . Oh, I beg your pardon, gov; I'm always buttin' in.

VIC: Think nothin' of it. Tell us somethin' funny.

RUSH: It's about a kid in my Physical Geography class. That's what I got under Miss Shade third hour, ya know.

VIC AND SADE: Uh-huh.

RUSH: Well, Miss Shade is one of the very few teachers that make a lesson assignment before kids get their text-books. She does that because we got so much to *cover* durin' the semester. Anyway, she made a lesson assignment yesterday an' we were s'posed to have it studied for today. So she asked this kid—his name is Gerald Snow— a question about the first paragraph. He said he didn't know the answer. She said didn't you read it. He said sure, he read it three times. *When* did you read it three times, says Miss Shade. "This semester, last semester, an' the semester before that," he says. [*Laughs*]

VIC AND SADE: [*Laugh without conviction*]

RUSH: Don'tcha get the joke?

SADE: He . . . didn't know his lesson?

RUSH: *No. Here's* the joke: the kid had read the lesson three times because he took the *course* three times. He'd *flunked* it twice, get the angle?

SADE: [*Still not quite clear on the matter*] Oh.

RUSH: "I read it this semester, last semester, an' the semester before that." [*Re-enjoys the joke*]

SADE: [*Laughs as much as she can*]

VIC: A splotch of butter for my bread perhaps, Mis' Jackson?

SADE: It's right there by ya. Behind the big dish.

RUSH: Mom, who ya think's in my Latin class?

SADE: Who?

RUSH: Mildred Tisdel.

SADE: Ain't she in all your classes?

RUSH: No, that's the only one. Latin.

SADE: You're . . . you're both *freshmen,* ain't ya?

RUSH: Sure, but there's *hundreds* of freshmen. They got four beginning algebra classes alone. In *my* algebra class there's not one single kid from Edwards school.

SADE: Well.

RUSH: Chances are I won't even *see* much of Mildred. Around *school,* that is. She's takin' different subjects than I am an' her classes are in different parts of the building. I never saw her at *all* this *morning.*

SADE: Thought you walked to school with her.

RUSH: I *did.* An' home too.

SADE: Whatcha know about that.

RUSH: Oh, it's an awful big place, that school. You just oughta see 'em pile in the Auditorium for Assembly.

SADE: I'd like to sometime.

RUSH: We'll *arrange* it for some Friday.

VIC: How about your ol' side-kicks Heinie an' Rooster? Are you in any classes with them?

RUSH: I'm in *every* class with *Rooster.*

SADE: Oh, *that* makes it nice.

RUSH: We got it fixed up with Superintendent Chinbunny. Rooster an' me wanted to be together, but the English class I was in was all full an' it looked like Rooster'd hafta take it second hour under Miss Tate. That would of thrown his whole schedule off, ya see?

SADE: Uh-huh.

RUSH: But I went to Mr. Chinbunny about it. At first he said he didn't favor the idea of close friends bein' in the same classes because they were apt to distract each other. But *I* talked him around.

SADE: Maybe he's *right* about close friends distractin' each other.

RUSH: Oh, no. Rooster Davis an' me are just like *that.*

SADE: Might be just what'd cause the trouble.

RUSH: *We'll* make out. Ya know Rooster made a great sacrifice in order to be with me in every class?

SADE: What'd he do?

RUSH: Agreed to take Latin. Agnes, his big sister, ya know, took Latin when she was in high school an' she usta come home nights an' bawl her head off. So Rooster's always been scared of it.

SADE: An' he's takin' it?

RUSH: In order to be with me. Ain't that a friend for ya?

SADE: Yes, I guess it is.

RUSH: To be right down frank with ya, I don't believe Latin's half as tough as it's cracked up to be. All ya gotta do is learn Latin words for English words. An' there's only about ten a day to learn. I know some already. "Puella" means girl. "Puer" means boy. "Agricola" means farmer. "Patria" means native country. "Hic" means this. Looks like a pipe to *me*.

SADE: I guess it's stringin' the words *together* that's *hard*.

RUSH: Don't see why it *should* be. If I feel like sayin' "Here is my shoe" in Latin, all I gotta know is the Latin words for "Here is my shoe."

SADE: Well, I don't know the first *thing* about it.

RUSH: I'll give you the interesting angles as they come along, mom.

SADE: All right.

RUSH: Yes, sir, boy, this high school dope sure is the life.

SADE: It's nice you like it so well.

RUSH: Can't *help* but like it.

VIC: You say you were in some classes with your pal Heinie?

RUSH: Heinie's in my gym class, my Physical Geography class, an' my fifth-hour Study Hall. So us three friends will be together *part* of the day at *least*. An' we oughta have some fun too. In the boys' room between second an' third hour we decided to . . . Mom, is your kitchen clock right?

SADE: I guess it is.

RUSH: Twelve twenty-five?

SADE: Uh-huh.

RUSH: Say, do you mind if I beat it?

SADE: Not time for school *yet*.

RUSH: No, but I got lotsa business to take care of. May I leave the table?

SADE: I s'pose so . . . if you must.

RUSH: Oh, I got *plenty* of business. Hafta switch lockers with a guy, reserve a book outa the library, notify the office about the changes in my schedule, put in an application for Assembly monitor, an' get my name on the Voluntary Usher list.

SADE: You won't be doin' this *every* noon?

RUSH: Oh, no. Maybe just a day or two till I get organized. [*Moves off*]

SADE: When'll ya be home s'afternoon?

RUSH: [*Off*] Prob'ly not till a quarter to five.

SADE: I'll want groceries an' things, ya know.

RUSH: O.K. I'll show up early as I can. [*Opens screen door*] So long, mom.

SADE: So long.

RUSH: So long, gov.

VIC: So long, sport.

RUSH: See everybody later.

[*Screen door slams*]

VIC: [*To Sade*] There goes a man that attends high school.

SADE: He attends high school just like you'd shoot off a ton of dynamite.

VIC: I never seen a guy so *full* of a thing.

SADE: Did you notice how much dinner he ate?

VIC: No. Couldn't of ate much an' done all *that* talkin'.

SADE: He didn't eat *any* dinner.

VIC: Not *any*?

SADE: Not a mouth-ful.

VIC: Not a bean?

SADE: Not one single bean.

VIC: Some guy.

SADE: An' the *funniest* thing is.

VIC: What?

SADE: He didn't even *know* he didn't eat any dinner.

END OF SCRIPT

ANNOUNCER: Which concludes a brief interlude at the small house half-way up in the next block.

1935

VIC, CHEF FOR DINNER, QUOTES PANTLEY ON PEANUTS

INTRODUCTION: Well sir, it's time for the noon-day meal as we enter the small house half-way up in the next block now, and here in the kitchen we discover activities in progress toward that end. And these activities are being conducted by no less a person than Mr. Victor Gook—who is wearing an apron and who is setting the table. Since his wife is standing over her ironing-board, we judge she's drafted her husband into service. Shall we listen to their talk? O.K.

VIC: The table is set, kiddo. I have done my best. An' looking *over* the work I cannot but feel a little proud.

SADE: Move over so I can see.

VIC: You'll notice that a symmetry of pattern has been striven for. You'll notice that the cutlery gleams an' shines. I have achieved an inviting atmosphere in my table-setting an' . . .

SADE: It's the *knife* an' spoon that go together. Not the *fork* an' spoon. The fork goes by itself.

VIC: A situation easily remedied.

SADE: You *have* got 'em right at *Rush's* place.

VIC: Of course. I never make the same mistake twice. Since this type of endeavor is new to me, I was careful to *feel* my way. Very very deliberately I . . .

SADE: You've got two yards more table-cloth hangin' down one end of the table than you have hangin' down the other end.

VIC: Yes, so I have. Well, a simple flick of the wrist will . . .

SADE: No, better leave it be. You'll knock things over. Why is it you put on the salt-shaker outa the dining-room set an' the pepper-shaker outa the kitchen set?

VIC: Have I done that?

SADE: You can see they don't match, can'tcha?

VIC: I like to inject variety in my work. The salt-shaker *contrasts* with the pepper-shaker. It eliminates the danger of gettin' 'em mixed up.

SADE: I don't see *how*. Neither one's *transparent*. An' there's no *printin'* on 'em.

VIC: If you feel that I should go get the other . . .

SADE: No, they'll do. You ready to dish up your corn an' things now?

VIC: You bet.

SADE: Use the blue-bordered saucers there on the stove.

VIC: I *will*. Or *die*.

SADE: I hear Rush talkin' to somebody out in the alley. Guess he's gonna show up on *time* for once.

VIC: It'll be a new thrill for him to eat a meal prepared by the expert hands of his father.

SADE: Yeah. How's your meat?

VIC: Done to a turn.

SADE: Put it on the plate then.

VIC: I thought I'd let it writhe a moment or two longer in its own rich juices.

SADE: [*Giggles*] All right.

VIC: Ain't you surprised to find out what a handy man I can be around the kitchen?

SADE: Uh-huh. Got bread cut?

VIC: I have. It's arranged neatly in the center of the table. An' a cleverly sliced chunk of butter sleeps close beside it.

SADE: I expect we oughta open a glass of jelly for sweet.

VIC: That *too* has been anticipated by the man in charge. A glass of jelly has been opened. If you look you'll see it lurking coyly behind the sugar bowl.

SADE: Thought of everything, huh? I'd dish up my meat now. I hear Rush outside.

VIC: You ready to sit down to dinner?

SADE: Just about. All I hafta do is finish this shirt.

VIC: Will you be through with your ironing then?

SADE: Lands, no. I'll be on the jump till two o'clock. See all I got left in my clothes-basket?

VIC: Yeah.

SADE: Maybe you an' Rush will do the dishes?

VIC: Maybe. This the knife you jab the meat with?

SADE: Uh-huh. Say, ya know that magazine that come yesterday?

VIC: Your woman's magazine?

SADE: Yes. Did you bother it?

VIC: I *never* bother women's magazines.

SADE: Looks to me like somebody . . . Watch out there ya don't splatter hot . . . *That's* all right . . . looks to me like somebody musta tore a *page* outa that magazine.

VIC: Why?

SADE: Because I was talkin' to Mis' Harris over the phone this morning an' she told me about a cake plate offer they got. Where you can get one for fifty cents. Exactly the cake plate I been wantin' so long. I leafed through *my* copy of the magazine an' couldn't find head or *tail* of it. An' it's the same magazine, I *know*.

VIC: Maybe *Rush* can throw some light on the matter.

SADE: I'll certainly *ask* him. If I can get a cake plate for fifty cents I wanta *know* about it. They're so handy an' good-lookin' a person'd be *foolish* not to take advantage of . . . Better use a *cloth,* Vic. That'll be terrible hot.

VIC: My hands are hard an' horny with toil. They . . . Ouch!

SADE: See. You'll find a little towel hangin' on the hook behind the stove.

VIC: What *become* of that guy you heard out in the alley just now?

SADE: Rush? He might of got talkin' with . . . Here he comes.

  [*Door opens*]

VIC: Get *out.*

RUSH: [*Laughing*] Who says so?

VIC: *I* say so, you scoundrel.

RUSH: C'mon out in the alley an' *fight* me then. [*Door closes*] Hi, mom.

SADE: Hi. Who'd ya talk with so long outside?

RUSH: Rooster Davis.

SADE: What's he doin' in *this* neighborhood at noon-time?

RUSH: Gonna eat dinner with his aunt.

SADE: Oh.

VIC: Clear the track. Here comes the waitress.

SADE: [*To Rush*] Your *father* got dinner today.

RUSH: That so? *Smells* good.

VIC: Gonna *taste* good too. Ladies an' gentlemen, dinner is announced.

SADE: How about your potatoes?

VIC: Coming up. Pray be seated, friends.

RUSH: [*To Sade*] Gov cook the meat?

SADE: Uh-huh.

RUSH: Didn't think he had it in him.

VIC: [*Off a little*] Am I bein' insulted behind my back?

RUSH: I'm throwin' bouquets at ya, gov.

VIC: Don't hit me in the eye with one while I'm carryin' this dish of potatoes. [*Closer*] Everybody settled an' happy?

SADE: Things *do* look good, Vic.

VIC: Things *are* good.

SADE: Here, I'll take 'em.

VIC: Dig in, George. You're due for new adventures in fancy flavor.

RUSH: [*Chuckles*] O.K.

SADE: Sit down, Vic. I think you got everything on.

VIC: Sure I have. Never-miss-a-trick Thompson they call me.

SADE: [*Giggles*] What on earth did you do to the jelly?

VIC: *There's* nothing amiss with the jelly.

SADE: Ya *slice* it?

VIC: I did.

SADE: Why?

VIC: Because I always got my nose out for new ideas. I never stand still. I scout around for the novel an' the revolutionary. Sliced jelly is my own invention. It may sweep the world. How's that bite of meat, Haile?

RUSH: *Good.*

VIC: Perhaps you mean *wonderful.*

RUSH: Round-steak never *is* what you'd call *wonderful.* It's *good,* but . . .

VIC: It's good but it'd be wonderful if it was anything besides round-steak. That what you mean?

RUSH: [*Chuckles*] Yeah.

VIC: I am appeased.

SADE: [*Approvingly*] Not bad at *all.*

VIC: Say it *positively* rather than negatively, kiddo. Instead of "Not bad at all," say "Good as can be."

SADE: [*Giggles*] All right—good as can be. See how it is to cook somethin' nice an' then fish for compliments? You always josh me about doin' that an' here you are doin' it yourself.

VIC: I wasn't fishin' for *compliments,* Sade. I was fishin' for justice. Have a slab of sliced jelly.

SADE: [*Giggles*] Sure.

RUSH: Say, did we have a swell assembly this morning. Best assembly we've had since I been goin' to high school.

SADE: What'd they have?

RUSH: They had an animal trainer. An', boy, was he a whiz. Well, I'll tell ya what he *done:*—he determined my life's work for me.

SADE: You gonna be an animal trainer?

RUSH: If I'm not a professional animal trainer, at least I'll be an amateur animal trainer.

SADE: What kind of animals did he have?

RUSH: Didn't have *any.* He didn't *need* any. I said he was an animal *trainer,* didn't I?

SADE: Uh-huh.

RUSH: Well, he ain't so much of an animal *trainer* as he is an animal *charmer*.

SADE: Charmer, huh?

RUSH: *Yeah*. He hypnotizes 'em.

SADE: Snakes?

RUSH: *Anything*. Doggone, ya oughta *see* his eyes bulge out. Enough to make ya sick.

VIC: Why don't you folks *eat?* Instead of wastin' your time with idle chatter.

SADE: *We're* eatin'.

VIC: You find things satisfactory?

SADE: Excellent.

VIC: Potatoes the way you like 'em?

SADE: Uh-huh. *See* how it is to be a cook? If you've taken any pains at *all* you hafta be told how *nice* everything is every minute.

VIC: The musician must have his applause.

SADE: Exactly.

RUSH: This animal-charmer-guy can work on *people too*.

SADE: Yes?

RUSH: Make 'em weak as a rag. It's the way he *looks* at 'em an' the way he *talks* to 'em.

SADE: How's he look at 'em?

RUSH: Put down your knife an' fork once an' gaze in my eyes.

VIC: Aw, shucks, Harry, you're crampin' my style. Let your mother enjoy her dinner.

RUSH: This'll only take a minute. O.K., mom, gaze in my eyes.

SADE: I don't think you washed your forehead very good when you left school this noon.

RUSH: Don't look at my *forehead*. Look in my *eyes*.

VIC: Who wants another shot of potato?

RUSH: One second, gov. Now concentrate.

VIC: Huh?

RUSH: Talkin' to *you,* mom.

SADE: What'll I concentrate about?

RUSH: Nothin' in particular. Just make your mind a blank.

SADE: You're gonna have a mole just under your left eye some day. You got exactly the same kind of a little spot that Uncle Fletcher had when he was younger.

RUSH: Don't look *under* my eye. Look *in* my eye.

SADE: Which one?

115

RUSH: *Both* of 'em.

SADE: You *can't* look in *both* a person's eyes, son. Hafta choose one or the other.

RUSH: O.K. *Choose* one.

VIC: Wish people around here'd *eat.* A man breaks his back building the dinner of the century.

RUSH: Just half a second, gov. Concentratin', mom?

SADE: Uh-huh.

RUSH: Are my eyes bulgin'?

SADE: No.

RUSH: Bulgin' a *little,* ain't they?

SADE: Look awful *stare*-y.

RUSH: Fine. *Now* we're gettin' there. Keep concentratin'.

VIC: I'll queer *your* act sometime, Pete. Some day you'll be showin' your girl how you can throw your knee outa joint an' I'll come along an' . . .

RUSH: This works better with silence, gov. Feel your brain slippin', mom?

SADE: No.

RUSH: Don't ya feel kinda hazy an' dreamy an' weak as a rag?

SADE: [*Giggles*] No.

RUSH: Try my *other* eye.

SADE: I guess I'll eat my dinner.

VIC: Sure. An' you better do the same thing, friend. Won't get another dinner like this prob'ly for the next forty years. Can I help you to potatoes, kiddo?

SADE: All right.

VIC: You haven't taken much of your *corn.*

SADE: I will though.

VIC: Taste suit you?

SADE: Taste is very good.

VIC: Notice a barely perceptible difference in flavor?

SADE: Why . . . I don't know. Did you fix it different than I told you to?

VIC: I brought into play a little notion of my own.

SADE: What was that?

VIC: I vigorously shook the can.

SADE: Why?

VIC: On the theory that corn, allowed to settle over a period of time, allows its more delicious elements to sink to the bottom.

SADE: [*Giggles*] Aw.

VIC: That theory might very well be true. By *shaking* the can, all the various little flavors are mixed deliciously together.

SADE: Canned corn's only *got* one flavor.

VIC: There's where you lack vision as a *cook,* Sade. Your *real* artist works along the line that *nothing* is impossible. When *I* was preparing this corn I made myself believe that it had *forty* flavors. I made it my aim to bring those forty flavors to the surface.

RUSH: *I* can only taste thirty-*eight* of 'em, gov.

VIC: Your levity is misplaced, Lester. Did you ever hear of Walter B. Pantly?

RUSH: No.

VIC: The dirt-track discus-dodger of Des Moines?

RUSH: [*Neg.*] Uh-uh.

VIC: His chief claim to fame was his discovery of the second flavor in peanuts.

RUSH: Second flavor in peanuts?

VIC: Yeah. *There's* two flavors in peanuts.

RUSH: I only know of one.

VIC: Look: you've eaten a batch of peanuts.

RUSH: O.K.

VIC: When you first *began* on the peanuts they had *one* flavor.

RUSH: Yeah?

VIC: After you've got down a whole *sack*ful they taste a little *different.* Ain't that right?

RUSH: Why . . . a . . . Yes, I guess it is.

VIC: The discovery of Walter B. Pantly.

RUSH: I don't see how you can call it a *discovery.*

VIC: I don't see why I *can't* call it a discovery.

RUSH: *Everybody* knows that about peanuts.

VIC: Yes, but who, besides Walter B. Pantly, had the courage of his convictions an' got his discovery registered at the Capitol building in Washington, D.C.?

RUSH: He do all that?

VIC: He did all that. *Now* when you go to Washington, D.C., you notice great crowds standin' in front of a metal tablet, sacred to the memory of Walter B. Pantly, discoverer of the second flavor in peanuts. Have another piece of steak?

RUSH: Sure.

VIC: You, Sade?

SADE: I believe I can stand just a smidgin.

VIC: Is this a good dinner or *ain't* it a good dinner?

117

SADE AND RUSH: Good dinner.

END OF SCRIPT

ANNOUNCER: And so we've sat at table with Vic, Sade, and young Rush Gook, who have been eating a meal prepared by the head of the family, and who have been talking about this, that, and the other thing.

1935

SADE AND HER
BEST FRIEND ARE
ON THE OUTS

THEME
ANNOUNCER: OPENING AND COMMERCIAL CREDITS
INTRODUCTION: Well sir, it's a few minutes or so past eleven o'clock in the morning as our scene opens now, and here in the kitchen of the small house half-way up in the next block we discover Mrs. Victor Gook industriously bending over her ironing-board. *Tuesday* is the time usually given over to this task, but the holidays have more or less thrown Sade off schedule. And so she irons. But there's a newcomer approaching apparently . . . because the back door is opening. Listen.

SADE: [*As door opens*] Grocery boy?

VIC: [*Off a little*] *Husband* boy.

SADE: Oh, h'lo there.

VIC: *I'll* say. Still at it?

SADE: [*As door closes*] Still at it.

VIC: [*Drawing closer*] Colder'n Billy Jackson out-doors.

SADE: You home for dinner already?

VIC: Nope. Just steppin' in for one second. The boss is waitin' for me out in front.

SADE: Oh, is he?

VIC: We're on our way to the court-house to file some papers. I left my brief-case home this morning. Some dope in it we hafta have.

SADE: Yes, I noticed you left it. I put it in the library table swing-back.

VIC: [*Moving off*] O.K. I'll trot in an' . . .

SADE: Wait a second, will ya?

VIC: Huh?

SADE: Vic, I . . . I think I'll call Ruthie *after* all.

VIC: [*Back again*] Thought you'd *done* that.

SADE: No.

VIC: You *said* you were going to.

SADE: Yes, but I told you I'd changed my mind.

VIC: When I talked to you on the phone at nine-thirty you said you'd changed your mind *back* again.

SADE: I changed it back again *again*.

VIC: Aw, for gosh sakes.

SADE: Well, what's a person to *do*? It was all Ruthie's fault. *She* started the squabble. It's *her* place to phone.

VIC: Wait till she *does* phone then.

SADE: But she *hasn't* phoned.

VIC: [*Moving off*] Well, you work it out for *yourself*. I hafta . . .

SADE: Wait, Vic.

VIC: Mr. Ruebush is sittin' out in the car. I can't keep him all day.

SADE: Will *you* phone Ruthie for me?

VIC: *Why?*

SADE: Because . . . Well, here's the way it is, Vic:—*Ruthie* knows that fight was all her fault. An' I bet she's just cryin' herself *sick* over there. But she's can't bring herself to call up because . . . Well, *you* know how a person is. They hate to *admit* they're in the wrong. I'd be the same way myself if I was her.

VIC: Well?

SADE: An' I hesitate from callin' *her* up because . . . well, because I'm the injured *party,* don'tcha see? It's not my bee's-wax to be phonin' somebody that was *mean* to me.

VIC: Tell ya what ya do: figure it all out an' decide what's best an' this noon when I come home you can . . .

SADE: Will *you* phone her?

VIC: *I* got nothin' to say to her.

SADE: No, but once you got her on the wire it'd give her a chance to ask if *Sadie* is there.

VIC: An' then what?

SADE: An' then she could do her *apologizin'* to me.

VIC: What if she don't *feel* like apologizin'?

SADE: That's what I *mean.* Don'tcha see? If *I* phoned an' she didn't feel like apologizin' I'd look like a ninny.

VIC: [*Moving off*] O.K. I'll take care of it this noon.

SADE: Why don'tcha do it *now?*

VIC: Because Mr. Ruebush is out by the curb freezin' his whiskers off.

SADE: Only *take* you half a *second.*

VIC: Kiddo, we're on our way to the *court*-house. *I* can't stall around here.

SADE: No, but think of poor Ruthie. She's had time to think things over an' I just bet she feels *awful.* I bet she's strainin' her *ears* listenin' for the phone bell to ring. [*Pleading*] C'mon.

VIC: [*Giving in*] What's the number—2572-X?

SADE: 2572-X.

VIC: I hope the boss don't . . . Hey, what'll I *say* to Ruthie when she answers?

SADE: Say . . . "This is Vic."

VIC: "This is Vic?"

SADE: Sure.

VIC: A very interesting telephone message. I'll ring her up an' say "This is Vic." After *that* thrilling statement I'll say good-by, huh?

SADE: Tell her . . . Ask her . . . Ask her if she got . . . if she got your Christmas card all right.

VIC: I never *sent* her any Christmas card.

SADE: *I* did.

VIC: O.K. I'll say, "This is Vic. Did you get Sade's Christmas card all right?"

SADE: For heavens' sake, don't mention *my* name.

VIC: Kiddo, *please*. I got to get *going*.

SADE: Well, *call*.

VIC: Tell me what to *say*.

SADE: Say . . . Oh, *I* don't know.

VIC: Look: you decide just how you want the matter handled an' when I come home for dinner I'll . . .

SADE: *No*. Poor Ruthie over there sobbin' her heart out.

VIC: I'll ask her if *Fred's* home. How's that?

SADE: Yeah. Yeah, ask her if Fred's home.

VIC: 2572-X?

SADE: 2572-X.

VIC: [*Lifting receiver*] Hope poor ol' Mr. Ruebush don't *die* out there in the terrible sub-zero . . . [To phone] 2572-X, please. Correct. [*To Sade*] . . . in the terrible sub-zero . . .

SADE: [*Quickly*] Hang up, Vic.

VIC: Huh?

SADE: Hang *up*.

VIC: What in the name of . . .

SADE: Hang *up*, I say.

VIC: [*Hanging up*] Sade, this is . . .

SADE: She answer?

VIC: She never had *time* to answer. The operator didn't get through pluggin' in . . .

SADE: I decided it's better not to phone her *after* all. It's not *my* place to do the patchin'. She insulted me when I was a guest in her house. I'm the one with the dirty end of the stick an' she's the one that's got to make the first move. Don't *you* think so?

VIC: Sure.

SADE: If she's cryin' her head off an' mad at herself it's no look-out of *mine*. What I really *ought* to do is . . . Where ya goin'?

VIC: [*Moving off*] In an' get my brief-case an' beat it.

123

SADE: Wait.

VIC: *No,* doggone it. I've had *enough* of this . . .

SADE: *I* don't want you to phone again. Listen, how'd it be if I sent Rush over there this noon with . . . [*Phone rings*] [*Excited*] There she is. There she is, Vic.

VIC: Swell. Expect me home for dinner about . . .

SADE: *You* gotta answer it.

VIC: *Me?*

SADE: Yes. An' listen . . . [*Phone again*] Don't answer it yet. Don't answer it yet. Look: I'll pretend I'm outa the kitchen. I'll pretend I'm upstairs.

VIC: Why?

SADE: *I* don't want her to think I'm hangin' around waitin' for the phone to ring.

VIC: Oh, shucks.

SADE: Well, I don't. She's been mean to me an' I'd just as soon she thought I let it all roll off a duck's back.

[*Phone*]

VIC: Women are just plain hay-wire.

SADE: Why don'tcha *answer* that?

VIC: You said you were going upstairs.

SADE: I'm just *pretending* I'm upstairs.

VIC: Shall I pick up the receiver?

SADE: *No. Yes,* I mean.

VIC: What *do* you mean? Yes or no. [*Phone again*]

SADE: *No. Yes.*

VIC: *Yes?*

SADE: *Yes.*

VIC: [*To phone*] Hello? Yes. Why . . . a . . . I *believe* so. Believe she's upstairs. Just a second. [*Ordinary tones*] Sade, you're wanted on the . . .

SADE: [*Hissing*] *Holler.*

VIC: Huh?

SADE: [*Hissing*] Put your hand over that transmitter.

VIC: *It's* covered. Whatcha *mean,* "holler"?

SADE: If I'm upstairs you got to holler loud so I can *hear* you.

VIC: Oh.

SADE: Now take your hand off the thing.

VIC: O.K.

SADE: [*Hissing*] Holler.

VIC: [*Hollers*] Sade. Oh, Sade. Come on down from upstairs.

124

You're wanted on the phone. [*To phone*] Hold the wire just a moment.

SADE: [*Low tones*] How's she sound?

VIC: O.K.

SADE: Got your hand over the transmitter business?

VIC: Yeah.

SADE: Does she sound like she's sorry?

VIC: Yeah.

SADE: How'd I better answer?

VIC: "Hello."

SADE: I mean . . . hadn't I better say "Yes" real bright till I find out it's Ruthie an' change my voice a little?

VIC: Good idea.

SADE: I'll say, [*Brightly*] "Yes?" An' then, [*Politely inquiring*] "Oh, yes, Mis' Stembottom?"

VIC: Great stuff. Here, take the receiver. *You've* had time to get downstairs.

SADE: No, it'd look like I *ran*.

VIC: Kiddo, *I* can't let my boss *freeze* to death out there at the curb.

SADE: [*Who is upset to begin with*] Oh, *forget* your boss five seconds.

VIC: [*Tough*] *Forget* him! I s'pose you'd have me put *this* silly nonsense ahead of *business*. I s'pose you'd . . .

SADE: Don't aggravate me, Vic. Got enough on my mind already.

VIC: As though *I* got nothin' on my mind. Holy smokes, I . . .

SADE: *Now* give me that phone.

VIC: *Take* it.

SADE: Stick around a minute.

VIC: I *can't* stick around a . . .

SADE: [*To Vic*] Hush. [*To phone—in her sweetest tones*] Mis' Gook Speakin'. What? Who *is* this? Oh. Oh. No, he hasn't. No. No, he hasn't showed up yet. Perfectly all right. Good-by. [*Hangs up*] [*Raises voice to call bitterly to her husband*] Vic, c'mere.

VIC: [*Off a little*] Kiddo, I *got* to get my brief case an' . . .

SADE: C'mere, I said.

VIC: [*Returning*] What the heck's wrong *now*?

SADE: Why didn't you *tell* me that wasn't Ruthie?

VIC: I didn't know it wasn't Ruthie.

SADE: It was Mis' Croucher at the grocery store.

VIC: What'd *she* want?

SADE: Wanted to speak with the grocery boy if he was here. [*Mad*] Such a lot of craziness I never seen before in my life.

125

VIC: I always *did* think Mother Croucher was a little bats. She . . .

SADE: I'm talkin' about *you.*

VIC: *Me?* What on earth have *I* done?

SADE: All that stuff about pretendin' I was upstairs.

VIC: That was *your* idea.

SADE: You should of found out if it *was* Ruthie on the phone or not.

VIC: [*Moving off*] O.K. O.K. *It's* all my fault. I *know* I'm to blame for . . .

SADE: C'mere.

VIC: Huh?

SADE: I'm *tired* of these monkey-shines. If Ruthie Stembottom ain't got the courage to call up an' admit she's wrong *I'm* not gonna be small about it. *Telephone* her.

VIC: Sade, Mr. Ruebush is out there in the bitter cold prob'ly writin' my discharge papers this very moment. *I* can't . . .

SADE: Let's get this over with.

VIC: *You* don't want me to lose my . . .

SADE: Number is 2572-X.

VIC: What'll I say to her?

SADE: Don't care *what* you say to her.

VIC: This is Vic?

SADE: Huh?

VIC: [*Stupidly*] This is Vic.

SADE: Oh, goodness, *baby*-talk—now of all times.

VIC: Shall I *say* "This is Vic?" To *Ruthie?*

SADE: Yes.

VIC: If I ever get mixed up in any half-wit didoes like this *again,* you can . . . [*Phone rings*]

SADE: There she is. There she is.

VIC: Want me to answer?

SADE: Of *course.* Of *Course.* Remember—I'm upstairs now.

VIC: [*Stupidly*] You're upstairs?

SADE: *Yes.* Like we done *before.*

  [*Phone*]

VIC: Shall I say . . .

SADE: Say that Sade is *upstairs* is all ya hafta say.

VIC: An' to hold the line a minute, huh?

SADE: Sure.

  [*Phone*]

VIC: Shall I . . .

SADE: *Answer* it, Vic. She's liable to think I'm not home.

VIC: [*To phone*] Yes? Oh, *hello* there. One second. (to Sade) Sade.

SADE: [*Hissing*] *Holler.*

VIC: [*Hollers*] Oh, Sade. You're wanted on the phone.

SADE: Now give me plenty of time to get *down.*

VIC: This is *Rush* on the . . .

SADE: Cover up that transmitter with your . . . Who?

VIC: Rush.

SADE: On the phone?

VIC: Yeah.

SADE: [*Irritated no end*] Oh, my heavens' sake's alive!

VIC: Well, you *told* me to holler. *Thunder,* I can't . . .

SADE: Gimme that. An' you stick around.

VIC: I *got* to go see if Mr. Ruebush is . . .

SADE: Stick around because you got to call up Ruthie for me. [*To phone*] Yes, Rush. What? Eat at the cafeteria this noon? Got money? When'll ya be home? Uh-huh—well, don't bring any boys with ya because there's errands to be run. Yes. All right. What? Where was I that gov had to holler. Oh, nowhere. No. You run on an' eat with your friends. Huh? Look, son, I hafta hang up now because I wanta use the phone for another call. Yes. Eat a nice hot dinner now. All right. Good-by. [*Hangs up*] [*To Vic*] He's gonna take lunch at the Greek's with . . . Vic. Where are ya? [*Calls*] Vic. [*Pause*] Oh, *Vic. Vic.* [*Pause*] [*And then hotly to herself*] *S*neaked *out* on me.

END OF SCRIPT

ANNOUNCER: Sade, being absolutely honest with you, we don't know as we blame him.

1936

VIC AND SADE
DISCUSS A
CLOSE FRIENDSHIP

THEME
ANNOUNCER: OPENING AND COMMERCIAL CREDITS
INTRODUCTION: Well sir, we *have* no scene as we enter the small house half-way up in the next block now, because within the largest upstairs bed-room where we are taking you it is pitch dark and al-most twelve o'clock midnight. But here's a *voice*. Listen.

SADE: [*Softly*] Vic?

VIC: [*With a bare edge of gruffness*] What?

SADE: Asleep?

VIC: Yeah.

SADE: *No,* you're not.

VIC: Yes, I am.

SADE: *Talk* to me a minute.

VIC: I'm very drowsy.

SADE. Vic, *I* don't wanta go to sleep mad.

VIC: Watcha mad about?

SADE: *I'm* not mad. But *you* are.

VIC: Me? Mad? Laughable. My soul never *was* so much at peace. I never *was* so serene.

SADE: *Fred* don't mean to be aggravating.

VIC: Sade, you'll kindly not mention that name to me *again.* I've *finished* with Fred Stembottom. I play no more Five *Hundred* with Fred Stembottom. I brush no more *elbows* with Fred Stembottom. Fred Stembottom an' I are *quits.*

SADE: *I* know you feel bad about tonight.

VIC: [*With spirit*] *Who* feels bad about tonight? *I* don't feel bad about tonight. I feel *good* about tonight. Tonight has taught me that a man can cherish a rattle-snake as a friend an' . . .

SADE: A little lower, Vic.

VIC: Huh?

SADE: You'll wake *Rush* up talkin' so loud.

VIC: Very well, I'll say no more. Let us sleep. I bid you good-night. [*With finality*] Good night.

SADE: [*After a brief pause*] It's just his *way.*

VIC: What's just who's way?

SADE: It's just Fred's *way* to get under a person's skin.

VIC: He didn't get under *my* skin. He might of *thought* he got under my skin, but he *didn't* get under my skin.

SADE: *Jokin'* is all it really *is. I* realize that kind of jokin' bothers a person.

VIC: It didn't bother *me* by a long shot.

SADE: [*Timidly*] You got kinda red in the face.

131

VIC: [*Tough*] What?

SADE: You . . . kinda squirmed in your chair when he was talkin'.

VIC: [*Louder than necessary*] Who *wouldn't* squirm around in their chair listenin' to such ignorant bunk? Who *wouldn't* . . .

SADE: Please, Vic—Rush.

VIC: [*Referring to Fred*] The fat-head.

SADE: [*Brief pause*] *It's* just Fred's *way*.

VIC: Just his *way*, hey? Some *way*, *I'll* say.

[*A poem*]

SADE: *I* know he's stubborn an' loud-talkin' but he's a wonderful husband to Ruthie an' *such* a good provider an' sends money to his folks an' just as soon give you the shirt off his back as . . .

VIC: I don't *want* the shirt off his back. I wouldn't *have* the shirt off his back. An' I'll tell ya *this*, Sade, I've been in that guy's house for the last time. The—last—time.

SADE: I bet if he had any idea you felt this way about it, he'd just *more'n* apologize. I bet he'd come over *a-kitin'* sayin' how sorry he . . .

VIC: If he come over a-kitin' I'd send him right *back* again a-kitin'. Listen, were we or were we not guests at his home tonight?

SADE: *'Course* we were guests in his home tonight an' that's why I say . . .

VIC: Let *me* say a minute . . . long as we're gonna lay in bed till morning *talking*. We were *guests* over there tonight. We were invited over there to play a sociable game of cards. What did our courteous *host* do? He lit right in an' told his guest his business was just so much hooey. He spent twenty minutes laughin' about his guest's . . .

SADE: *No*, he didn't, Vic. He . . .

VIC: [*Exercised*] He *didn't?* He didn't? Fred Stembottom didn't sit there at that card-table with that big wide dumb half-wit grin on his face an' snort over how funny my job down at the Plant . . .

SADE: Vic, *please*. You're talkin' terrible loud. Rush's got to have his sleep.

VIC: O.K. *I* didn't ask to discuss this. *You're* the one that wanted to have a pleasant chat in the middle of the night.

SADE: Couldn't you bring your voice down just a little?

VIC: I'll bring my voice down to *nothin'*. I need sleep *myself*. I bid you good-night. Good-night.

SADE: [*Ignoring this*] Fred didn't laugh at your job, Vic.

VIC: Oh, he *didn't*, huh? Where were *you?* In Canada? He sat there with that monkey-face grin an' went on for twenty minutes about the Kitchenware Industry. [*Mocks Fred*] "How do they *get* men to go in Kitchenware, Vic? Do they pick 'em out of insane asylums or do they stunt the brains of new-born babies?"

SADE: He just meant that to be *funny.*

VIC: Did *you* think it was funny?

SADE: No, but . . .

VIC: I should think it'd burn you *up* to hear cheap cracks like that about you husband's work.

SADE: I didn't think it was very smart of Fred to go *on* like that, but just the same I realized he was only . . .

VIC: We make our *living* out of Kitchenware. The food we *eat* comes from Kitchenware. Our money in the *bank* comes from Kitchenware. I've spent going on twenty years of my *life* in Kitchenware. All the future I *got* is Kitchenware.

SADE: No, I didn't think it was very smart of Fred to go on like that but just the same I realized . . .

VIC: An' who the heck is Fred Stembottom? Nothin' but a rotten little thirty-two-dollar-a-week clerk that only hangs on to his job because his bosses are too kind-hearted to . . .

SADE: [*Reproach*] Oh, *Vic.*

VIC: Oh, I wouldn't tell that to *him.* I wouldn't tell it to *nobody.* But what if I *had* said things like that tonight? *He* did. To *me.*

SADE: [*Small voice*] Only foolin' though.

VIC: [*Scornfully*] "Only foolin'." "Only foolin'."

SADE: Well, he *was* only foolin'. I know Fred's a little stupid when it comes to lots of things but I know as sure as there's a man in the moon that he wouldn't set *out* to hurt . . .

VIC: What surprises *me,* Sade, is that you didn't get mad *yourself. That's* what surprises *me.*

SADE: I *did* get a little mad. I . . .

VIC: Certainly *acted* it. You an' Ruthie *both* sat there an' giggled while Fred was hittin' up the two-bit comedy. Laughed out *loud* when he called me "The Prince of Pots an' Pans" an' the "Sweetheart of the Fryin' Skittle."

SADE: I laughed because . . .

VIC: *Never* mind. *It's* O.K. *It* won't happen again. I've been in Fred Stembottom's house for the last time an' you can put that in your pipe an' smoke it. Now let's go to sleep. Must be going on one o'clock.

SADE: Vic, don't get mad, but . . .

VIC: *I'm* not mad.

SADE: Don't you . . . Can't you kinda see where . . . Don't get mad now at what I say, will ya?

VIC: I'm not mad. *I'm* not mad. Can't I kinda see *what?*

SADE: Can't you kinda see where maybe *you* were a little bit half to blame tonight?

VIC: How?

SADE: Fred didn't start his joshin' till . . . till after you give *him* a little joshin'.

VIC: Did I run down his job? Did I make fun of the way he makes a living? Did I poke him in the spot where it hurts the worst?

SADE: No, but . . . [*Halts*]

VIC: But what?

SADE: You kinda went after *his* goat early in the evening there.

VIC: When?

SADE: Well—remember when Ruthie served the ice cream?

VIC: I do.

SADE: Remember what was bein' said?

VIC: I complimented Ruthie on her ice cream, stated it was delicious, announced it was my favorite flavor, an' in every way behaved like a guest is *s'posed* to behave.

SADE: Do you remember—I may not get this exactly right—but do you remember sayin' you liked ice-cream served in round chunks like baseballs?

VIC: I do.

SADE: An' then you recollect what *Fred* said?

VIC: Somethin' insulting, I imagine. What'd he say?

SADE: He said speakin' of baseball it wouldn't be long now before . . . Izzy Bean, is it?

VIC: Dizzy Dean.

SADE: He said speakin' of baseball it wouldn't be long now before Dizzy Dean would be fannin' out National League batters like sick flies.

VIC: I recall the remark, yes.

SADE: An' then *you* said Dizzy Dean was just so much wet gunpowder an' oughta be plowin' corn down on the farm.

VIC: *Sure.* That's *right.* Dizzy Dean's a flash in the pan.

SADE: That got under Fred's skin.

VIC: What did?

SADE: The things you said about Dizzy Dean. He thinks Dizzy Dean is marvelous. Keeps a scrap-book about him an' everything. Listens to the radio. Thinks the sun rises an' *sets* on Dizzy Dean.

VIC: That's *another* example of Fred's stupidity.

SADE: But you were trompin' on his *toes* with the things you said.

VIC: Good.

SADE: Trompin' on 'em good an' *hard.* I saw his neck get red as fire one time there when you said you'd rather have one pitcher from the bush league than all the Dizzy Deans in the world.

VIC: I was tellin' the *truth*. I would.

SADE: But it made Fred *mad*.

VIC: Excellent.

SADE: An' you went right *ahead* makin' him mad. You were talkin' about his *car*. Said you'd bet him three to one the transmission wouldn't hold up five hundred miles.

VIC: An' it *won't*. I was statin' *facts*. *Everybody* knows that make of automobile is so much junk.

SADE: But after all it's *his* car. He paid good *money* for it. He's as proud of it as Adam. Goes over it with a damp cloth every night of the universe.

VIC: If he was smarter he'd drive it into Sugar Crick.

SADE: But don't you *see,* Vic?

VIC: See what?

SADE: He didn't make you any madder than you made *him*. It was just one thing leading to another. Till finally he got on the subject of Kitchenware.

VIC: Well, he won't get on the subject of Kitchenware any *more*. Not with *me*. I'm *through* with the fat-head.

SADE: But won't you admit you were *partly* to blame for . . .

VIC: Kiddo, it's gettin' on for *morning*. Let's get some *sleep*.

SADE: All right.

VIC: Good night.

SADE: Good night.

  [*Pause*] [*More pause*]

SADE: Vic.

VIC: I'm asleep.

SADE: It's *Ruthie* that *I'm* thinkin' of.

VIC: What about her?

SADE: She's my best friend.

VIC: Well?

SADE: I wouldn't lose her for *anything*.

VIC: *You* don't hafta lose her.

SADE: [*Pause*] When you an' Fred have these flare-ups, *naturally* the wife sticks to the husband. I noticed it tonight. I was peeved when Fred was laughin' at your work an' Ruthie was peeved when you were makin' fun of Fred's baseball players an' his auto. We just couldn't *help* it. We *tried* to, but it was *bound* to show a little. Like I said, Ruthie is my best friend. My *very* best friend. I'm with other ladies a lot, *yes*—Mis' Donahue an' Mis' Harris an' Mis' Brighton an' Mis' Applerot—but it's not the same. Maybe it's because they're a little *older* than I am. Maybe it's because they're a little brighter in the head an' got more education. *I* don't know what it is. But I'm not the *same* with them as I am with Ruthie. With Ruthie I can laugh an' cry an' fight an' gossip an' talk nonsense an' just get along marvelous. With other ladies I sorta feel like here I am a woman that ain't a girl any longer an' got a fourteen year old boy to boot. See?

VIC: Um.

SADE: Ruthie an' I get along a lot like *kids* get along. It's *hard* for married ladies with families to have close friends where you can just take your *hair* down. An' Ruthie's the only close friend like that I *got*. The only one I ever *will* have probably . . . because I'm getting along to an age where women don't *make* close friends. [*Pause*] Awake?

VIC: Yeah—*I'm* listenin'.

SADE: You . . . see what I mean?

VIC: Uh-huh.

SADE: Don't you think . . . If you *tried* don't you think you an' Fred could hit it off better?

VIC: *I* guess so.

SADE: Mean it?

VIC: Sure. *Fred* ain't beyond redemption. Not a bad egg at *all* if ya don't take him serious.

SADE: Would it . . . Would it be all right if . . .

   [*Low giggle because she's afraid to say it*]

VIC: Would it be all right if what?

SADE: If I asked 'em over tomorrow tonight for more cards?

VIC: Fred an' Ruthie?

SADE: Yes.

VIC: Sure.

SADE: You're not just talkin'?

VIC: *No.* Go ahead—ask 'em over.

SADE: Thanks, Vic.

VIC: Hey, kiddo, don'tcha think we oughta settle down an' get some *sleep?*

SADE: Yes.

VIC: Good-night.

SADE: Good-night.

END OF SCRIPT

ANNOUNCER: Which concludes another brief interlude at the small house half-way up in the next block.

1936

**FOURTH OF JULY PICNIC
WITH OLD FRIENDS
OR STYLISH ONES**

THEME

ANNOUNCER: OPENING AND COMMERCIAL CREDITS

INTRODUCTION: Well sir, it's about three thirty o'clock in the afternoon as our scene opens now, and here in the kitchen of the small house half-way up in the next block we discover Mrs. Victor Gook all by herself. The lady has just answered the telephone and we hear her saying . . .

SADE: [*To phone*] No we haven't, Ruthie. No, no special plans at all. We did talk a little about takin' the train to Chicago for the day but finally decided not to. Vic's got some business at the office first thing in the morning and Rush an' the boys want to go to the Park an' watch the soldiers shoot off the cannon so we just thought we'd stay around home an' kinda take it easy . . . maybe go to the movie show in the evening. Uh-huh. Ah—were *you* thinking of . . . ? A picnic? Who—you an' Fred an' us? Oh sure, an' Melvin. Why I don't know, Ruthie—sounds grand to *me*. *Yes*. Dillman Dells? Uh-huh. Yes, I *know* they have. Long picnic tables an' little ovens where you can build a fire. Yes. Oh, sounds just fine to *me,* Ruthie. We'd be away from the Fourth of July noise too. Oh, *fun*. Well, look, lady, 'course I don't know whether *Vic's* got anything up his sleeve or not, but I'm real sure he hasn't an' . . . Say, wait—here he comes now, I think. [*Calls*] Vic?

RUSH: [*Out on porch*] No—me.

SADE: Seen your father along the alley any place?

RUSH: [*Opening screen*] I haven't *been* along the alley. I just come from Rooster Davis's house.

SADE: How'd ya like to go on a picnic tomorrow?

RUSH: Fine. Where?

SADE: [*As screen door slams*] Dillman Dells.

RUSH: Who all's in on it?

SADE: Just the Stembottoms an' us. It's Mis' Stembottom I got here on the phone. [*To phone*] Hello, Ruthie?

RUSH: Just a second, mom.

SADE: Whatcha want?

RUSH: I'm tied *up* from eight o'clock till ten o'clock tomorrow. I have an engagement to go to the Park with my various friends to . . .

SADE: We won't be startin' till early afternoon. [*To phone*] Ruthie? It was *Rush* just come in; *he'd* like to go on a picnic. [*Laughs*] Oh sure. Uh-huh. Of *course* baseball. [*Laughs*] Well, let's see now; what all we got to do?—I'll fix a basket for *my* fellas, huh? All right. Oh, *'course* we don't hafta make any monstrous big elaborate preparations. I'll just throw some sandwiches in a hamper an' wait for you folks to pull up to the curb an' away we go for a Fourth of July picnic. [*Laughs*] *Sure*. What? Why . . . a . . . would you have *room?*

He's right by my elbow here; I'll ask him. [*To Rush*] Mis' Stembottom says how would you like to bring one of your friends along—somebody to play baseball with at the picnic grounds.

RUSH: That'd be great.

SADE: Who could you get?

RUSH: *Any* of my various friends would accept a cordial invitation. Rooster Davis or Milton Welch or Smelly Clark or Heinie . . .

SADE: Well, you decide on somebody. [*To phone*] Ruthie? Rush thinks that'd be lovely. What? [*Laughs*] That's right: what's a picnic without kids. [*Laughs*] Oh, we'll have oceans of fun. Sure. What time ya think we oughta get started?—little before noon, maybe. Uh-huh. Sure, an' be good an' hungry for . . . Sure. Well, all right, Ruthie, we'll go ahead like that then. I'll prob'ly phone you back a little later on. Yes. What? No, *I* won't go to any enormous bother—just toss some eatables in my little basket. [*Laughs*] Sure. All right, Ruthie,—good-by. [*Hangs up*] [*Briskly to Rush*] We'll hafta pitch in an' get busy now, kiddie. That picnic basket's got to be dug out from behind that junk down cellar. I'll want you to help me wash out you an' gov's white duck pants sometime this evening. The store won't be open in the morning so we'll hafta get our groceries tonight. There's *loads* of stuff to be looked after. You stick around close so you'll be handy when I need ya. *First* thing I'm gonna do is go upstairs an' find my little blue middie-blouse an' skirt. [*Moves off*] While I'm doin' that you can go down in the basement an' . . . *I'll* tell ya what *you* can do. You can call your father.

RUSH: What for?

SADE: [*Moving off*] Tell him we're going on a picnic with Mr. an' Mis' Stembottom tomorrow. Say maybe he oughta come home soon as he can because there's so many things to do.

RUSH: O.K.

SADE: [*Off*] I expect what I *oughta* do is fix up a list of things for him to bring from town.

RUSH: [*Calls*] Go ahead. I'm gonna call Rooster Davis first anyhow. He's the one I'm gonna invite.

SADE: [*Off*] All right.

RUSH: [*To phone*] 2572-X, please. Correct. [*Calls*] Oh, mom, how'd it be if I issued Rooster a cordial invitation to . . .

SADE: [*Far away*] I can't hear ya, son. Wait'll I come back down.

RUSH: [*Almost to himself*] O.K. [*Whistles a few seconds*] [*To phone*] Hello, Mrs. Davis? Rush, Mrs. Davis. Is Roost . . . Edwin there? If you please.

　[*Whistles in low tones a few seconds*]

VIC: [*Opening screen door*] Get away from that telephone, you wretch, or I'll tear you to pieces.

RUSH: Oh, h'lo, gov. Happy Third of July.

VIC: Same to you, honey, an' here's a diamond wrist-watch to remember me by. [*Screen door slam*] Where's your mother?

RUSH: Just went upstairs. Hey, I was just about to telephone you.

VIC: Why don't ya hang up the receiver then? You prob'ly won't hear my voice at the other end because here I am in person.

RUSH: [*Chuckling*] I'm not telephonin' ya *now*. I'm endeavoring to get in touch with Rooster Davis. He's out in the back yard; his mother just went to call him. We're going on a *picnic*, gov.

VIC: Who is?

RUSH: You an' me an' mom an' Mr. an' Mis' Stembottom an' Melvin an' maybe Rooster.

VIC: *No.*

RUSH: Sure.

VIC: No *arrangements* have been made, have they?

RUSH: Sure. Mis' Stembottom just phoned mom an' they doped out . . .

VIC: Ya say your mother's upstairs?

RUSH: Yeah. She . . . [*To phone*] Oh hello, Rooster. How are ya, fella?

VIC: [*Calls*] Sade. *Oh* Sade.

RUSH: Pipe *down,* gov. I'm *talkin'*.

VIC: Hold it a second. [*Calls*] Oh, Sade.

RUSH: [*To phone*] Hold it a second, Rooster. [*To Vic*] Shucks, gov, when a person is conversing over the . . .

    [*Ad lib*]

SADE: [*In the distance, over Rush*] Callin' me?

VIC: [*To Rush*] *Will* you keep that clam closed?

SADE: [*Off*] That you, Vic?

VIC: [*Calls*] Yeah. Can ya come down right away?

SADE: [*Off*] What's the matter?

VIC: [*Calls*] Got somethin' to tell ya.

SADE: [*Off*] All right.

VIC: [*To Rush*] How long ago did your mother an' Mis' Stembottom talk to each other?

RUSH: Just before you come in. *Now* may I be permitted to continue my conversation over the telephone with Rooster . . .

VIC: Who all'd you say was going on this picnic?

RUSH: Us an' Mr. an' Mrs. Stembottom an' Melvin an' maybe Rooster.

VIC: That why you're callin' Rooster—to invite him?

RUSH: [*Tough*] That's why I'm *tryin'* to call him. Looks like I ain't got much *chance* to . . .

VIC: Well, *don't* invite him. Stall him off. Tell him something else. This business has got to be talked over.

RUSH: Mom *asked* me to invite a friend to go with us on . . .

VIC: I said tell him something else. [*Calls*] Sade.

SADE: [*Much closer than before*] *I'm* comin'. What's the matter?

VIC: [*Calls*] We got somethin' of a mix-up.

SADE: [*Closer*] I'll be there as fast as I *can*. Is somebody *murdered*?

RUSH: [*Tough, to his father*] *Now* may I talk to Rooster Davis that's been sittin' holdin' the telephone receiver to his head for half an hour?

VIC: Don't invite him on any picnic *yet* awhile.

RUSH: Why?

VIC: Do like I say.

RUSH: [*To phone*] Hello, Rooster? Sorry to keep you waitin', fella. How ya feelin'? Uh-huh.

SADE: [*Almost up*] What's the commotion?

VIC: Wait'll Andy here gets through.

RUSH: [*To phone*] It's nice to hear you're feeling no pain, Rooster. Uh-huh. Oh, I . . . just called to ascertain the state of your health. Uh-huh.

VIC: Hurry it up, George.

SADE: What *is* all this?

VIC: I'll tell ya in a second.

RUSH: [*To phone*] That was all I wanted, Rooster. Yes. Be seein' ya tomorrow at the Park for the cannon explosion, perhaps? Fine. All right, fella. So long. [*Hangs up*] He prob'ly thinks my *brains* have folded up. Shucks, I try to carry on an intelligent conversation with . . .

VIC: Pipe down, Rush. Sade, this Stembottom picnic business ain't all *set,* is it?

SADE: Ruthie phoned just a few minutes ago an' asked would we . . .

VIC: Yeah, Pete was just tellin' me. But it ain't so ya can't get *out* of it, is it?

SADE: Why, *no*. All we said was we'd . . .

VIC: Well, listen, *I've* made arrangements to go on a picnic.

SADE: Just you or all of us?

VIC: All of us.

SADE: With who?

VIC: [*Elated*] Kiddo, you'll jump through the ceiling when I tell ya.

SADE: Well, tell me.

VIC: Mr. *Ruebush* an' his friends.

SADE: [*Bewildered*] Mr. *Ruebush.*

VIC: Mr. Ruebush. Here's what happened. I was sittin' in my office about half an hour ago an' in walked the boss. He says, "How you an' the family gonna spend the Fourth, Vic?" I says, "Thought we'd just kinda stick around the house. Maybe take in a picture show an' shoot off a firecracker or two." He says, "A bunch of *us* is gonna drive up to White's Lake for a little picnic. How'd ya like to come along?" I hesitated a minute an' then says, "Sounds *fine.*"

SADE: Who else is . . .

VIC: Lemme tell ya the rest of this. I hesitated a minute an' then says, "Sounds fine." "O.K.," says Mr. Ruebush, "Let's consider it a date. We'll be by an' pick you up along about eleven or eleven-thirty."

SADE: Who *else* is going . . .

VIC: [*Proud and happy*] Whatcha think of *them* onions, kid?

SADE: I'd like to know . . .

VIC: What *you* think about picknicking with the blue-bloods, Oscar?

RUSH: One picnic's the same as another to *this* chicken. I'm the type of an individual that . . .

VIC: Sade, we're gettin' *up* in the world. *Think* of us hobnobbin' with that crowd?

SADE: Who's gonna *be* in the crowd?

VIC: Well, Mr. Ruebush's sister's in town. She'll be along with her boy, a kid around Rush's age. Then there's Mr. an' Mrs. T. R. Freeman.

SADE: [*Tight-lipped*] From the Prairie Hill Addition?

VIC: [*Gleefully*] *Sure* from the Prairie Hill Addition. Where they pull ten-dollar bills outa *trees.*

SADE: Who else is going?

VIC: Mr. an' Mrs. Roy Floriman.

SADE: Roy Floriman that's head of the bank?

VIC: Sure.

SADE: Who else?

VIC: Those are the only parties the boss mentioned. But I know there's gonna be four car-loads.

SADE: How's it happen *we* got invited?

VIC: *You* know how the boss is, *kiddo.* Good as gold. Fine as silk.

SADE: He's *always* been good as gold an' fine as silk but he's never invited us to *picnics* before.

VIC: You're not tellin' me ya don't wanta *go?*

SADE: Vic, *we* don't belong in a crowd like that.

VIC: Why *not?*

SADE: Just because we don't.

VIC: That's foolishness. Listen, we're going to White's *Lake.* That's the toniest place there is. There's gonna be an orchestra concert in the afternoon under the trees an' a dance in the evening.

SADE: We haven't danced in *years.*

VIC: What's the *difference?* Hey, kiddo, what's *eatin'* on ya?

SADE: We don't belong in a crowd like that.

VIC: Oh, bosh. I s'pose you'd rather go with Fred an' *Ruthie* on a picnic.

SADE: Lots rather.

VIC: I bet that *Melvin* guy'll be along.

SADE: Yes, he will.

VIC: Pete here was just invitin' the Davis kid. Were we going in Fred's car?

SADE: Yes.

VIC: Wouldn't *that* be fine. Let's see: you an' me an' Rush an' Rooster an' Fred an' Ruthie an' Melvin. Seven people. In *that* little go-cart. Where'd we *sit?*

SADE: We'd make out.

VIC: Whereabouts did ya *plan* your picnic?

SADE: Dillman Dells.

VIC: Oh, my, my, my. Dillman Dells. Where there's flies an' kids an' cows. Look: we got a chance to go to White's *Lake.* Where the picnic grounds have been gone over with a *lawn*-mower. Where there's *waiters* an' colored lanterns an' . . .

SADE: We just can't go, Vic.

VIC: *Why* can't we?

SADE: Because we can't.

VIC: We've been *invited.* They *want* us to go. Why would they invite us if they didn't want us to go?

SADE: I never said they didn't want us to go. I said *we* don't want to go.

VIC: *Sure* we wanta go. *You're* just *timid.* Mr. Ruebush invited you especially.

SADE: Invited Rush especially too, didn't he?

VIC: *Sure.*

SADE: Because they got a boy fourteen years old an' thought it'd be nice for him to have another boy fourteen years old to play with, I bet.

VIC: Oh, come now, Sade. That's ridiculous.

SADE: We can't go.

VIC: *Why* can't we go?

SADE: We wouldn't fit. How'd we be with Mr. Ruebush an' his stylish sister an' Roy Floriman an' his wife from the bank an' Mr. an' Mrs. T. R. Freeman from the Prairie Hill Addition?

VIC: Fine.

SADE: We'd be all tight inside.

VIC: Bunk.

SADE: *I'd* be all tight inside. I wouldn't know what to say. Wouldn't know what to do. *It* wouldn't be any Fourth of July picnic for *me*. I'd be miserable from the minute we started till the minute we got back.

VIC: [*Pause*] That . . . a . . . puts another light on the matter—if *you* wouldn't have a good time.

SADE: You *know* I wouldn't have a good time.

VIC: You'd . . . rather go with Fred an' Ruthie?

SADE: Oh, *my!* What if we *do* hafta crowd seven of us in a little tiny automobile an' sit on baskets? What if we *do* hafta spread our eatables on an ol' broken table in the woods where we get ants down our neck? We'll play baseball an' wade in the crick an' get dirty an' have *fun. That's* a *picnic.*

VIC: [*Slowly*] Whatever you say, kiddo.

SADE: Don'tcha think I'm right?

VIC: I guess so.

SADE: You won't be disappointed not going with the fancy folks?

VIC: Naw. [*Chuckles*] Shucks.

RUSH: You folks have had a darn interesting discussion. I enjoyed every minute of it.

END OF SCRIPT

ANNOUNCER: Which concludes another brief interlude at the small house half-way up in the next block.

1936

**SMELLY CLARK
TO CHANGE HIS AGE
FROM 16 TO 21**

THEME

ANNOUNCER: OPENING AND COMMERCIAL CREDITS

INTRODUCTION: Well sir, supper has been over just a little while as we enter the small house half-way up in the next block now, and here in the living-room we find Mr. and Mrs. Victor Gook and their son Mr. Rush Gook. Mr. and Mrs. Victor Gook are reading sections of the evening paper, while their son Mr. Rush Gook is removing his overcoat because he's just come in from out-doors. Listen.

RUSH: May I attract your attention a few moments? [*Pause*] May I attract your attention a few moments?

VIC: Tell it to your mother, Axle-grease. I'm right in the middle of an article.

RUSH: I do not wish to *tell* anything, gov. I wish to *ask* something.

VIC: Ask your mother.

RUSH: This is a matter where I wish to ask *both* of you. Mom.

SADE: [*Looking up*] What?

RUSH: May I attract your attention a few moments?

SADE: I told you at supper-time you weren't gonna scrunge any twenty-five cents outa *me*. I give you twenty-five cents just last Monday. I'm not *made* of twenty-five centses, ya know. Twenty-five centses don't grow on trees.

RUSH: [*Patiently*] No mention was made of any twenty-five centses, mom.

SADE: Whatcha want then?

RUSH: Merely to attract your attention a few moments.

SADE: Um.

RUSH: I wish to attract your attention also, gov.

VIC: *You* got it attracted. What's the commotion?

RUSH: Do I have *your* attention attracted, mom?

SADE: [*Impatient giggle*] Yes.

RUSH: [*Quietly*] You continue to read your newspaper.

SADE: What ails this child, Vic?

VIC: Couldn't tell ya. Perhaps the cold weather has worked its way into his slender skull so empty an' fragile.

RUSH: Now that I have both your attentions attracted, I'd like to state my case.

VIC: Go ahead.

RUSH: I'm expecting some company to drop in an' see me pretty soon.

VIC: That's great.

RUSH: Smelly Clark.

149

VIC: Oh, boy.

RUSH: Are *you* expecting any callers, mom?

SADE: [*Neg.*] Uh-uh.

RUSH: Then perhaps you'll be willing to cooperate with me in *entertaining* Smelly.

SADE: *Entertaining* him?

RUSH: Exactly.

SADE: [*Giggling*] Why should *I* entertain him?

RUSH: There's a great *change* takin' place in Smelly's life, mom.

SADE: Is there?

RUSH: I'll explain if you'll let me.

SADE: All right.

RUSH: Will you listen *too,* gov?

VIC: I'm listening.

RUSH: [*Quietly*] You continue to read your newspaper.

VIC: [*A hint of impatience*] Oh gosh, what *is* this?

RUSH: I'd love to *explain* if you'll give me two cents' worth of attention.

VIC: Shoot.

RUSH: Smelly Clark is gonna pay us a short visit this evening.

VIC: Yeah, you said that.

RUSH: I'd like to have you an' mom co-operate with me in entertaining him.

VIC: You said that also.

RUSH: The reason I'm askin' this favor is because Smelly Clark is takin' a very important step in life. He's takin' a step prob'ly nobody else in the world ever took before.

VIC: What step is that?

RUSH: [*With dramatic simplicity*] He's having his *age* changed.

SADE: His *what* changed?

RUSH: His *age.*

SADE: Havin' it *changed?*

RUSH: Havin' it changed.

VIC: You must be thinkin' of a half-dollar, Snake-bite. Smelly's havin' a half-*dollar* changed.

RUSH: Smelly is havin' his *age* changed.

VIC: How is he going about *that,* pray?

RUSH: By means of lawyers, courts, an' the United States government.

VIC: You awake in my heart a mild interest.

RUSH: I *thought* I would.

VIC: Tell all.

RUSH: Will ya cooperate with me in entertaining Smelly when he gets here?

VIC: Sure.

RUSH: Will *you,* mom?

SADE: Sure.

RUSH: That's fine, an' thank you. Now I'll explain about how he's havin' his age changed.

SADE: Yeah, do that.

RUSH: Well, as you know, Smelly is about a year older than I am.

SADE: Uh-huh.

RUSH: He's going on sixteen.

SADE: Uh-huh.

RUSH: But sixteen is still fairly young.

SADE: Yeah.

RUSH: It's *quite* young for the average human being, in fact.

SADE: Sure.

RUSH: An' Smelly finds himself *handicapped* by that. See, he quit school an' went out in the world to make his living, but it seems like a sixteen-year-old individual has difficulty getting *respect* from people. They insist on thinkin' he's a young *kid.*

SADE: Uh-huh.

RUSH: Smelly can't shave anybody there in the barber shop because he's not old enough to get a barber's license. All he can do is shine shoes an' sweep *up* the place an' stuff.

SADE: Uh-huh.

RUSH: So his salary remains low an' he has trouble gettin' rich.

SADE: Yeah.

RUSH: Therefore he's havin' his age officially changed.

SADE: Officially changed to what?

RUSH: Twenty-one years.

SADE: He's gonna be twenty-one years old?

RUSH: If this thing goes *through* he is.

SADE: [*Mildly*] My, my. He won't *look* twenty-one.

RUSH: No, but he'll be twenty-one *officially.* Anybody that doubts it can look it up on the record in the White House in Washington, D.C.

VIC: How does a person go *about* gettin' their age officially changed?

RUSH: Same way people go about gettin' their *names* changed.

VIC: Oh.

RUSH: You've heard about people gettin' their *names* changed, haven't ya?

151

VIC: Sure.

RUSH: You told me about a case *yourself*. You said you knew a fella back in Dixon, Illinois, by the name of Walter Squish. He didn't *like* the name Squish so he arranged it with the United States government to be called Walter *Henderson*.

VIC: That's right.

RUSH: Ya do the same thing when ya get your *age* officially changed. I don't know all the ins an' outs of it, but I suppose ya submit your case to the president or the secretary of the Navy or somebody an' they okay it.

VIC: Yeah.

RUSH: Anyway, if all this works out Smelly Clark'll be twenty-one years old instead of fifteen in the eyes of the world an' he'll be entitled to apply for a barber's license. Also he'll be entitled to vote in all elections. He'll even be able to get *married*.

SADE: Does he *want* to get married?

RUSH: He's got no *woman* in mind right *now*. But if a woman comes along that suits him, all he's got to do is take her around to the preacher's an' slap down two dollars.

VIC AND SADE: [*Laugh a little*]

RUSH: [*Chuckles*] Pretty high-class stuff, huh?

VIC: Yeah.

SADE: I believe *I'll* do that. Have *my* age officially changed. Only I'm gonna go the *other* way. I'll have it fixed so I'm *sixteen*. Be a *girl* again.

RUSH: [*Approvingly*] Uh-huh.

VIC: I'm gonna have my age officially changed to ninety-six. Then I can draw a Civil War pension. Or *no*—I'll have my age changed to three hundred an' fifty. Then I can get a job in the circus.

RUSH: Oh, I don't imagine a person can play fast an' *loose* with the idea. Liable to get the United States *government* after ya.

SADE: Smelly's comin' over here after a bit, huh?

RUSH: I expect him very shortly.

SADE: How old will he be? Fifteen or twenty-one?

RUSH: Fifteen. See, he hasn't got this proposition *started* yet. Maybe by the middle of next *week* he'll be twenty-one.

SADE: Oh.

VIC: You said somethin' about your mother an' *myself* entertaining Smelly, Sam. What was that?

RUSH: That's what I want to *talk* to you folks about. Smelly's already started to *act* like he's twenty-one, so he wants people to *treat* him like he's twenty-one. Appreciate the angle I'm attempting to put across?

152

SADE: You want *us* to treat him like he's twenty-one?

RUSH: Exactly. Will ya do it?

SADE: Sure.

RUSH: Will you, gov?

VIC: Sure.

RUSH: Thank you very much. It'll buck Smelly up considerable.

VIC: How do you *treat* a guy when ya wanta treat him like he's twenty-one?

RUSH: Well, I got a few *hints* to pass along to you an' mom.

VIC: Fine.

RUSH: In the first place, forget that nickname "Smelly."

VIC: Is he havin' "Smelly" officially changed to something else?

RUSH: No, but he's *droppin'* his nickname. Nicknames ain't *dignified* for a man aged twenty-one years.

SADE: Whatcha want us to *call* him?

RUSH: I think *you* oughta address him as Mister Clark, mom.

SADE: Mister Clark, huh?

RUSH: Yes.

SADE: All right. [*Giggles*] Mister Clark.

RUSH: An' please don't do it in a *comical* way. If ya do you'll hurt his *feelings*. Say things like, "How is the weather out, Mister Clark?" "Mister Clark, take *this* chair: it's more comfortable."

SADE: All right.

RUSH: See, when Smelly gets here he's not gonna stand out by the back porch an' *holler* like he generally does. He's comin' right up the front steps an' ring the bell.

SADE: Um.

VIC: Shall *I* address him as Mister Clark?

RUSH: No, gov, *you* call him "T. W."

VIC: T. W.?

RUSH: Yeah. "By the way, T. W., I see where they voted a new street-car system in Akron, Ohio." "T. W., what do you think of the European situation?"

VIC: O.K.

RUSH: Call him old *man* once in a while too.

VIC: O.K.

RUSH: "Old man, we're moving a lot of merchandise in Minnesota these days." "Who's your tailor, old man? That's a nice lookin' suit ya got on."

VIC: Uh-huh.

RUSH: An' mom.

SADE: Yes?

RUSH: Don't say, "How's mama," will ya?

SADE: [*Giggles*] No.

RUSH: You wouldn't say "how's mama?" to any *other* guy aged twenty-one.

SADE: No, I wouldn't.

RUSH: An' don't offer him a cookie.

SADE: He *likes* cookies awful well. That is, he did when he was a *boy*.

RUSH: Yeah, but the point is he *ain't* a boy any longer.

SADE: All right.

RUSH: You can say, "Mister Clark, would you care for a little refreshment?" Or, "Mister Clark, perhaps you'll wait while I make some coffee."

SADE: Uh-huh.

VIC: How are *you* gonna treat Mister Clark, Pete?

RUSH: The way I'd treat *any* older person. See, Smelly's twenty-one. *I'm* only *fourteen*. I'll be very courteous towards him.

VIC: Sure.

RUSH: An' he'll treat me like *any* twenty-one-year-old man would treat a youngster. He'll say to you folks, "My, my, Rush is just *sproutin'* up."

VIC: Uh-huh.

RUSH: He'll say, "How ya gettin' along in school these days, son?" I'll say, "Very well, thank you, Mister Clark."

VIC: Uh-huh.

RUSH: An' when he leaves he's gonna give me a nickel to buy candy with.

VIC AND SADE: [*Laugh a little*]

RUSH: [*Chuckling*] 'Course he owes me a nickel already so he won't be out anything.

VIC: Could you tell me a little more about the *procedure* of gettin' your age officially changed, Walter?

RUSH: Well, I imagine ya get a-hold of a *lawyer first*. He draws up the proper documents an' sends 'em to Washington, D.C., an' the President signs his name an' . . . [*Door-bell*].

SADE: There's Smelly now.

RUSH: Mister *Clark*, mom.

SADE: Yeah, Mister Clark. Go let him in.

RUSH: [*Moving off*] You won't forget all I told ya?

SADE: No.

RUSH: [*Moving off*] Just keep in mind we got an *adult* visitin' us.

SADE: Sure.

VIC: [*To Sade*] Ya s'pose Mister Clark would like a cigar?

SADE: Don't you *dare*.

VIC: Maybe he'll be good enough to go on my note at the bank for ninety thousand dollars payable February nineteen-thirty-eight.

SADE: [*Giggles*] Say, what if he needs a *handkerchief*? He generally *does*. I can't say, "Here, Mister Clark, use *mine*."

VIC: You can say, "Mister Clark, I . . ."

RUSH: [*Approaching*] Father. Mother.

VIC AND SADE: [*Raise voices*] Yes?

RUSH: [*Closer*] Here's Mister T. W. Clark come to see us.

SADE: Good evening, Mister Clark.

VIC: How *are* ya, T. W.?

END OF SCRIPT

ANNOUNCER: Which concludes another brief interlude at the small house half-way up in the next block.

1937

**RUSH TO HAVE
A STRANGER
FOR A BED-MATE**

THEME

INTRODUCTION: Well sir, it's early evening as we enter the small house half-way up in the next block now—about eight o'clock—and here in the living-room we find Mr. Victor Gook all by himself. He's seated in his easy chair under the floor-lamp and he's arrived at the very last page of his newspaper. But our friend looks up at this moment because his wife is coming in from the kitchen. Listen.

VIC: Where *you* been?

SADE: Over to Donahue's.

VIC: I wondered what the dickens had *become* of ya.

SADE: *I* hollered an' told ya I was going over there.

VIC: Did ya? I guess I was so interested in the paper I never paid any attention.

SADE: Where's Rush?

VIC: Upstairs.

SADE: Studyin'?

VIC: Uh-huh.

SADE: [*Calls*] Son. [*To Vic, giggling*] I'll prob'ly hafta have a big argument with *him*.

VIC: Why?

SADE: Because . . .

RUSH: [*Upstairs*] You holler, mom?

SADE: [*Calls*] Yeah. Will ya come down here?

VIC: [*To Sade*] Why will ya prob'ly have a big argument?

SADE: [*Giggles*] I hafta send him to bed.

VIC: Rush?

SADE: Uh-huh. Them *people* came.

VIC: What people?

SADE: Don't you listen to *anything* I say?

VIC: Sure, but I don't recall . . .

SADE: Them people *Donahue's* were expecting. *I* told you they were expecting an automobile-load of old friends to . . .

RUSH: [*Upstairs*] Want me right this minute, mom?

SADE: [*To Vic*] What?

VIC: "Want me right this minute."

SADE: [*To Vic*] Holler yes.

VIC: [*Calls*] Yeah.

RUSH: [*Upstairs*] I'll hafta put my pants on.

SADE: [*To Vic*] Don't you *remember* at the supper-table me tellin' about these people comin'?

159

VIC: Yeah.

SADE: They're old friends of *Mr.* Donahue. From Grand Crossing, Wisconsin. They're drivin' to Kentucky an' they're gonna stop overnight next door.

VIC: I see. What was that about sendin' Rush to bed?

SADE: [*Giggles a little*]

VIC: What's the matter?

SADE: [*Giggles*] He'll go through the roof.

VIC: Who, Rush?

SADE: Uh-huh. [*Giggles*] *Is* kinda silly.

VIC: I don't *follow* you very well. Why don'tcha whip out the . . .

SADE: Well, Mis' Donahue's got accommodations for four of the people. There's five of 'em altogether. *We're* gonna take care of *one* fella.

VIC: Yeah?

SADE: The fella that drives the car. I'm gonna put him in with Rush.

VIC: Oh.

SADE: [*Giggles*]

VIC: You afraid Sam'll *kick* about havin' to share his bed?

SADE: No, but . . . [*Giggles*]

VIC: I'm not *gettin'* all this humor.

SADE: This fella that's gonna sleep with Rush is comin' over at nine o'clock an' pile in bed. See, he's tired from drivin' the car all day an' they're gonna start out again at five o'clock in the morning so he hasta have all the rest he can get. The other four people are gonna sit up kinda late an' chat with Mr. an' Mis' Donahue, but *this* young fella wants to get to sleep as soon as he can. Sensible way to work it too.

VIC: Yeah.

SADE: Well . . . [*Giggles*] . . . in order for this fella to get lots an' lots of rest an' not be disturbed, I told Mis' Donahue I'd send Rush to bed right *now* so . . . [*Raises voice*] Were ya through studyin'?

RUSH: [*Approaching*] I wasn't studyin'. I was tapin' a baseball.

SADE: I bet you're kinda *tired,* ain't ya? Had such a busy day.

RUSH: [*Up*] Wasn't any busier'n *usual.* H'lo, gov.

VIC: H'lo.

RUSH: What'd ya want with me, mom?

SADE: I want you to . . . [*Has to giggle*] . . . go to bed.

RUSH: Huh?

SADE: [*Doesn't want to laugh, but has to*]

RUSH: [*Little chuckle*] What's the joke, gov?

VIC: [*Little chuckle*] I'm in the dark.

RUSH: [*Chuckles*] Shucks. [*Washes his hands of this trivial business*] Was that all ya wanted of me, mom?

SADE: [*Straightening up*] Them people of Donahue's come.

RUSH: Did they?

SADE: Yes. There's five of 'em an' Mis' Donahue's only got accommodations for four, so *we're* havin' a young fella.

RUSH: Yeah?

SADE: He's gonna sleep with *you*.

RUSH: O.K.

SADE: He's a very nice young man. I met him just now when I was over there.

RUSH: O.K. *There's* plenty of room for two. Well, I'm going back upstairs an' . . .

SADE: Wait a minute?

RUSH: Yeah?

SADE: He's the driver of the automobile. I guess they come several hundred miles today. An' they're gonna start at five o'clock in the morning an' drive *another* great big long ways. This fella hasta have all the rest he can get.

RUSH: *I* see. Well, O.K., when he gets here I'll . . .

SADE: So you hafta go to bed.

RUSH: *I* hafta go to bed?

SADE: Yes. Now.

RUSH: *Now*?

SADE: See, he'll be along pretty soon an' he'll wanta hop right *in*. He won't wanta be bothered by *you* turning on lights an' jostlin' around later *on*. So I told Mis' Donahue you'd be in bed an' settled for the night.

RUSH: When's the guy comin'?

SADE: Oh, quarter to nine or in around through there.

RUSH: It's only about eight-*fifteen* or so *now*.

VIC: Eight-fifteen on the *head*.

RUSH: I'm not going to bed at eight-fifteen.

SADE: Yes.

RUSH: No.

SADE: Don't you *say* no to me like that.

RUSH: Well, if you think I'm gonna . . .

SADE: If it's eight-fifteen now you only got half an hour to get settled in bed.

RUSH: No.

SADE: I said *yes.* An' be sure the *lights* are all out. He's gonna sneak up an' crawl in with ya an' go right off to sleep.

RUSH: Mom, this is *ridiculous.* Why should I inconvenience myself for the benefit of a total stranger that . . .

SADE: Oh, "inconvenience yourself." Who are you anyway? The governor of Peoria? *You* can use a little extra sleep.

RUSH: You'd actually make me go to bed . . .

SADE: Sure.

RUSH: . . . at eight o'clock in the evening . . .

SADE: Sure.

RUSH: . . . like a two-year-old kid . . .

SADE: [*Imperturbable*] Sure.

RUSH: . . . just for the benefit of some guy ya never set eyes on before?

SADE: Sure.

RUSH: Gov, I appeal to you.

VIC: Count me outa this, George.

RUSH: Mom, I wish to repeat this is ridiculous.

SADE: Repeat it all ya want to. The boy that's gonna sleep with you has been drivin' an automobile since early this morning. He's dead tired. An' he's gonna get up at five o'clock tomorrow an' drive some more. He wants his rest. If you come slammin' to bed at ten-thirty or eleven you'd wake him up.

RUSH: [*Bitterly*] An' wouldn't *that* be terrible.

SADE: Sure it would. Now scoot. Get outa your clothes an' pile in an' be sure the lights are turned out.

RUSH: Is this guy gonna undress in the *dark?*

SADE: He'll be *already* undressed.

RUSH: Comin' over here from Donahue's *Naked?*

SADE: He'll have on pajamas an' bath-robe an' slippers.

RUSH: Mom, when are you gonna realize I'm fourteen years old. When are you gonna realize . . .

SADE: Let's talk about all that some *other* day.

RUSH: Gov, *you* got a good head on your shoulders. I'd like to have *your* opinion . . .

VIC: I'm afraid I'll hafta remain neutral, Adolph.

RUSH: No, but look here: mom says she's invited a guy to come over an' sleep with me. Do I kick? *No.* I say *sure. Then* she says *I* got to go to bed. At eight-*fifteen.* When it ain't hardly *dark* yet.

SADE: *It's* dark enough. Now trot along.

RUSH: Sometimes, mom, I wonder how you can *face* yourself.

SADE: [*Giggles*] I'd hafta be an *acrobat* to do *that*. If I could *face* myself I'd get a job with Ringling Brothers Circus . . .

RUSH: An' *laugh* at me to boot.

SADE: *I'm* not laughing at you. *Goodness,* what a hullabaloo you stir up over a little tiny thing. *You* got no plans for this evening. Might as well be in bed as anywhere else. An' it's a favor to Mis' Donahue. She's been terrible, terrible nice to *you,* don't forget.

RUSH: It's the *idea* that burns me up, mom. Here I am a human *being,* an' I get shoved around like a dirty sock. I don't even get *consulted.*

SADE: You'll get consulted enough when you're twenty-one years old. Now hike.

RUSH: Hey!

SADE: What?

RUSH: I won't even get to *see* this guy that's gonna sleep with me.

SADE: Why not?

RUSH: Didn't you say he's gonna sneak up an' crawl in bed in the *dark?*

SADE: Sure. But you'll see him in the morning.

RUSH: How ya *figure?* He's gettin' up at five *o'clock*. I'll be dead to the world. Why, *I* won't see that son-of-a-gun.

SADE: [*Laughs*]

RUSH: [*Tough*] What do you think of *this* feature, gov?

VIC: [*Little chuckle*] Well, I . . .

RUSH: [*Tough*] Here's a guy gonna crawl up an' slide in bed with me like a thief in the night an' I won't even get to *see* him.

SADE: [*Giggles*] Oh, what do *you* care whether ya see him or not?

RUSH: How would *you* like the sensation of bein' in bed with a party an' ya had no idea of what the party looked like?

SADE: [*Laughs*] I don't think I'd . . .

RUSH: *I* won't be asleep when he sneaks in my room. I'll be wide awake. An' I'll feel this strange presence. Pretty soon a human being gets under the covers beside me. I wonder . . .

SADE: Don't you start any conversation with him.

RUSH: Can't even *talk* to this unknown creature in the darkness, huh?

SADE: No. He won't wanta chew the rag. He'll want his rest.

RUSH: Why, I'm liable to get *frantic,* mom.

SADE: [*Not worried*] Well, get frantic *quiet* if ya get frantic.

RUSH: I'll hear this guy's deep breathing. I'll wonder if he's got a mustache. I'll think of picture shows I've seen where people wake up in the middle of the night an' here in bed beside 'em is a great big green monster belchin' fire that . . .

SADE: This young fella is not a great big green monster belchin' fire. An' he hasn't got any mustache. He's about twenty years old an' looks somethin' like Rooster's big brother Harold.

RUSH: Gov. I appeal to you.

VIC: Don't bother. I couldn't do you the slightest bit of good.

RUSH: What's this individual's name, mom?

SADE: The young fella's?—I don't remember.

RUSH: *That's* a fine note.

SADE: Oh, what difference does it make what his name is?

RUSH: Suppose sometime I'm called up before the Supreme Court. The judge says, "Mr. Gook, where were you on the night of March 16, 1937?" "I was home in bed, your honor." "Anybody with you?" "Yes." "Who?" "I don't know." Wouldn't *that* be swell. Why, I'd be in Sing Sing jail in five minutes. Shucks, . . .

SADE: You prob'ly won't be called up before the Supreme Court for a week or two. Anyway I'll find out from Mis' Donahue tomorrow what his name is.

RUSH: He's gonna come skulking over here in his pajamas, huh?

SADE: Yes. Figured that'd save him time an' also make it more convenient for us. See, he can light out first thing in the morning without botherin' us an' do his dressing next door.

RUSH: I hope when he's prowlin' around outside half-naked, he gets arrested.

VIC: I hope he gets the right *house*. Be a shame if he went in Drummond's by mistake an' crawled in bed with Bull-dog.

SADE: Rush, he'll *be* here in a minute. Why don'tcha get *goin'?*

RUSH: [*Tough*] Bed at eight-thirty.

SADE: Scoot.

RUSH: Sleepin' with a guy I don't even know what his name is.

SADE: Scoot.

RUSH: Don't even know what he *looks* like. By gosh, if I done right I'd sprinkle a few *tacks* on his side of the bed.

SADE: Don't you dare even *think* about such shenanigans.

RUSH: *Picture* me up there: I lay quivering in bed, my ears straining to catch the slightest sound. I hear the door open softly; here's the form of a human being; my muscles contract; I'm in an agony of terror; the veins stand out on my forehead. This monster approaches. I scream. A low guttural chuckle like that of a fiend comes from the throat of . . .

SADE: Rush, are you gonna get going?

RUSH: [*Tough*] What?

SADE: Are you gonna get going?

RUSH: [*Tough*] O.K., *I'll* get going.

SADE: *Get* going then.

VIC: Good night, Pete.

SADE: Good night.

VIC: I say good *night,* Pete. [*To Sade*] Guess he don't care to answer.

SADE: [*Neg.*] Uh-huh.

VIC: [*Little chuckle*]

SADE: [*Little chuckle*]

VIC: [*Bigger chuckle*]

SADE: [*Bigger chuckle*]

VIC: [*Little laugh*]

SADE: [*Little laugh*]

RUSH: [*Through clenched teeth*] That's O.K. That's O.K.

END OF SCRIPT

ANNOUNCER: Which concludes another brief interlude at the small house half-way up in the next block.

1937

THIRD LT. CLINTON
STANLEY: BRIGHT
KENTUCKY HOTEL

THEME
ANNOUNCER: OPENING AND COMMERCIAL CREDITS
INTRODUCTION: Well sir, it's late afternoon as we enter the small house half-way up in the next block now, and here in the living-room we find Mr. Victor Gook and his son Mr. Rush Gook. The gentlemen arrived home from the office and Tatman's vacant lot about five minutes ago, and after settling themselves on the davenport the younger sought to entertain the elder with excerpts from a volume of vigorous fiction he's currently reading. Listen.

RUSH: [*Reads*] Third Lieutenant Stanley gave the villainous crew of counterfeiting smugglers one supercilious glance. Then his eyes softened as he turned and gazed at the oval face of Lady Margaret. The beautiful woman smiled bravely, revealing twin rows of perfect teeth the rich color of old ivory. Her hand trembled slightly as she twirled her dainty pink parasol and her small foot in its fashionable French spat tapped nervously. Third Lieutenant Stanley touched her arm. "Let us share a hug an' kiss before we fight these miserable wretches," he grunted. Nothing loath, the beautiful woman lifted her veil an' thrust her lovely head forward. Jabbering amongst themselves, the counterfeiting smugglers watched the exchange of tender caresses an' there was a burst of rude laughter as Third Lieutenant Stanley . . .

VIC: Somebody's in the kitchen.

RUSH: Huh?

VIC: Back door just opened. [*Calls*] Hi.

SADE: [*Off*] Hi.

RUSH: [*Briefly, and not loudly*] Hi, mom. [*Reads*] Jabbering amongst themselves, the counterfeiting smugglers watched the exchange of tender caresses an' there was a burst of rude laughter as Third Lieutenant Stanley began to cry. "Sweetheart," he blubbered, "Five minutes from now I may be dead. But, sweetheart, I want you to know that . . .

VIC: [*Little chuckle*] Oh heck.

RUSH: " . . . my love for you transcends everything in . . . " [*To Vic*] It'll get exciting in a minute.

VIC: Let's play rummy.

RUSH: Wait'll I come to the place where the counterfeiting smugglers attempt to . . .

VIC: [*Raises voice a little*] Greetings, Sadie. It's *grand* having you home again.

SADE: [*Coming up*] Uh-huh. Who tracked dirt in on the kitchen linoleum?

VIC: Rush.

169

RUSH: [*Chuckles*] I did not. *Gov's* the guy. *I* wore my *rubbers* today.

SADE: [*Who is not in the best humor*] Just makes extra work for a person is all.

VIC: You seem out of sorts.

SADE: Do I?

VIC: Instead of the aura of sweetness which generally . . .

SADE: [*Briefly*] Mis' Appelrot riled me up again.

VIC: Indeed. How was Thimble Meeting?

SADE: *Thimble* Meeting was all right. But she button-holed me afterwards. [*Tough*] Why is it always *me* she hasta button-hole? Prob'ly figures I'm soft like putty an' can be talked *into* trash. Appreciates if she button-holes Mis' Hettles or Mis' Trogel or Mis' Harris—they'll tell her no an' *mean* no.

RUSH: Gov, here's the place where the counterfeiting smugglers attempt to murder Third Lieutenant Stanley by . . .

VIC: Your *mother's* talking, Arthur.

RUSH: Um.

VIC: [*To Sade*] What'd Ma Appelrot have up her sleeve this trip?

SADE: Oh . . . [*Pauses because she doesn't know whether or not she wishes to spend time on a disagreeable matter*] . . . just silliness.

VIC: I bet she wants you to go to Washington, D.C., an' call on Congress an' demand that they . . .

SADE: [*Little giggle*] Just about as *bad*.

RUSH: [*In low but piercing tones*] My *gosh!*

VIC: [*To Sade*] Yeah?

SADE: [*To Vic*] Talk about your big enormous lah-de-dah *stunts.* That woman manufactures 'em out of thin air.

RUSH: [*Amazedly*] Holy *smoke!*

VIC: [*To Sade*] What's she got on the fire *now?*

SADE: Thimble Club ladies put on a monstrous campaign to have the city tear down the Bright Kentucky Hotel.

VIC: [*Chuckles*] Oh, shucks.

SADE: [*Giggles*] Ain't that just like her?

VIC: [*Chuckles*] Uh-huh.

RUSH: [*Low piercing tones*] Great *snakes!*

SADE: [*Sharply*] What's eatin' you, Willie?

RUSH: [*Dramatically*] The counterfeiting smugglers try to murder Third Lieutenant Stanley by tying him to a tree an' smearing melted marshmallow all over his clothes an' releasing two grizzly bears from a cage. Grizzly bears are very fond of melted marshmallow so it looks like curtains for Third Lieutenant Stanley.

SADE: Will you read to yourself, please?

RUSH: I thought you people would be excited about . . .

VIC: You will read to yourself please, William, an' you will also refrain from giving voice to loud ejaculations. I warned you a moment ago, I've just now warned you again, an' if I hafta warn you a third time there will be gnashing of teeth an' tearing of hair an' the cries of a boy in pain.

RUSH: Um.

VIC: You may continue, Sadie.

SADE: *That's* all there is to it. Mis' Applerot cornered me after Thimble Meeting an' give me all this talky-talk an' trash about getting' the city to tear down the Butler House Hotel.

VIC: *Butler* House Hotel!

SADE: Bright Kentucky, I mean. [*Giggles*] See, how upset I get?

VIC: What's she want the Bright Kentucky torn down for?

SADE: It's so old it's liable to topple over on its *own* accord one of these days. People might get hurt. Also, it's ugly. Passengers going through town on stylish Chicago an' Saint Louis trains hafta look at it an' they're apt to think its typical of the *city*. Oh, *I* s'pose there's sense to Mis' Applerot's fol-de-rol. Darn Bright Kentucky Hotel *is* old an' ugly an' an eye-sore. But that's not the *Thimble Club* ladies' bees'-wax. Like I *told* her s'afternoon:—"Mis' Applerot," I says, "Us ladies get together to sew an' chat an' have good *times*. Idea behind the organization never *was* to mix up in politics an' the government an' this, that, an' the *other* thing."

VIC: What was her rejoinder to *that*?

SADE: Oh, she tossed her head an' snapped her nose-glasses that come in an' out of her chest on a chain back an' forth an' talked about how up-to-date progressive women oughta take an interest in different junk an' so on an' so on an' so on. I stood there an' listened an' listened an' wished I could go home. Kept gettin' madder an' madder inside all the time but hadda smile an' nod an' agree an' fidget an' stand on one foot an' then on the other. Ruthie waited for me about fifteen minutes a little distance away but finally buttoned her coat an' left. [*Giggles, because after all the incident was trivial*] Oh, well.

VIC: Ma Appelrot is a fat-head.

SADE: Just lah-de-dah is all. Person hasta make allowances, I guess.

RUSH: Hey, if they tore down the Bright Kentucky Hotel Mr. Gumpox would lose his home.

SADE: [*Giggles*] Yeah. He would.

RUSH: An' he *likes* living there.

SADE: Um.

RUSH: He *complains* about the Bright Kentucky a good deal. *Always* belly-achin' about fast trains going right past his bedroom at night to where he can't sleep an' freight trains lettin' off steam an' soot an' chunks of coal that come right in his window. But pin him down once an' he'll admit he *enjoys* residing there. He's used to the noise an' clatter.

SADE: [*Giggles*] What would he think of his good friend Mrs. Gook if she went bustling down to the City Hall an' demanded the mayor an' everybody get their axe an' chop his home right out from under him?

RUSH: [*Chuckles*] He'd prob'ly stop *speakin'* to Mrs. Gook.

SADE: [*Giggles*] Don't know as I'd blame him.

RUSH: Tear down the Bright Kentucky Hotel an' *another* fella we know would be miserable.

SADE: Who's that?

RUSH: Smelly Clark's Uncle Strap.

SADE: Oh.

RUSH: He's night *clerk* at the Bright Kentucky. Tear down the Bright Kentucky an' he'd lose his *job* at the Bright Kentucky. A guy couldn't be night clerk at the Bright Kentucky if there *wasn't* any Bright Kentucky.

SADE: [*Little giggle*] No, they couldn't.

VIC: What's the name of that hotel again, Lawrence?

RUSH: Bright Kentucky.

VIC: [*Dryly*] Thanks.

RUSH: [*Chuckles*] Not at all.

SADE: [*Rather dismally*] No, but it's ridiculous. The Thimble Club ladies get together to sew an' chat an' gossip an' eat little refreshments an' *enjoy* theirself. *They* don't get together to change the world around an' stir up the government an' all such axle-grease. Take ladies like Ruthie Stembottom an' Mis' Husher an' Mis' Tice. *They* don't even read the *news*paper. *They* don't care about passing a law in Michigan people have got to wear their stockings inside out. All *they* want is a sociable afternoon with maybe a dish of ice-cream an' somebody read a nice poem out loud or something.

VIC: Is Ma Appelrot agitating for a law that'll compel inhabitants of Michigan to wear their stockings inside out?

SADE: *You* know what I mean. [*Quotes Mrs. Appelrot*] "We of this City should demand *so*-and-so. Us voters here in Illinois should see to it that lah-de-dah congress lah-de-dah is forced to lah-de-dah go 'way back an' sit down." *That's* all right. That's *fine*. But it's not for our little *Thimble* Club.

VIC: Um.

SADE: [*Contemptuously*] Demand that the City tear down the Bright Kentucky Hotel.

VIC: Um.

SADE: Can you see timid little Ruthie Stembottom marching into the mayor's office down town an' roaring an' shouting an' pounding on the table?

VIC: [*Little chuckle*] No.

SADE: Or Mis' Husher or Mis' Tice or Mis' Williams or Mis' Freeze?

VIC: No.

SADE: Or *me,* for *that* matter.

VIC: [*Neg.*] Uh-huh.

SADE: Mis' *Appelrot* could do it probably. Or Mis' *Brighton.* But they're the only two in the whole Club that could even come *close* to doing it. Or *thinking* about it far as *that* goes.

VIC: Um.

SADE: Makes a person *tired.*

VIC: Um.

RUSH: I was just thinkin' of something Mr. Gumpox told me the other day that backs *up* Mis' Appelrot's idea they oughta tear down the Bright Kentucky.

SADE: What was that?

RUSH: The place is so old an' rickety it trembles when trains go past.

SADE: Does it?

RUSH: Oh, awful. Especially the fast passenger trains, the stream-liners. Mr. Gumpox says his bed walks right across the room when some of them late-at-night limiteds roar by.

SADE: His bed *walks?*

RUSH: *You* know how a bed or a table or a chair will do when something makes it vibrate. Our wash-bench down cellar, for instance, when we got the wash-machine going. It *walks.* Catch on how I mean?

SADE: Yeah.

RUSH: Well, same thing with Mr. Gumpox. He'll be asleep an' a fast passenger train'll flash by the Bright Kentucky sixty or seventy miles an hour an' by George the building starts to shake from the vibration an' he'll ride all around the room in his doggone bed just like you'd ride around in an automobile. One time he rode right outa the bedroom into the hall-way. Woke up the next morning in the hall by the fire-escape, thirty-five feet from the spot where he'd retired. He jokingly passed the remark he thought he'd attach a speedometer to the foot of his bed in order to keep track of the mileage.

VIC: A rather tall story, Margaret, if you'll permit a little mild skepticism.

RUSH: *I* don't doubt it any.

SADE: Oh well, lands, *I'm* not gonna bother my head about Mis' Applerot. She upsets a person but there's no sense in losing any *sleep*.

VIC: Naw.

SADE: [*Giggles*] Let her go buy a hatchet an' chop down the Bright Kentucky Hotel by *herself*.

VIC: Sure.

RUSH: That'd throw Mr. Gumpox out of a home an' Smelly Clark's Uncle Strap out of a job.

SADE: Uh-huh.

RUSH: Smelly Clark's Uncle Strap is night clerk at the Bright Kentucky. Tear down the Bright Kentucky an' he'd lose his *job* at the Bright Kentucky. A guy couldn't be night clerk at the Bright Kentucky if there *wasn't* any Bright Kentucky.

SADE: No, they couldn't.

VIC: What was the name of that hotel again, Ralph?

RUSH: Bright Kentucky.

VIC: [*Dryly*] Thanks.

RUSH: Not at all.

SADE: [*Briefly*] You hafta trot to Croucher's after groceries, son.

RUSH: O.K.

SADE: [*Moving off*] I'll see what we need.

RUSH: *Sugar* for *one* thing.

SADE: [*Moving off*] Yes, sugar, an' other stuff besides. Come when I holler.

RUSH: O.K.

VIC: [*To Rush*] Believe I'll stretch out for a short snooze before supper.

RUSH: Wanta hear the exciting way the counterfeiting smugglers attempt to murder Third Lieutenant Stanley?

VIC: No.

RUSH: Thrilling as a horse.

VIC: Not interested.

RUSH: [*Reads*] The handsome young officer faced death valiantly. "You fellows can go jump in the creek, I'm not scared," he growled to the leader of the counterfeiting smugglers. But for Lady Margaret he had a sweet smile an' eyes that twinkled merrily. "Give me one more kiss an' one more hug before I kick the bucket, sweetheart," he gloated. The beautiful woman simpered and coquettishly pretended that the mother-of-pearl buttons on her fashionable French spats had come unbuttoned. Finally, blushing furiously, she lifted her veil an' thrust forward her lovely head. "Just *one* hug an' *one* kiss now," she warned an' Third Lieutenant Stanley howled loudly his satisfaction an' approval.

END OF SCRIPT

ANNOUNCER: Which concludes another brief interlude at the small house half-way up in the next block.

1940

MR. GUMPOX AND
HIS BRIDE

ANNOUNCER: OPENING AND COMMERCIAL CREDITS

INTRODUCTION: It is late afternoon as we enter the small house half-way up in the next block now, and here in the kitchen we find Mrs. Victor Gook sitting in her little rocking chair by the window busy with her sewing. She looks up expectantly at this moment, because she's just heard a foot-step on the back porch and she knows the door is about to open. It *does* open—to admit *Mr. Victor Gook.* Who says . . .

VIC: Hi, Mrs. Abrams.

SADE: Hi. Thought that was *Rush* comin' up the steps.

VIC: I believe I noticed *that* person over in Seymour's vacant lot as I come past. I judged he an' his associates were playing Duck-on-the-rock.

SADE: What brings *you* home so early?

VIC: The boss didn't come down s'afternoon an' the girls were makin' so much noise I thought I'd finish my reports where it was quiet. Would I be in the way if I pulled a chair up to the kitchen table?

SADE: No. I'll be glad for company.

VIC: *Warmer* out.

SADE: I *thought* it must be. Noticed school-kids comin' along the alley with their sweaters over their arm. You can throw your overcoat on a chair, Vic. *I'll* be goin' in the other room in a minute.

VIC: O.K.

SADE: I hollered out the window to Mis' Agle while ago.

VIC: How's she?

SADE: Much better she says. It's Albert now that's ailin'.

VIC: What's bitin' *him?*

SADE: *Teeth* again.

VIC: Thought he only had one tooth left.

SADE: I know, but that tooth's givin' him trouble.

VIC: *I* heard a little gossip today myself.

SADE: Oh, ya did?

VIC: Mr. Gumpox's bride got in town.

SADE: *No.*

VIC: Miss Kleeberger—Ike Kneesuffer's secretary—was down to the depot this noon to meet her mother, an' there was Brother Gumpox takin' a lady off the same train.

SADE: Well, whatcha know. Miss Kleeberger say anything about what she looked like?

VIC: She may have. I just picked up that much information as I was walkin' through the main office.

SADE: Well, well, well. Mr. Gumpox has been writin' to matrimonial agencies for *years* an' at last he's got a wife.

VIC: Uh-huh.

SADE: I'd give my hat to see her.

VIC: Don't imagine she's any ravin' *beauty*—woman that a garbage man got through a matrimonial bureau.

SADE: Mr. Gumpox is a very nice fella, Vic—garbage man or *no* garbage man.

VIC: Rush says he don't wear socks.

SADE: Rush exaggerates. Gee, I wish you'd asked Miss Kleeberger *more* about it. Was Mr. Gumpox all dressed up an' did he look happy an' was the lady big or little?

VIC: Personally I didn't attach much *importance* to the matter. Gumpox an' myself have little more than a speaking acquaintance.

SADE: Well, *I* think of him as somebody I know right well. I see him twice a week regular as the clock, an' he's *always* got a smile an' a happy *word* to say. When anybody don't feel well he always asks how they're gettin' along; if he sees me havin' trouble with my clothes-line he hops right off his wagon an' helps; he's been good about *lots* of things to me.

VIC: Uh-huh.

SADE: I hope his wife is real nice because I *know* he'll be a good husband—so kind an' considerate. Tomorrow's his day to come for the garbage. I wouldn't be out of place *askin'* him about it all, would I?

VIC: Really couldn't say.

SADE: What time did Miss Kleeberger say the train got in?

VIC: It was the 11:52 from Chicago.

SADE: Oh—*Chicago* lady, huh?

VIC: Not necessarily. She mighta come from any place in the world.

SADE: Yeah, that's right. Well, if she arrived at 11:52 I expect they're all *married* by *now*. Prob'ly the first thing they done.

VIC: Yeah.

SADE: Must be a funny feelin' for a woman to get off a train in a strange town an see a man she's never set eyes on before an' marry him right off without an aye, yes, or no.

VIC: Be just as strange for the *guy*.

SADE: Yes.

VIC: Far as *that* goes, Miss Kleeberger might be mistaken. The lady might not of been any bride at *all*. Mighta been his sister or aunt or grand-mother or somebody.

SADE: Oh, no. Miss *Kleeberger* could tell. *She's* a woman. *She'd* know by the way they acted whether . . . [*Phone*] Sit still. I'll get it.

VIC: Prob'ly Ike Kneesuffer.

SADE: [*Off a little*] Prob'ly Ruthie. She *said* she'd . . . [*To phone*] Hello? Oh, hello, Mis' Feeley. What? Why, *yes,* my husband was just now *tellin'* me . . . uh-huh. What? Oh, is that *so?* Really? [*Laughs delightedly*] Well, what's she look like? Oh, she is? [*Laughs*] [*Aside*] Vic, Mis' Feeley says . . . [*To phone*] Whatcha say, Mis' Feeley? [*Laughs*] Oh, I am too. Feel like it was somebody in the *family* gettin' married almost. Yes. Well, Vic an' I were just now talkin' about it. One of the girls from the office saw Mr. Gumpox take the woman off the train. Yes. What? Oh, that so? Uh-huh. Well, I certainly wish 'em all the good luck in the world. Yes, indeed. Thanks for callin' Mis' Feeley. We'll be watchin' out the window. [*Laughs*] Uh-huh. Good-by. [*Hangs up*] Vic, Mr. Gumpox an' his bride are comin' down the *alley.*

VIC: Yeah?

SADE: Just now passed Mis' Feeley's back yard. Oughta be by here in ten minutes or so.

VIC: Are they *walkin'?*

SADE: No, they're *ridin'.*

VIC: Well, *that's* a hot way to treat a new wife. Ride her down the back alley in a *garbage* wagon.

SADE: He's prob'ly showin' her his *route.*

VIC: Shucks.

SADE: *That's* all right. *Any* new wife oughta be interested in her husband's work. Mis' Feeley says she's right handsome—near as she could tell from her kitchen window. Kinda *fat*—but real red in the complexion an' wearin' a nice cloth coat an' laughin' so jolly. Mr. *Gumpox* was laughin' *too.*

VIC: The happy bridegroom.

SADE: I'm gonna sit here in the window till they go past. Wouldn't miss it for a silver dollar.

VIC: We could throw some ol' *shoes.*

SADE: [*Pleased with the notion*] Sure. An' we could . . . [*Thinking better of it*] No, guess we better not. Mr. Gumpox might think we meant the old shoes for his garbage wagon. Hurt his feelin's.

VIC: How'd it be to drape some orange blossoms around the garbage bucket an' . . .

SADE: [*Raps on window*] Hi-tye-tye.

VIC: Gumpox an' spouse?

SADE: No, Rush.

VIC: Sade, how'd it be to drape some orange blossoms around the garbage bucket? That way we could convey delicate sentiments of best wishes an' happy . . .

SADE: Vic, don't you dare make *fun* of Mr. Gumpox if you happen to see him. He's been good to *me* an' . . .

[*Door opens*]

RUSH: [*Coming in*] Hey, guess who's comin' up the alley.

SADE: Mr. Gumpox an' a lady?

RUSH: [*Closing door*] Yeah, an' ya know who the lady *is?*

SADE: *Mrs.* Gumpox.

RUSH: Yeah—how'd ya know?

SADE: Mis' Feeley just telephoned. Where *are* they?

RUSH: Just passin' Kane's house. Hi, gov.

VIC: Hi.

SADE: You get a good look at the lady, Rush?

RUSH: Sure. I stood right beside the garbage wagon.

SADE: You *say* anything to Mr. Gumpox?

RUSH: Sure. An' he introduced me to his wife.

SADE: Really?

RUSH: I said, "hello there, Mr. Gumpox." He said, "Hello, Rush, want you to meet *Mrs.* Gumpox." I said, "How do you do, Mrs. Gumpox?" She said, "Very well, thank you." Mr. Gumpox said, "Josephine, this is Rush Gook from down on Virginia Avenue. We'll be *passin'* his house directly."

SADE: *Well.* Josephine, huh?

RUSH: Yeah. He offered to give me a lift but there was no room on the seat an' I'd hafta ride back with the garbage so I declined.

SADE: You should of declined even if there *was* room on the seat. People that just got married like to be *alone.*

RUSH: That *did* cross my *mind.*

SADE: Was Mis' Gumpox fat?

RUSH: Oh, boy, *I'll* say. I *liked* her though. One of these kinda ladies that *laugh* easy, ya know?

SADE: Uh-huh.

RUSH: Ya know Mr. Gumpox got that wife just by writin' in to a mail-order house?

SADE: Yes, I *knew* that.

RUSH: Pretty good system, seems to *me.* You take a guy all of a sudden feels like gettin' *married:* he whips out his fountain pen, sends his order in, an' by gosh on the next train here comes his good ol' wife.

SADE: Oh, it's not as simple as *that.* The people *correspond* first

182

an' find out if they *like* each other. If they *do* then they . . . Who's *that* in the alley?

RUSH: [*Looking*] Dirty Johnson an' his fish truck.

SADE: Say, Vic.

VIC: Uh-huh?

SADE: How'd it be to have Rush run out with the garbage bucket? It's not Mr. Gumpox's *day,* but if he *sees* it he'll stop an' *take* it. Give me a chance to get a glimpse of the bride.

VIC: Certainly O.K. by me.

SADE: *That* wouldn't hurt anything would it?

VIC: Guess not.

SADE: Rush, do that, will ya? Garbage bucket's beside the bottom step.

RUSH: Mom, I'm personally *acquainted* with Mrs. Gumpox. If ya *want* me to I'll notify her when she comes past you'd like to form her acquaintance an' . . .

SADE: No, that might look funny. Do like I say.

RUSH: [*Moves off*] All right.

SADE: [*After him*] An' I'd try not to let 'em see you.

RUSH: [*Opening door*] O.K.

SADE: An' come back in yourself.

RUSH: Sure.

[*Closes door*]

SADE: [*To Vic*] I s'pose I'm pokin' my nose in other people's business doin' things like this, but I just can't help it. When somebody I know gets married I get excited as a horse. Just like when somebody I know has a *baby.* Even when somebody I *don't* know has a baby an' I just *hear* about it I hafta know all the details an' . . . [*Giggles*] Rush is puttin' the garbage bucket right out in the open where Mr. Gumpox can't miss it.

VIC: Poor ol' bridegroom Gumpox. He can't even take his wife out for a honeymoon on his garbage wagon but what somebody makes him stop for potatoe peelin's.

SADE: [*Tartly*] If that's the way you feel about it why didn't you say so when I *asked* ya?

VIC: [*Chuckling*] I take it back, kiddo.

SADE: Goodness, a person can . . . [*Door open*] [*Raises voice*] They comin?

RUSH: Yeah.

SADE: Where are they?

RUSH: [*Closing door*] Right by Harris's.

SADE: They see you?

RUSH: No.

SADE: Vic, c'mon, let's peek out the window.

VIC: [*Getting up*] If the lady is lovely enough I don't know but what I'll step outside an' ask to kiss the bride.

RUSH: Mom, ya know where Mr. an' Mrs. Gumpox gonna *live?*

SADE: No, where?

RUSH: 702 West Chestnut—little bungalow.

SADE: [*Approvingly*] Oh, *that's* good. Mr. Gumpox told me *several* times he gets so tired of it there at the Bright Kentucky hotel. Trains goin' by his window all night . . .

VIC: Move over, folks. I, too, would love to see the wedding procession.

RUSH: It ain't come yet.

SADE: [*Giggles*] I bet Mr. Gumpox stopped his horse there by Drummond's barn so they could have a little *kiss.*

RUSH: [*Laughs*] Mr. Gumpox an' his wife or Mr. Gumpox an' his horse?

VIC: [*Joins in this laughter*]

SADE: Don't make a lotta noise now so they *hear* ya.

RUSH: Hey, Mr. *Montgomery* is garbage man over on Chestnut Street. I wonder if Mr. Gumpox plans on takin' his *own* garbage or do the professional rules state that . . .

SADE: Here they come. Here they come.

VIC: If *I* was a bridegroom I think *I* would pick out a horse for my wedding chariot that weighed at least ninety pounds an' could keep his head . . .

SADE: [*Delighted*] There's the bride. There's the bride.

VIC: Move *over*. Thunder.

SADE: Oh, she *is* a fatty. Wish she'd look *this* way once. Don't stick your head outa the window so they *see* ya, Rush.

RUSH: Well, heck, gov's pushin' me in the back an' . . .

SADE: Mr. Gumpox sees the garbage. He's callin' his horse to whoa.

RUSH: Hey, they have diamond weddings and silver weddings an' golden weddin's . . . Even have paper weddings. If they have *garbage* weddings I bet Mr. an' Mrs. Gumpox can celebrate until the . . .

SADE: She's lookin' this way, Vic. She's lookin' this way.

VIC: Uh-huh. Not a bad lookin' dame.

SADE: She's a *handsome* woman. Just like Mis' Feeley said. [*Delighted*] Well.

VIC: [*Chuckles*] Hey, the ol' boy's showin' her how he handles garbage.

RUSH: He's puttin' on a demonstration.

VIC: Know what he's sayin'?

RUSH: What?

VIC: Just a simple twist of the wrist.

RUSH: [*Laughs*] Yeah, or else he's sayin' . . .

SADE: Vic, that's a real good cloth coat she's got on.

VIC: Uh-huh.

SADE: *All* her clothes show she's got refinement.

VIC: Um.

SADE: Look at her laugh at him.

   [*Giggles*]

VIC: Um.

SADE: Look at him laugh at her.

   [*Giggles*]

VIC: Um.

SADE: Ain't that sweet?

VIC: Um.

SADE: Yes, sir, I believe Mr. Gumpox done all right. You can tell a nice person by their looks even from this distance.

RUSH: Gov, I wish you'd get your elbow outa' my back an' quit pushin' so I could . . .

SADE: *Stop* that, will ya. Want them people to . . . they *do* see ya', Rush.

RUSH: *I* couldn't help it, mom. Gov's elbow . . .

SADE: Mr. Gumpox is *wavin'*. Vic, open the window.

VIC: Open it?

SADE: Yes. Hurry up.

VIC: [*Opening it*] It's always been my fault when things go wrong. I'm the poor unfortunate . . .

SADE: Now get outa the way.

VIC: *I'm* outa the way.

SADE: [*Calls*] Mr. Gumpox. Mr. Gumpox . . . Will you an' your wife come in the house a minute . . . an' . . . an' have coffee. Please do.

END OF SCRIPT

ANNOUNCER: Throw our congratulations and best wishes in your garbage wagon too, Mr. Gumpox. From what we've heard we gather you have taken unto yourself one dandy wife.

1937

LOOKING FORWARD
TO A SPIN IN
STEMBOTTOM'S MACHINE

THEME

ANNOUNCER: OPENING AND COMMERCIAL CREDITS

INTRODUCTION: Well sir, it's early evening as we approach the small house half-way up in the next block now, and here on the front porch we find Mrs. Victor Gook and her son Mr. Rush Gook. Sade is sitting rather gingerly in the swing: she's dressed in her best and doesn't want to become disarranged. Young Rush is established on the top step but one. He too is attired in his best, and his attitude suggests rigidity and restraint. Listen.

SADE: I wouldn't lean against the railing with my clean white shirt, Rush.

RUSH: Can I take my shoes off till Fred an' Ruthie get here?

SADE: No. An' how many times have I told you not to say "Fred an' Ruthie"?

RUSH: They pinch my feet.

SADE: They shouldn't. We bought 'em plenty big enough.

RUSH: What time'd they say they'd be around for us?

SADE: Fred an' Ruthie? Oh—around seven or seven-fifteen or kinda half way around in through there.

RUSH: I'll be melted down to a low gravy if they don't show up pretty quick. Sittin' around in your good clothes is like bein' in a straight-jacket.

SADE: I imagine you'll live. Where'd your father go?

RUSH: I guess he's out in back by the garbage box chattin' with Mr. Razorscum or Mr. Donahue or somebody.

SADE: Fred an' Ruthie'll come along an' honk an' he won't be here an' we'll hafta wait on him.

RUSH: Sure wish I could take my shoes off.

SADE: Them shoes are *plenty* big enough. It's just your imagination.

RUSH: Yeah, prob'ly is. My imagination gets to going ninety miles an hour when I'm all dressed up. My back itches an' my shoes pinch an' the perspiration runs down my forehead an' my collar feels too tight an' . . .

VIC: [*Approaching*] Hi-de-hi, ho-de-ho.

SADE: Rush, I told you *no*. That railing's *dirty*. Stay *away* from it. You don't wanta look like a *tramp* when they get here, do ya?

VIC: [*Almost up*] Hi-de-hi, ho-de-ho.

RUSH: [*To Sade*] They've seen me look like a tramp plenty of times.

SADE: *I'll* say. [*To Vic*] Where *you* been?

VIC: [*Up*] Out in the alley chewin' the fat with Razorscum.

189

SADE: If Fred an' Ruthie'd come along an' honked we'd of had to go hunt for ya.

VIC: I wouldn't of been hard to find. I was by the garbage box. Razorscum tells me . . .

SADE: Sit on the step by Rush, why don'tcha? If ya crowd in here with me you'll rumple my dress.

VIC: Seems to me we're puttin' on a lotta dog just to go for an automobile ride.

SADE: I s'pose you'd wear your overalls.

VIC: We don't dig out the glad-rags when we play Five *Hundred* with Fred an' Ruthie.

SADE: This is different. They asked us to go for a spin in their car. For decency's sake it's up to us to dress half-way civilized.

VIC: [*To Rush*] Shove over, Ink-eraser.

RUSH: I'm very uncomfortable.

VIC: You look it.

RUSH: I was just tellin' mom, it's like bein' in a straight-jacket to sit around with good clothes on.

VIC: [*To Sade*] Where we gonna ride to?

SADE: Oh, prob'ly around by Hudson an' over to Chenoa an' back down through Lexington an' Towanda.

VIC: I get awful sick of that same old route. Why don't Fred go somewhere else for a change?

SADE: He likes the concrete.

VIC: *There's* other concrete roads. Route whatever-it-is to *Peoria* is concrete.

SADE: Peoria's too *far* to drive in one evening.

VIC: We wouldn't hafta go clear *to* Peoria. We could go half way an' then turn around.

SADE: It's Fred's automobile. He's got a right to steer it wherever he wants to.

VIC: Kappa, Hudson, El Paso. Chenoa, Lexington, Towanda. I've made that trip so many times I know every bump in the road.

SADE: Beggars can't be choosers, ya know. If we had our own machine we could ride any place we pleased. Rush, what'd I tell you about leaning against that railing?

RUSH: I keep forgetting. Heck, it'll be *dark* pretty *quick*. Nobody can *tell* whether I look like a tramp or not.

SADE: When we get to Lexington Fred'll suggest ice-cream cones. You'll be the one to go in the confectionary an' get 'em.

RUSH: Ump.

VIC: *That* old ritual.

SADE: What?

VIC: I say, "*that* old ritual." We go to Kappa, then Hudson, then El Paso. Then Chenoa an' then Lexington. At Lexington Fred always turns around like he's springin' a great big jolly surprise an' says, "Hey, folks, how about a *cone* all around."

SADE: [*Crisply*] What's your objections to that?

VIC: [*Chuckles*] It's always the same old *thing*.

SADE: Listen, I don't want you to *antagonize* Fred tonight.

VIC: I don't plan on antagonizin' him.

SADE: I mean bring up things ya know he disagrees with.

VIC: [*Chuckles*] O.K.

SADE: An' let's not have that same old argument about where people's gonna sit.

VIC: *Fred's* the one that always goes through *that* business. [*Quotes Fred*] "You can sit anywhere ya want to. There's room for two in the front seat an' three in the back seat. Ya wanta sit in the front or ya wanta sit in the back? Which ya want it to be? The back or the front? Just suit yourself. Vic, you wanta sit in the front seat? Or would ya prefer to sit in the back seat?"

SADE: [*Tiny giggle*] *I* know he does that. But there's no need to egg him *on*.

VIC: *I* don't egg him on.

SADE: Ya do too.

VIC: I don't either.

SADE: Don't *wait* for him to put on that performance about the back seat an' the front seat. Just crawl in the auto. *You* know the husbands always sit in front an' the wives in back.

VIC: Rush, be Fred.

RUSH: [*Chuckles*] O.K. [*Quotes Fred*] "Where ya wanta sit? Front seat or back seat?"

VIC: Don't make a bit of difference, Fred.

RUSH: There's room for two in front an' three in back. Decide for yourself where you'd like to sit.

VIC: Front seat's all right with *me*.

RUSH: You can sit in the *back* seat if you'd *rather*.

VIC: O.K., I'll sit in the back seat.

RUSH: You can *see* more in the front seat.

VIC: O.K., I'll sit in the front seat.

RUSH: There's more leg-room in the back seat.

VIC: O.K., I'll sit in the back seat.

RUSH: Easier to *talk* back an' forth in the front seat.

VIC: O.K., I'll sit in the front seat.

RUSH: It's smoother *ridin'* in the back seat.

VIC: O.K., I'll sit in the back seat.

SADE: Yes, an' that's the way you egg him on.

VIC: [*Chuckles*] All I do is *agree* with him.

SADE: When they drive up tonight just crawl in the front seat an' don't *wait* for him to start that business. Last time they took us for a spin you an' Fred stood out on the curbing ten *minutes* talkin' that foolishness. Ya both know good an' well you sit up with Fred an' I sit back with Ruthie.

VIC: Um.

RUSH: I sure am uncomfortable.

SADE: [*To Vic*] You close the upstairs windows like I said?

VIC: Yeah.

SADE: Lock the back door?

VIC: Yeah.

SADE: When they come by an' honk we're all ready to jump up an' run then, huh?

VIC: Yeah.

RUSH: Gosh, but I'm uncomfortable.

VIC: You *should* be very, very *happy*.

RUSH: Why?

VIC: You're going to travel to Kappa an' then to Hudson an' then to El Paso an' then to Chenoa an' then to Lexington an' then to Towanda.

RUSH: Ump.

VIC: [*To Sade*] Ya s'pose there's any way Fred could be talked into drivin' a little *faster?*

SADE: He feels *safer* drivin' slow.

VIC: He don't hafta drive that *slow*. Plugs along at fifteen miles an hour. That Hudson-Chenoa circle he takes is less than twenty miles. It shouldn't take us all evening.

SADE: He had an uncle to get bad scratches in an auto accident years ago. That's why he's timid about burning up the road.

VIC: [*With some bitterness*] Ya can't burn up the road with the speedometer at fifteen miles an hour. After about ten minutes of it I feel like screaming. Makes the *other* motorists mad at us too.

SADE: They got no *right* stickin' their heads out an' hollerin' at Fred the way they do.

VIC: *I* don't blame 'em for gettin' sore. Fred chugs along the middle of the highway barely crawling an' when they honk for him to pull over an' let 'em past he takes all day doin' it.

SADE: *He* pays his taxes. What's the big hurry *anyway?*

RUSH: [*Chuckles*] "Drive it or sell it," they holler.

VIC: "Whatcha burnin'—kerosene?"

RUSH: "Look out there, Oldfield, you'll hurt somebody."

SADE: Don't you dare *antagonize* Fred now.

RUSH: Gee, but I'm uncomfortable.

VIC: Be patient. In just a few minutes you'll be in heaven . . . Dashing wildly up the road at break-neck speed.

RUSH: Uh-huh.

SADE: Fred's got *one* annoying habit I wish he'd cut out.

VIC: What's that?

SADE: Oh, that trick of his of turning around every couple seconds an' makin' Ruthie an' me break up our conversation while he points out something along the way we've seen a million times before.

VIC: Yeah.

SADE: [*Quotes*] "We're coming into Hudson now. That farm over there belongs to a man by the name of Cooney. I had a puncture one day right about here."

VIC: Yeah.

SADE: Ruthie an' I can't get in nine consecutive words.

VIC: [*Chuckles*] Uh-huh.

SADE: An' that business of makin' Ruthie hang out the side every little bit to see if the tires is flat. [*Quotes*] "Ruthie, take a look at my rear left, will ya?" Means she's got to crawl all over that back seat an' lean over to where she risks her life.

VIC: [*Little chuckle*] Uh-huh.

SADE: Fred's as good as gold but he can be exasperating.

VIC: Yeah.

RUSH: Golly, but I'm uncomfortable. Sittin' around in good clothes is just like bein' in a straight-jacket.

VIC: You'll forget all that when we've arrived in Lexington an' you're eatin' an ice-cream cone.

RUSH: Fred's the same way about ice-cream cones as he . . .

SADE: [*Dangerously*] Who?

RUSH: Fred. He's the same . . .

SADE: [*Dangerously*] Who?

RUSH: Mr. Stembottom.

SADE: [*Tough*] "Fred." There's *some* people close enough to hit with a rock think they're great big grown-up men aged twenty-one.

RUSH: Um.

VIC: What'd ya start to say, Pete?

RUSH: Started to say Mr. Stembottom's the same way about the ice-cream cones as he is about the front seat an' the back seat.

193

VIC: Worse. Be Fred.

RUSH: [*Chuckles*] O.K. Well, Vic, what'll it be?—vanilla flavor or strawberry flavor?

VIC: All the same to me.

RUSH: Vanilla O.K.?

VIC: Vanilla's fine.

RUSH: It's my treat. Have a *strawberry* cone if ya feel like it.

VIC: All right, I'll have strawberry.

RUSH: Maybe you'd rather have chocolate.

VIC: O.K., I'll have chocolate.

RUSH: Or pineapple.

VIC: O.K., pineapple.

RUSH: How about orange?

VIC: O.K., orange.

RUSH: I'm spendin' the money an' I want everybody to be satisfied. Whatcha want—chocolate?

VIC: Yeah.

RUSH: Pineapple?

VIC: Yeah.

RUSH: You're the doctor. How about Tutti-fruitti?

VIC: Gimme Tutti-fruitti.

SADE: That's the way you egg him *on,* Vic.

VIC: I only try to be *agreeable.*

SADE: When he asks ya what kind of an ice-cream-cone ya want say, "I want *vanilla.*"

VIC: Yes, an' then he'll say, "How about Chocolate."

SADE: You *encourage* him to go through that big elaborate talky-talk.

VIC: [*Chuckles*] I do not.

SADE: Ya do too. It's the same as makin' fun of him.

VIC: Aw.

SADE: It is so. An' *Ruthie* knows it. You're not foolin' her a parti-cle. I just wonder what she *thinks* of your smart actions.

VIC: [*Chuckles*] Aw heck, Sade, I'm only . . .

RUSH: Hey, here they come, I think.

SADE: [*Looks*] Yeah.

VIC: [*Mildly*] Hi-de-hi, ho-de-ho. Now for a reckless dash to Kappa, Hudson, El Paso, Chenoa, Lexington, an' Towanda. Hold on to your hat, Egg-white, because we won't spare the horses.

RUSH: Boy, I sure am uncomfortable.

SADE: Only one of Fred's headlights is workin'.

RUSH: Sittin' around in good clothes is like bein' in a straight-jacket.

SADE: Now, Vic, crawl in the front seat right away an' don't let's start this big long palaver about the front seat an' the back seat an' the front seat an' the back seat an' the . . .

[*Sound of auto horn*]

VIC: [*To Rush in low tones*] Drive it or sell it—drive it or sell it.

RUSH: [*Little chuckle*] Yeah.

[*Auto horn again*]

SADE: [*Calls*] All right, Peoples—we'll be right with ya. [*To her family*] C'mon.

END OF SCRIPT

ANNOUNCER: Which concludes another brief interlude at the small house half-way up in the next block.

1938

ROOSTER DAVIS'
NEW SPECTACLES

THEME

INTRODUCTION: Well, sir, it's a few minutes past twelve o'clock as we enter the small house half-way up in the next block now, and the noon-day meal should be in full swing. But we find our friends not in the kitchen but the living-room. Immediately we surmise the meat's not done. Which is exactly the case. Listen.

VIC: I am glowering at you, Sade.

SADE: Um.

VIC: I am baring my teeth at you, Sade.

SADE: [*Giggles*] Hey, I'm tryin' to read Bess's letter.

VIC: *Yes.* You are trying to read Bess's letter. I, on the other hand, am reflecting bitterly that the meat's not done. I have labored all morning at the office an' I feel that I deserve . . .

SADE: *I* explained why dinner's not ready. Croucher's delivery truck broke down . . . *All* the grocery orders got slowed up.

VIC: I guess I'm just a poor miserable football of fate. Life kicks me around like a . . .

SADE: Walter's knee-cap's been on the rampage again.

VIC: Yeah.

SADE: Give him severe twinges all last week.

VIC: I am desolate at this startling news.

SADE: Bess says [*Reads*], "Walter's knee-cap went off the reservation last Tuesday. For five days in a row it bothered him to where he was grumpy as an old bear. I tell him he ought to . . ."

VIC: The patter of little feet.

SADE: What?

VIC: Some interloper just opened the kitchen door. [*Calls*] We don't *want* any fish.

RUSH: [*Approaching*] Hi.

SADE: Big Christmas doin's in Carberry this year.

VIC: Um?

SADE: Three different parties besides the monstrous *church* affair.

VIC: Um.

SADE: Bess says [*Reads*], "Looks like we're going to be pretty much on the go this Christmas. Invitations have come from . . ."

RUSH: [*Almost up*] Meat's not done, huh?

VIC: No.

RUSH: I could eat a fried horse, harness an' all.

SADE: Something went wrong with the grocery wagon. The boy didn't show up until almost eleven o'clock.

199

RUSH: Um.

SADE: Will ya die if ya don't eat in the next ten minutes?

RUSH: I'll die if I don't eat in the next *eleven* minutes.

SADE: Here, Vic . . . Bess's letter.

VIC: Just lay it on the library table. I'll savor its rich contents after dinner when I can revel in each burnished phrase.

SADE: Smartness?

VIC: [*Neg.*] Uh-uh.

SADE: You don't hafta bother with the little old letters my sister writes. *There's* no policeman around to put you in prison if you're not interested in what she's got to say.

VIC: [*Getting off this dangerous subject*] What's new in higher-education circles, Smoke-screen?

RUSH: Plenty.

VIC: Principal Chinbunny has no doubt run away to the Western Ocean. Your algebra teacher . . .

RUSH: Everything's in a turmoil.

VIC: Ya don't say so.

RUSH: The high school don't know whether it's standing on its head or on its feet.

VIC: [*Mildly*] Hey, hey.

RUSH: A *bomb*-shell hit civilization this morning.

SADE: [*Who hasn't been listening*] What's all this?

VIC: A bomb-shell hit civilization this morning.

RUSH: [*To Sade*] I was just tellin' gov here there's big excitement up at school.

SADE: Um.

RUSH: A bomb-shell hit civilization.

SADE: Wanta read Aunt Bess's letter?

RUSH: Huh?

SADE: There's a letter from Aunt Bess on the library table.

RUSH: I'll get around to it later on. Gov, you'll never in the wide world guess who *threw* the bomb-shell that hit civilization.

VIC: [*Guessing*] J. Speewack Hook? U. U. Jibe? Yorick Q. Nix? Hamilton W. Hunkermanlystoverdelmagintoshfer.

RUSH: Rooster Davis.

VIC: Who?

RUSH: Rooster Davis.

VIC: Rooster threw the bomb-shell that hit civilization?

RUSH: Yep. The last individual on *earth* you'd expect to set the world on fire. Rooster's been in the *background* for the last few months. Smelly Clark an' Blue-tooth Johnson an' various parties have been *out-shining* him. It looked very much like ol' Rooster had lost his zip. Looked like he couldn't stand the gaff. Looked like he was all washed up. Why, LeRoy Snow told me this morning he had just recently advised Rooster to retire from public life. An' here by golly that doggone Rooster throws the whole *high*-school in a turmoil.

SADE: [*Mildly interested*] What'd he do?

RUSH: He showed up in first-hour algebra class wearing *glasses*.

SADE: Glasses?

RUSH: Glasses.

SADE: Eye-glasses?

RUSH: Eye-glasses.

SADE: What's so wonderful about *that?*

RUSH: It hit civilization like a bomb-shell.

SADE: Oh my. You kids certainly have a lot to get worked *up* about. Read Aunt Bess's letter: she says some nice things about *you* in it.

RUSH: No, but let me make this *clear* to ya. I wanta explain it so you'll get the terrific *significance* of it.

SADE: Terrific significance of a boy wearing spectacles to school, huh?

RUSH: Exactly.

SADE: Rooster havin' trouble with his eyes?

RUSH: Not *serious* trouble. He just figured he wasn't seein' as good as he ought to an' told his mother it an' she took him to the doctor an' the doctor give him glasses to wear while he's in school. He don't hafta wear'em *other* times. Only when he's in school or home reading or studyin' or in the picture show an' all like that.

SADE: Um.

RUSH: I just can't get *over* old Rooster turning the population upside down. *I* thought he'd sunk into oblivion.

VIC: You swiped that right out of Third Lieutenant Clinton Stanley.

RUSH: No, but it's the *truth*. I *did* think he'd sunk into oblivion. An' here by golly he goes to work an' hits civilization with a bombshell.

VIC: Is he the only kid in *school* that wears glasses?

RUSH: No, there's *plenty* kids in school wear glasses.

SADE: Eunice Raypole wears glasses, don't she?

RUSH: Sure.

SADE: An' that boy with the real thin little legs you had here the other afternoon. *He* was wearing glasses.

RUSH: Wilmore Stuffle. Yeah, *he* wears glasses. Been wearin' glasses ever since he was born.

SADE: Well then, what's so remarkable about Rooster wearin' . . .

RUSH: I'll be delighted to make it plain as a horse.

VIC: [*To Sade*] I wish the meat was done.

SADE: *I* told ya it'd be at least ten minutes.

VIC: Um.

SADE: Not *my* fault if the delivery wagon breaks down.

VIC: Um.

RUSH: I'll be delighted to make it plain as a horse why Rooster's glasses threw a bomb-shell that hit civilization.

VIC: Go ahead.

RUSH: [*Slowly and impressively*] Rooster showed up in first-hour algebra class this morning with glasses that had a ribbon on 'em.

SADE: Ribbon?

RUSH: Yes, ribbon. Eunice Raypole's glasses an' Wilmore Stuffle's glasses got *hooks* on 'em. *You* know. Hooks that run beside their head an' hook back of their ears.

SADE: Uh-huh.

RUSH: But *Rooster's* glasses didn't *have* any hooks. They had a *ribbon*. A big thick black ribbon. This ribbon was attached to one of the eye-glasses an' run down the side of Rooster's face an' ended up 'way down at the bottom button of his coat where it was attached to a brooch of his mother's about twice the size of a silver dollar.

SADE: Um.

RUSH: A *breast-pin,* ya know.

SADE: Uh-huh.

RUSH: You've seen 'em.

SADE: I've *got* one upstairs.

RUSH: Oh, sure. Well, Rooster's is lots bigger'n yours an' it's all covered with fake diamonds.

SADE: Um.

RUSH: He wears it 'way down at the bottom button of his coat.

SADE: Um.

RUSH: The ribbon itself is about six feet long. It goes from his glasses to his face, past his chest, past his stomach, down to his knees an' then loops back to this great big breast-pin. Ya' know the kinda spectacles Mis' *Brighton* wears.

SADE: Uh-huh.

RUSH: Come in an' out of her chest on a chain.

SADE: Uh-huh.

RUSH: Well, Rooster's glasses work on the same principle except instead of a chain he's got a black silk ribbon an' instead of a little gold round thing he's got this *brooch.*

SADE: Um.

RUSH: Can'tcha *see* how a bomb-shell like that'd hit civilization?

SADE: Um.

RUSH: [*Chuckles*] The American public just about had the idea Rooster Davis was on the shelf. *He* showed'em.

VIC: Did the algebra teacher instruct Rooster to leave the room an' get rid of the masquerade an' come back lookin' like a decent . . .

RUSH: She *did* not. Rooster was wearin' glasses on advice of his physician.

VIC: Just the same . . .

RUSH: It wasn't any of *her* bee's-wax what *kinda* glasses Rooster was wearin'. He was wearin' glasses on the advice of his physician. The algebra teacher's hands were tied.

VIC: Um.

RUSH: They say it was wonderful to *watch* him. Mis' Monroe, she's the teacher, would ask him a question. "Edwin," she'd say, "what result did you obtain in problem three of your home-work?" Rooster'd take off his glasses an' tap his teeth with 'em.

VIC AND SADE: [*Chuckling*] Aw.

RUSH: [*Chuckling*] That's an absolute *fact.* Rooster'd scrounge 'way back in his chair an' close his eyes an' open his mouth an' tap his teeth with his glasses. After while he'd open his eyes an' say very aristocratic, "My result was three hundred an' sixty-seven, Miss Monroe."

SADE: I should think she'd throw a dictionary at him or something.

RUSH: She was *tempted* to all right. Oh, an' *another* thing he done in first-hour algebra. He passed his glasses across the room to Milton Welch. Milton Welch wanted to try'em on. Well, Rooster's seat is the first seat in row one an' Milton's seat is the last seat in row seven. Rooster passed the glasses but he didn't disconnect the silk ribbon. By golly, that silk ribbon was stretched clear across the whole room. I said a while ago it was six feet long. It musta been at least *fifteen* feet long.

SADE: [*Some distaste*] Oh my.

RUSH: [*Chuckles*] Old Rooster Davis that everybody thought had shot his bolt.

VIC: [*To Sade*] I wish the meat was done.

SADE: Just a few more minutes. I been watchin' the clock.

VIC: Sometimes I weep great salt tears when I reflect on my wretched lot. Seems like the fates conspire against me. The meat's not done an' . . .

RUSH: I wanta tell ya what Rooster done in second-hour English Class.

VIC: What'd he do?

RUSH: He showed up with a *stick* on his glasses.

VIC: A stick?

RUSH: Remember the other evening when we went to the Bijou an' saw Gloria Golden in "I Leave You Now, Sweet Hawaii"?

VIC: Yeah.

RUSH: Remember the fat lady at the fancy ball that was so rich an' had the white hair an' talked la-de-da I'm charmed to see you lookin' so healthy, Mr. Hooker, an' all that?

VIC: Yeah.

RUSH: Remember her glasses?

VIC: They had . . .

RUSH: They had a little *handle* on 'em.

VIC: [*Chuckles*] Oh, uh-huh.

RUSH: Whenever she wanted to look at something she'd just take hold of the handle an' lift her glasses up in front of her eyes.

VIC: [*Chuckles*] Uh-huh.

RUSH: [*Imitates the movie dowager*] "Oh, slush, General Simpson, ain't this a peachy evening. Have another jolt of raspberry sherbet."

VIC: [*Chuckles*] Rooster have a handle on *his* glasses?

RUSH: Yeah. He'd disconnected the big silk ribbon an' attached this *stick*. Whenever Miss James—she's the English teacher—called on him he'd put his glasses up in front of his eyes an' stare at her like a baboon.

VIC: Didn't she jump down his throat?

RUSH: She *attempted* to. She says, "Edwin, I guess we've had sufficient nonsense. I suggest you put your play-things away an' settle down to business."

VIC: Um.

RUSH: Rooster merely said, "These glasses are not play-things, Miss James. I'm wearing 'em on the advice of my physician." What could she *do?* Her *hands* were tied.

VIC: Um.

RUSH: All *morning* it was like that. Civilization rocked back an' forth like a feather in the breeze.

VIC: Um.

RUSH: [*Chuckles*] Old Rooster Davis that everybody thought was through. Old Rooster Davis, that'd sunk 'way back in the background an'd been advised to retire from public life.

VIC: Um.

RUSH: Old Rooster Davis.

VIC: Um.

SADE: All right, fellas.

VIC: [*Brightly*] Meat done?

SADE: *Oughta* be. C'mon.

END OF SCRIPT

ANNOUNCER: Which concludes another brief interlude at the small house half-way up in the next block.

1938

BESS' LETTER:
THE GUMPOX PETITION

THEME

ANNOUNCER: OPENING AND COMMERCIAL CREDITS

INTRODUCTION: Well, sir, it's about seven-thirty o'clock as we enter the small house half-way up in the next block now, and here in the living-room we find Mr. and Mrs. Victor Gook and their son, Mr. Rush Gook spending a quiet evening at home. Vic is in his easy-chair, young Rush is on the davenport, and Sade—at the library table—prepares to read from a letter. Listen.

SADE: [*Reads*] "Dear Sister an' all. Thought I would write an' see how you are feeling." [*Brief pause*] If I'm gonna read this I'd like to have your divided attention.

VIC: *I'm* listening. My newspaper's folded in my lap.

SADE: Yeah, but ya got it folded at some particular piece. You keep glancing down at it.

VIC: You can *blindfold* me if ya *wanta*.

SADE: No, but Bess don't write letters just to hear herself *think,* ya know.

VIC: Um.

SADE: Means you too, Willie. Put your book off to one side.

RUSH: You told us *most* of the things Aunt Bess said in her letter at the supper table.

SADE: [*Eyeing him*] Smartness?

RUSH: *No,* but, heck. Individuals always . . .

SADE: Better *not* be smartness.

RUSH: Um.

SADE: [*Brief pause*] "Dear Sister an' all. Thought I would write an' see how you are feeling. We are fine an' Walter's knee-cap is on the up-grade again, not giving him a single twinge during the whole month of February. I expect Rush is having big times at school."

RUSH: *I'll* say.

SADE: What?

RUSH: [*Little chuckle*] Aunt Bess says that in every letter she writes.

SADE: [*Gently*] You don't like it?

RUSH: I *like* it all right, only she's . . . [*Chuckles*] . . . always expecting I'm havin' big *times.* "I expect Rush is having big times now that it's Christmas vacation." "I expect Rush is having big times in the snow." "I expect Rush is having big times shooting off firecrackers."

SADE: [*Gently*] You object to that?

RUSH: *No.*

SADE: It might be better if children waited till they got to be

209

twenty-one years old before they gave out monstrous big opinions like the King of Peoria.

RUSH: Um.

SADE: "I expect Rush is having big times at school. Our kids haven't missed a day this winter. Eunice is improving just wonderful on the piano. She can play four pieces now without looking at the music. I expect Vic is having big times at the office."

VIC: [*Chuckles*] Oh boy.

SADE: What?

VIC: Next time you write assure her that I *am* having big times at the office. I put roses in my hair an' dance barefoot the whole day through.

SADE: [*Gently*] Smartness, huh?

VIC: [*Chuckles*] What's she think I *do* at my office . . . sing songs an' eat grapes?

SADE: [*Gently*] *All* right, *I'll* put the letter away.

VIC: [*Little chuckle*] No, but "I expect Vic is having big times in his office" sounds like my office was a roller-coaster or a picnic grounds where bright-faced girls an' happy boys . . .

SADE: [*Gently*] I'll put poor Bess's miserable little letter away.

VIC: [*Little chuckle*] Aw heck, kiddo, why do you always have a *chip* on your shoulder every time you read one of Bess's letters?

SADE: [*Gently*] *I* wasn't aware I had a chip on my shoulder.

VIC: *Invariably*

RUSH: That's the truth, mom.

SADE: [*Gently*] I guess it's because I can't bear to sit still an' listen to people criticize my only sister.

VIC: We were only tryin' to have a little *fun*.

SADE: [*Gently*] Yes . . . at poor Bess's expense.

VIC: Oh, go ahead . . . read.

SADE: [*Gently*] I'll just put the letter away in the library table drawer.

VIC: No . . . I wanta hear the rest of it.

SADE: [*Sad giggle*] I'll say.

VIC: I *do*.

SADE: All right.

VIC: Um.

SADE: [*Reads*] "I expect Vic is having big times at the office." [*Pause*] Have you laughed at that all you care to?

VIC: Go ahead.

SADE: [*Reads*] "Walter stayed home from the shop all last Friday

210

making a new garbage box. He isn't much of a carpenter an' the garbage box looks like . . ." [*Thinks of something*] Oh, *say*.

VIC: Um?

SADE: Mr. Gumpox is thinking of resigning from his position.

VIC: Yeah?

SADE: This reference to garbage made me think of it. Yes, he was here s'afternoon an' made quite a spiel to me about it. He don't think the city pays him enough salary an' he's just about decided to tender his resignation.

VIC: Can he make another connection?

SADE: Says he can go to any one of a dozen different cities an' be taken on.

VIC: Um.

RUSH: Mr. Gumpox claims he's got a reputation that extends all over Central Illinois.

SADE: Yeah. Told me that s'afternoon.

RUSH: [*Quotes Gumpox*] "I've grown *up* with garbage. I've been associated with garbage my entire life. It's only *natural* that I should gain some small reputation. In Streator and Dwight they call me the Grand Old *Man* of Garbage."

SADE: Made exactly the same speech to *me*.

VIC: I'm sorry to hear he's *leaving* us. I've grown *used* to seein' him perched up on that wagon-seat with his big shoes hangin' over the side an' not wearin' any socks.

SADE: He hasn't *left* us *yet*. An' I have a kinda half-way semi-notion in my noodle he don't even *intend* to. *I* think he's got an *axe* to grind.

VIC: How ya mean?

SADE: I think he's just tryin' to pull off a little stunt so the city'll raise his salary.

VIC: What's the stunt?

SADE: He wants me to go around town with a petition an' get everybody's name.

VIC: A petition?

SADE: . . . requesting the city not to *accept* his resignation.

VIC: Oh.

SADE: See?

VIC: [*Little chuckle*] Uh-huh.

SADE: He's not gonna tender his resignation until I've got the petition all filled with names an' that's the reason I think he's just tryin' to pull off a cute scheme.

VIC: Pretty cute scheme at that.

SADE: Sure it is. The mayor or whoever handles the garbage department will receive this resignation. Very next day he'll receive a petition with six hundred names on it askin' him not to accept the resignation. Here's all these citizens an' voters askin' him a special favor. What else can he *do* but raise Mr. Gumpox's salary?

VIC: [*Chuckles*] Uh-huh.

SADE: [*Giggles*] Pretty slick, huh?

VIC: Yeah.

RUSH: You gonna do it, mom?

SADE: Get six hundred people to sign a petition? I *am* not.

RUSH: Mr. Gumpox is a good *friend* of yours.

SADE: Yes, he is. Done me many an' *many* a favor. [*Giggles*] But that'd be a little *too* much.

VIC: Six hundred names is a lotta names.

SADE: *I'll* say. [*Giggles*] Take me ten years.

VIC: Consider the noble *cause* you'd be workin' for though.

SADE: Yeah. People'd say, "What ails that Mrs. Gook from over there on Virginia Avenue? She come to the door today wantin' me to sign a paper askin' the mayor to raise her garbage-man's pay."

[*Laughs*]

VIC: [*Laughs a little*]

RUSH: There ain't six hundred people on Mr. Gumpox's whole *route*.

SADE: *No.* An' that's the thing *about* it. Why on earth should folks on the east an' west side be interested in whether the garbage-man in *this* neighborhood quits his job or not. They got their *own* garbage-man.

RUSH: Did you point that *out* to Mr. Gumpox?

SADE: Sure I did.

RUSH: [*Little chuckle*] What'd he say?

SADE: He said he wanted six hundred names on the petition or he wouldn't tender his resignation.

VIC: Believes in havin' a sure *thing*.

SADE: Exactly. Refuses to take any chances.

VIC: How does that fit in with his statement that he can get taken on in a dozen different cities.

SADE: [*Giggles*] It don't *fit* in.

VIC: Um.

SADE: An' the petition *itself* is worded so ridiculous. He showed it to me. Why, I wouldn't any more ask people to sign such a thing than a rabbit.

VIC: How'd it read?

SADE: Oh . . . [*Tries to recollect it*] . . . something about "we, the undersigned, being in sane mind an' sound body, do hereby command, request, an' implore that Francis Gumpox be retained by the . . .

VIC: Francis?

SADE: [*Giggles*] Uh-huh.

VIC: Very pretty.

SADE: [*Giggles*] First time I ever knew what his first name *was.* I like to fell over.

RUSH: Frances is a *girl's* name.

SADE: [*Neg.*] Uh-uh.

RUSH: Sure. Up at school we got Frances Otto, Frances Sprague, Frances Meeker, an' Frances Johnson. Also my English teacher's first name is Frances.

SADE: It's a girl's name when it's [*Spelling*] F-r-a-n-c-e-s, an' a boy's name when it's F-r-a-n-c-i-s.

RUSH: Um.

SADE: We had a Francis back in Dixon. Francis Kleek. Remember him, Vic? Always had shoe-horns in the heel of his shoes stickin' up the back of his socks?

VIC: Yeah.

RUSH: Why'd he do that?

SADE: Very absent-*minded* fella.

RUSH: Used shoe-horns to get his shoes on with an' then forgot to take them out.

SADE: Yeah. Let's see. I think I can remember *most* of that petition. "We, the undersigned, being in sane mind an' sound body, do hereby command, request, an' implore that Francis Gumpox be retained by the city. As home-owners with a passionate love for a beautiful town in which to live we feel that this community could never stand to lose the services of Francis Gumpox, who knows and loves garbage like no other man on earth."

VIC: [*Laughs*] Oh, for gosh sakes, does the guy . . .

SADE: Wait a second, I left *out* a word. "Who knows and loves garbage *disposal* like no other man on earth."

VIC: [*Chuckles*] Thunder.

SADE: [*Giggles*] The other way sounds *funny* . . . "knows an' loves *garbage* like no other man on earth."

RUSH: [*Chuckles*] It *all* sounds funny.

SADE: Yeah.

VIC: You turned him down on the proposition, huh?

SADE: Oh, sure.

VIC: Did he put up a holler?

SADE: He made several pretty fancy *speeches*.

RUSH: [*Quotes*] "I flatter myself I have done more for garbage than any other one individual east of the Mississippi."

SADE: [*In some surprise*] Yeah. He tell *you* that too?

RUSH: Told quite a *bunch* of us one time.

SADE: [*Quotes*] "Garbage has been my great love through life. I've been up to my ears in garbage since I was nineteen years of age an' I expect to die in harness."

RUSH: "The citizens of Dwight and Streator have dubbed me the Grand Old Man of Garbage. An *Emperor* could be no prouder of his title."

SADE: [*Giggles*] Yeah. Well, lands, I hope he *does* get his pay raised. Been awful nice to *me* during the years we've lived here. Just *jumps* at the chance to do a person a favor. Why, I bet five cents if he's helped me string my clothes-line on Mondays once he's done it fourteen thousand times.

SADE: [*Brief pause*] Well . . . Bess's letter?

VIC: [*Little chuckle*] *See,* kiddo, how you always get a chip on your shoulder when ya got a letter of Bess's to read?

SADE: [*A touch of acid*] *I* haven't got any chip on my shoulder.

VIC: Sure ya have.

SADE: The trouble *is* I just can't stand around an' let people take digs at my sister.

VIC: Nobody's takin' any digs at your sister. You just *imagine* they are. Two seconds ago when we were talkin' about Gumpox you were jolly as a horse. The minute you whip out Bess's letter you start givin' Rat-trap an' myself suspicious glances.

SADE: It's too bad about Rat-trap an' yourself.

SADE: [*Reads*] "Dear sister an' all: Thought I would write an' see how you are feeling. We are fine an' Walter's kneecap is . . ."

RUSH: [*Very low tones*] Ya read that.

SADE: [*Sharply*] What?

RUSH: [*Meekly*] Nothin'.

SADE: You *said* something. What was it?

RUSH: [*Meekly*] Um.

SADE: [*Tough*] What was it?

RUSH: [*Meekly*] I guess I was just callin' your attention to the fact you'd already *read* the first part.

SADE: You don't wanta hear it read again?

RUSH: [*Meekly*] Sure.

SADE: [*Brief pause*] "Dear sister an' all: Thought I would write

214

an' see how you are feeling. We are fine an' Walter's kneecap is on the up-grade, not giving him a single twinge during the whole month of February. I expect Rush is having big times at school." [*Pause*]

RUSH: *I* didn't say anything.

SADE: "I expect Rush is having big times at school. Our kids haven't missed a day this winter. Euncie is improving just wonderful on the piano. She can play four pieces now without looking at the music. I expect Vic is having big times at the office." [*Hostile pause*]

VIC: [*Meekly*] *I* didn't say anything, Sade.

SADE: [*Pause*] "Walter stayed home from the shop all last Friday making a new garbage box. He isn't much of a carpenter an' the garbage box looks like something the cat drug in. Ha-ha. Mr. an' Mrs. George Eppler dropped in the middle of last week. They asked after you folks an' bet Rush was as big as his papa. I expect people in your city are having big times with colds an' influenza."

[*Hostile pause*]

VIC AND RUSH: [*Meekly, after a pause*] *I* didn't' say anything.

END OF SCRIPT

ANNOUNCER: Which conclues another brief interlude at the small house half-way up in the next block.

1939

ROOSTER'S BLOCK
OF THEATER SEATS

THEME

INTRODUCTION: Well, sir, the evening meal has been over only a few minutes as we enter the small house half-way up in the next block now, and here in the living room we find Mr. Rush Gook all by himself. The young man is at the telephone talking earnestly with a close associate, one Rooster Davis. We're just in time to get in on the tail end of the conversation. Listen.

RUSH: [*To phone*] I'll make every possible effort to be there, Rooster. I won't leave a single stone unturned. No. Well, it might be a *little* difficult:—like a fat-head I let drop at the supper table we're gonna have an algebra quiz tomorrow an' my mother'll prob'ly insist pretty strong I hafta stay home an' study. But I'll do everything that's humanly possible to be on deck. You bet. O.K., fella. O.K. So long. [*Hangs up*]

VIC: [*Coming up*] I believe your mother's ready for you to help her with the dishes, Straight-edge.

RUSH: Listen, gov, will you co-operate with me on a . . .

SADE: [*In kitchen*] All right, sonny.

RUSH: [*Calls*] Mom.

SADE: [*In kitchen*] Your towel's all ready an' waitin' for ya.

RUSH: [*Calls*] Will you step in here a moment, please, mom?

SADE: [*In kitchen*] What?

RUSH: [*Calls*] Will you step in here a moment, please?

SADE: [*Off*] Why?

RUSH: [*Calls*] Something of the greatest importance has come up.

VIC: Seems to me that if something of the greatest importance has come up you'd go out to where the *lady* is rather than ask the lady to come where *you* are.

RUSH: I wanta talk to you people as a *group*.

VIC: That so? How *fine*. *I* usta talk to my mother as a group *myself* when I was a lad. What happy days those were. My hair was burnished gold an' by some odd quirk of fate I wore shoes on my feet. I'll never forget . . .

SADE: [*Coming up*] What's the matter?

RUSH: That was Rooster Davis I talked to on the phone just now, mom.

SADE: [*Up*] You make me come all the way in here just to tell me . . .

RUSH: He's gonna do it *again*.

SADE: Do what again?

RUSH: Rock the foundations of civilization.

SADE: Rush, did you make me walk clear from the kitchen just to . . .

RUSH: Listen—there's gonna be something take place at the Bijou Theater tonight that's never happened before in the history of the United States. Sit down on the davenport;—let me tell ya about it.

SADE: [*Wearily*] Guess I will sit down . . . after that long tramp clear from the kitchen just to listen to foolishness.

RUSH: Put your newspaper off to one side, gov.

VIC: Is that a command?

RUSH: You'll scream like a *panther* when ya hear what Rooster's gonna do tonight.

VIC: [*Very mildly screams like a panther, and then observes . . .*] Hear me scream like a panther, kiddo?

RUSH: [*Addressing his parents as a group*] People, at ten minutes to seven this evening the audience in the Bijou Theater will receive the greatest shock they ever . . .

SADE: [*Warningly*] Hey, now.

RUSH: . . . received in . . . [*To Sade*] Beg pardon?

SADE: Is this some monstrous big elaborate scheme to get permission to go to the show?

RUSH: Mom, after I've described the events scheduled to take place a little later on you'll *urge* me to go to the . . .

SADE: [*Dryly*] I *will,* huh? Didn't I hear some boy at the supper table say there was gonna be an algebra examination up at school tomorrow?

RUSH: *Forgetting* that for the moment, may I . . .

SADE: [*Little giggle*] Yeah, "forgetting that for the moment." *You'd* forget your lessons for the rest of your *life* if people didn't stand *over* ya like policemen. Goodness gracious, you'd think an enormous big man aged fourteen years would . . . [*Telephone*]

VIC: [*Mildly*] Telephone is ringing, telephone is ringing.

SADE: Probably Ruthie.

RUSH: Might be Blue-tooth Johnson.

SADE: Answer it an' see. If it's some chum of *yours* don't get in any long involved conversations. We hafta get at them dishes.

RUSH: [*To phone*] Hello? Oh *yes* Smelly.

SADE: [*To Vic, giggling*] Made me walk clear in here from the kitchen just to tell me Rooster Davis called him on the phone.

RUSH: [*To phone*] I know all *about* that, Smelly. Yeah. Well, I'm gonna make every possible *effort* to be there.

SADE: [*To Vic*] You gonna let him run off to the picture show when there's a test tomorrow?

220

VIC: I'll leave the matter in your hands. I'll take the role of innocent bystander an' . . .

RUSH:[*Gently*] Please, people.

SADE: [*Dryly*] Excuse us for livin'.

RUSH: [*To phone*] It will be a *tremendous* sensation. Yes, *sir.* By George, an' they said ol' Rooster Davis was *through.* By George, certain individuals even advised him to retire from public life. By George, it's ridiculous. By George. Yeah. Well, I'm gonna make every possible effort to be there that's humanly *possible,* Smelly. Yeah. O.K., fella. You bet. So long. [*Hangs up*] [*To his folks*] By George.

VIC: Before you begin any campaign to obtain permission to attend the Bijou it might be well to advise you that your mother has a few rather strong *notions* on the matter. She feels . . .

RUSH: [*Pleadingly*] Will you people *listen* to me a minute?

SADE: [*Briefly*] Let's go do the supper dishes.

RUSH: Listen one minute. *Two* minutes. Three at the outside.

SADE: [*Wearily*] Oh my.

RUSH: [*Tensely*] Tonight at the Bijou there's gonna be a block of twenty-five seats roped off. These twenty-five seats are in the center section down front. There's gonna be a big sign in the middle. This sign's gonna say, "Reserved for Mr. Davis."

VIC AND SADE: [*No answer*]

RUSH: [*After a pause*] Ain't you *startled?*

VIC: Just confused.

RUSH: I'll boil it down in a nutshell. Rooster Davis . . .

   [*Phone*]

SADE: [*Mildly*] Telephone is ringing.

VIC: Say hello to it, Road-map.

SADE: [*To Vic*] If it's Ruthie, ya feel like Five Hundred?

VIC: Suits me.

RUSH: [*To phone*] Hello? Oh *yes,* LeRoy.

SADE: [*To Vic*] My dish-water gettin' colder every minute.

VIC: Um.

RUSH: [*To phone*] I know all *about* it, LeRoy. Yeah. Talked to Rooster *himself* a while ago. Why, it's gonna be the *biggest* thing that ever *happened* to civilization. Sure. Well, I'm gonna make every possible effort that's humanly *possible* to be there. You bet. All right, fella. I just called to make sure you . . . what? Oh, that's right, you called *me.*

VIC: [*To Sade*] Our little boy has a fine mind.

SADE: Yeah.

RUSH: [*To phone*] O.K., LeRoy. O.K. You bet. So long, fella. [*Hangs up*]

SADE: C'mon, Willie, otherwise it'll be midnight before we get that kitchen straightened around to where . . .

RUSH: [*Pleading*] Mom, *please.*

SADE: [*Little weary sigh*]

RUSH: Tonight at the Bijou there's gonna be a block of twenty-five seats roped off. These twenty-five seats are in the center section down front.

VIC: [*Briefly*] You *said* that.

RUSH: Well, let me *explain.*

VIC: Explain.

RUSH: In the middle of these twenty-five roped-off seats there's gonna be a big sign sayin', "Reserved for Mr. Davis."

VIC: How come?

RUSH: It's like this: The Bijou management had some carpenters in the theater this morning to do some work. They didn't get through with what they started. Matinee begins about two o'clock so they roped off the twenty-five seats they'd been fixin' an' knocked off for the day. Those seats are *still* roped off. Rooster Davis discovered the situation an' had a chat with the manager. The manager's a friend of his. Begin to catch on?

VIC: Rooster's gonna shock the Bijou audience by strolling in the show an' sittin' down in the middle of the whole block of reserved seats?

RUSH: You've hit it right square on the *head.*

VIC: [*Chuckles*] For Pete's sake.

SADE: [*Interested*] This is the truth, Rush?

RUSH: The absolute break-my-back-and-holler-die truth or I don't want my correct change.

SADE: He's gonna be all *alone* in that big section of seats?

RUSH: All alone. An' like I say it's in the center section right down front. An' it's roped *off.* An' gonna have this *sign* on it, "Reserved for Mister Davis." You ever hear of such a thing in all your life?

SADE: [*Neg.*] Uh-uh.

RUSH: *You* know how it is at the Bijou. They start sellin' tickets at six-thirty. At quarter to seven there's a big crowd outside. People like to come early an' stare at each other an' see who's with who an' let their kids run up and down the aisle an' like that. You've seen it nine million times.

SADE: [*Giggles*] Uh-uh.

RUSH: Well, Rooster plans to make his entrance at ten minutes to seven on the dot. He'll be escorted to his block of seats by two ushers.

VIC: *Two* ushers, huh?

RUSH: Two. See, the manager caught the spirit of the thing an' no holds is barred.

VIC AND SADE: Um.

RUSH: An' he's gonna wear his brother's overcoat.

VIC: Rooster is?

RUSH: Yeah. *You* know Rooster's brother Rotten, don't ya?

SADE: Know him when I see him.

RUSH: Ever notice him when he had his overcoat on?

SADE: Don't think so.

RUSH: It's a *long* overcoat. An' *awful* long overcoat. Comes 'way down to Rooster's heels. An' it's got a big fur collar.

SADE: Yeah?

RUSH: A *real* big fur collar.

SADE: [*Giggles*] He'll walk down the aisle with . . .

RUSH: . . . this long coat on, yeah. Escorted by two ushers. He'll arrive at his block of seats, lift the rope an' take a chair right in the exact center. There won't be anybody within ten feet of him. He'll be just like an island in an ocean.

SADE: Lands.

RUSH: Can't you just *hear* the hush fall over the audience when this thing takes place? *You* know how it is at the Bijou ten minutes before the picture starts. There's about a million separate conversations going on an' kids yellin' back and forth an' nine thousand *other* noises. But there won't be a *sound* when Rooster gets half-way down the aisle.

VIC: I bet there won't at that.

RUSH: *Now* do you begin to understand why I . . .

    [*Telephone*]

SADE: Telephone ringing.

VIC: Prob'ly for you, Smoke-screen.

RUSH: Yeah. *Now* do you begin to understand why I said civilization would get rocked back an' forth like a feather in the breeze tonight?

VIC AND SADE: Um.

RUSH: [*To phone*] Hello? Oh *yes,* Milton. *I* know what you're callin' up about. I know *exactly* . . . what? Yeah. I talked to Rooster *himself* while ago. Ain't it though. By George, yes. Well, I'm sure gonna make every possible effort that's humanly *possible* to be there. You bet. O.K., Milton, thanks for callin'. Good-by. [*Hangs up*]

[*To his folks*] Just *visualize* the scene. The audience at the Bijou are sittin' there wonderin' why a whole section of seats is roped off. They wonder who the heck Mr. Davis is. At ten minutes to seven a guy in a long overcoat with a big fur collar starts down the aisle escorted by two ushers. The buzz of conversation begins to die. People begin to crane their necks. Rooster Davis struts to his block of roped-off seats, picks up the sign, hands it to one of the ushers, an' proceeds to the exact *center* of the roped-off seats. He carefully removes his overcoat. He gazes around at the sea of faces, a slightly *contemptuous* expression on his face. He waves, condescendingly to some acquaintance he spots in the gallery. From his pocket he produces a sack of salted peanuts. He starts tossin' salted peanuts in his mouth. He gets a peanut stuck in his tooth. He screws his jaw around until he gets the peanut loose. He spits it out very irritated an' fashionable. His *back* itches. He reaches around an' . . . [*Telephone*] [*Briskly*] *I'll* get that.

VIC AND SADE: Um.

RUSH: Wouldn't be surprised but what it's . . . [*To phone*] Hello? Oh, *hello,* Orval. Yeah, know all about it. I'm sure gonna *try* to. You bet. Well, I'll see ya there if it's humanly *possible* for me to. Sure. O.K., Orval, thanks for calling. Yeah. So long. [*Hangs up*] [*To his folks*] Orval White.

VIC AND SADE: Um.

RUSH: [*Taking up his story where he left off*] His *back* itches. He reaches around very stylish an' scratches. Pretty quick he gets impatient. He twists around an' stares tough at the little booth where the movie-show operator sits. He makes irritated *signs* at the movie-show operator. Like, "Hey, let's get *going* here." The audience is speechless an' pop-eyed. Civilization rocks back an' forth like a feather in the breeze. [*Takes a long breath*] By *George!*

VIC: [*After a pause*] What's on at the Bijou tonight?

SADE: I don't know.

VIC: What's on, Harry?

RUSH: I don't know.

VIC: Whatcha say we go, kiddo?

SADE: You couldn't *keep* me away.

END OF SCRIPT

ANNOUNCER: Which concludes another brief interval at the small house half-way up in the next block.

1939

**VIC MEMORIZES
THE LODGE RITUAL**

THEME

ANNOUNCER: OPENING AND COMMERCIAL CREDITS

INTRODUCTION: Well sir, the evening meal has been over only a little while as we enter the small house half-way up in the next block now, and here in the living-room we find our friends assembled. Vic is established beneath the floor-lamp, his attention riveted on a typewritten document spread out on his knees. Sade and young Rush—seated on opposite sides of the library table—compete in a sluggish game of rummy. Listen.

SADE: There I go again: played a diamond for a spade.

RUSH: I don't see how you can get mixed up on diamonds an' spades, mom. One is red an' the other is black.

SADE: I mean hearts an' clubs.

RUSH: [*Chuckles*] Hearts are red, clubs are black.

SADE: I mean . . . [*Little giggle*] . . . oh, *you* know what I mean.

RUSH: You mean you get diamonds mixed up with hearts an' clubs mixed up with spades.

SADE: Sure.

RUSH: Straightened out now?

SADE: Yeah. Go ahead: your turn.

RUSH: I've got a difficult *decision* to make. I'm afraid to draw that jack you discarded an' I'm also afraid *not* to . . .

SADE: You *memorizing* something there, Vic?

VIC: Yeah.

SADE: I noticed ya gazin' up at the ceiling an' moving your lips. What is it?

VIC: Part of the ritualistic conduct of lodge meetings.

SADE: [*To whom this is Greek*] Oh.

VIC: Headquarters sent all us Exalted Big Dippers letters the other day instructing us to commit to memory certain portions of the Scroll.

SADE: Um.

RUSH: O.K., mom, play.

SADE: Take my jack?

RUSH: Uh-huh, an' discarded the nine of spades.

SADE: [*Examining her cards*] Nine of spades, huh?

VIC: Up till now it's always been the custom of Exalted Big Dippers to *read* the Scroll. Headquarters got this new bee in their bonnet an' now we hafta learn it by heart.

SADE: [*To Rush*] Here's the nice three of clubs.

RUSH: Thanks. I can use it in my business. [*Thoughtfully*] Let's see what I got here now.

SADE: *Next* week at this time you'll be havin' fun in *Carberry*.

RUSH: Yeah.

SADE: You'll be on the tail-end of your visit.

RUSH: That's right, I will. Discardin' the ten of hearts.

SADE: Ten of hearts, huh? [*To Vic*] Are you able to do any memorizin' with us fellas jabberin' over our rummies?

VIC: I do work that requires concentration down at the office all day long in a hubbub worse'n they got in the C&A round-house.

SADE: Um.

VIC: Besides, this stuff is pretty easy to learn. I've read it at lodge meeting every week for the past three years.

SADE: [*To Rush*] *I* played.

RUSH: [*Chuckles*] *I* never said ya didn't play.

SADE: You looked at me like, "Whatcha waitin' for?"

RUSH: The expression on my face was a *puzzled* expression.

SADE: How ya mean?

RUSH: You drew that deuce of clubs only about two minutes ago. Here you are *discarding* it again.

SADE: I imagine a person's got the privilege of discardin' whatever they please.

RUSH: Sure, but I don't catch on how ya expect to *win*. You're not gettin' any place . . .

SADE: You just keep your eyes on your *own* rummies. *I'll* look after *mine*.

RUSH: [*Chuckles*] O.K.

SADE: An' prob'ly give you a good lickin'.

RUSH: [*Chuckles*] O.K. Here's the queen of diamonds.

SADE: Queen of diamonds, huh?

RUSH: [*Chuckles*] You sure got peculiar ideas about *rummy*.

SADE: [*Giggles*] You just wait. I'll *surprise* ya with my rummies.

RUSH: [*Chuckles*] You surprise me with every *play* ya make. I'm astonished ya . . .

VIC: Hey, you guys, wanta help a fella?

SADE: [*Glad for something different*] Sure.

VIC: I think I've got this pretty well in my head. If one of you catbirds'll take this paper I'll speak my piece out loud an' you can follow along an' check my mistakes.

SADE: Hand it over.

RUSH: How about our *game*?

SADE: I'm kinda tired of rummies.

RUSH: Ya can't quit *now*. I just about got ya *beat*.

SADE: I'll forfeit myself the game.

RUSH: You mean you'll forfeit *me* the game.

SADE: *All right.* [*To Vic*] Whatcha want me to do?—read this out loud?

VIC: No, just read along while I *recite* out loud.

SADE: An' if ya recite something that ain't . . .

VIC: . . . on there, holler.

SADE: All right, start reciting.

VIC: [*Clears throat preparatory to holding forth*]

SADE: Pull up your *chair* if ya wanta be in on this, Rush. Gives me the willies to have somebody standin' directly behind me breathin' their breath on my neck.

RUSH: Um.

VIC: [*Sundry coughs and throaty acrobatics*]

SADE: [*After a time*] Ready?

VIC: Yeah. I wanta put some eloquence an' *color* into this. It's a beautiful speech an' can be made impressive if I deliver it right. Some Exalted Big Dippers stand up on their rostrum an' *mumble* their doggone words.

SADE: Well—let's hear ya.

VIC: Start me off.

SADE: [*Giggles*] You must have it memorized just *grand*—if ya can't remember how it *begins*.

VIC: [*A touch of irritation*] *I* remember how it begins.

SADE: How?

VIC: "Hurry to the plashing fountain, maidens."

SADE: I was gonna *say*.

VIC: [*After a brief pause*] Sade, if you're not interested in this an' are disposed to take a *sour* attitude perhaps . . .

SADE: Looks like *you're* the party on pins an' needles to take a sour attitude. You asked me to help an' I said I would. Go ahead: let's hear ya recite.

VIC: [*After a pause*] "Hurry to the plashing fountain, maidens. Dabble your pale feet in the crystal water an' weave garlands of roses. The heroes have returned from the fray an' will . . .

SADE: [*Puzzled*] What'd you say this was?

VIC: [*Politely*] We do not *progress* very fast, *do* we?

SADE: [*Puzzled*] No, but . . . didn't you say this was part of your *lodge* junk?

VIC: I can't quite make myself believe I said "junk."

SADE: It talks about "maidens."

VIC: [*Politely*] Well?

229

SADE: You're *talking* to maidens. "Hurry to the plashing fountain, maidens," you say.

VIC: [*Politely*] Well?

SADE: [*Restraining a giggle*] I wondered . . . all them big hulks of *men* in your lodge . . . callin' 'em maidens an' . . .

VIC: [*Gently*] I do not call the *men* maidens.

SADE: It says *here* . . .

VIC: [*Gently*] Let me explain, Sade.

SADE: All right.

VIC: The word "maidens" is *figurative*.

SADE: [*Giggles*] I was gonna *say*. You standin' up in front of great big scalawags like Hank Gutstop an' Ike Kneesuffer an' callin' 'em maidens an' askin' 'em to paddle their pretty toes in the fountain an' . . .

VIC: [*Gently*] Give Rush the paper.

SADE: Rush?

VIC: [*Gently*] Give him the paper please.

SADE: [*Giggles*] Don't want me any more, huh?

VIC: [*Gently*] I think Rush might be a trifle more helpful.

SADE: [*Giggles*] Here y'are, Willie.

RUSH: Um.

SADE: [*Giggling, to Vic*] You've hurt my feelings something fierce.

VIC: [*Politely*] Ready, Rush?

RUSH: Shoot.

SADE: [*Cajolingly*] Don't be mad at me, Vic, I was just *jollyin'* ya.

VIC: You're forgiven. [*To Rush*] Check me for errors now, Turpentine.

RUSH: Shoot.

VIC: "Hurry to the plashing fountain, maidens. Dabble your . . .

RUSH: "Scurry" to the plashing fountain, maidens.

VIC: Scurry?

RUSH: Yeah—instead of hurry.

VIC: Funny I mis-read *that*.

RUSH: Scurry. S-c-u-r-r-y. Scurry.

VIC: O.K., scurry. "Scurry to the plashing fountain, maidens. Dabble your . . .

RUSH: Should that be "splashing?"

VIC: What?

RUSH: Shouldn't it be "splashing" instead of "plashing?"

VIC: No.

RUSH: Looks like their oughta be an *ess* on there.

VIC: "Plashing" is correct. If I want any editing done on the ritual of the Sacred Stars of the Milky Way which was written by a body of highly educated college professors I'll *ask* for it.

RUSH: [*Low tones*] I never heard of "plashing."

VIC: *Lots* of things young punks like you never heard of. Shall we proceed?

RUSH: Um.

VIC: "Dabble your pale feet in the crystal water an' weave garlands of roses. The heroes have returned from the fray an' will shortly squat before the camp-fire to pow-wow an' parley."

RUSH: Bow-wow an' barley.

VIC: What?

RUSH: It's bow-wow an' barley.

VIC: It is not.

RUSH: It is too. Look right here on the . . .

VIC: Miss Gregg made a typographical error. She copied this off on her machine an' did it in a rush an' there's *several* mistakes you'll run across. Use your *head,* Pipe-cleaner. One doesn't squat before the camp-fire to bow-wow an' barley. One squats before the camp-fire to pow-wow an' parley.

RUSH: [*Little chuckle*] *I* don't do either *one.*

VIC: [*Coldly*] We seem to have *two* humorists in the family.

RUSH: Um.

SADE: [*Interested*] You say Miss Gregg typewrote that for ya?

VIC: Yeah—out of my official lodge manual.

SADE: Is it . . . open to the public?

VIC: [*Coldly*] One's wife speaks in riddles. Is *what* open to the public?

SADE: That . . . *ritual* business. I had the notion it was s'posed to be *secret.*

VIC: I'm sayin' it out loud to you an' *Rush,* ain't I?

SADE: *We're* in the *family* though.

VIC: [*Almost tough*] Sade, do you imagine I'd reveal anything to my own *mother* that was of an esoteric nature? I've taken solemn vows. Would I be apt to come home here an' tell my wife an' son the secrets which my fraternal order . . .

SADE: Oh, *I* don't care. Just *asked* was all.

VIC: Please don't be offended, Sade, but your question was very foolish. *Very* foolish.

SADE: [*Why argue?*] All right.

VIC: [*To Rush, politely*] Shall we proceed, son?

RUSH: Sure.

231

VIC: I'll commence down where I left off.

RUSH: O.K.

VIC: "The heroes have returned from the fray an' will shortly squat before the camp-fire to pow-wow an' parley."

RUSH: [*Low tones to Sade*] See, mom, how it's written? Bow-wow an' barley.

SADE: Uh-huh. Sloppy typewriting.

VIC: [*Politely*] I suggest, Rush, that you pay attention to what you're doing. Otherwise the whole *point* of this is lost.

RUSH: [*Cheerfully*] Shoot.

VIC: "Ah, here they are now! An' our Exalted Little Dipper leads them. Sky-brother Franklin Gutstop, take your station. Instruct your followers to throw their tired bodies on the grass an' rest. Sing a song of . . .

RUSH: Glass.

VIC: Huh?

RUSH: It's glass instead of grass.

VIC: [*Annoyed*] Oh, it is not.

RUSH: "Throw their tired bodies on the glass." Look for yourself. I guess . . .

VIC: It's another typographical error. *You* oughta know that. Who'd throw theirself down on *glass?*

RUSH: [*Chuckles*] A *Chinese* individual maybe. "I thlow body on glass. Me heap big Chinee . . ."

VIC: [*Coldly*] Very, very witty—ha, ha, ha. [*Sharply*] Listen, now, Charley, you gonna get down to business?

RUSH: [*Yes*] Um.

SADE: [*Little giggle*] You an' me ain't very popular this evening, sonny.

VIC: [*To Rush*] Shall we try again?

RUSH: Shoot?

VIC: "Instruct your followers to throw their tired bodies on the grass an' rest. Sing a song of courage an' forget the . . .

RUSH: "College."

VIC: [*Gently*] College?

RUSH: Yes. Instead of "courage." It says "college" here. Unless Miss Gregg made another typographical . . .

VIC: [*Gently*] Give me that piece of paper.

RUSH: Look for *yourself:*—"Sing a song of *college.*" You told me to stop you when . . .

SADE: Where ya going, Vic?

VIC: [*Moving off*] Upstairs.

SADE: [*Giggles*] *Wait* now: no sense in gettin' *mad*. I . . .

VIC: [*Moving off*] *I'm* not mad. I just need a little privacy in order to accomplish this job of work. I'm sure you'll excuse me.

SADE: [*After a pause, to Rush*] *Well*.

RUSH: Might as well finish our rummy game.

SADE: All right.

RUSH: I kept the hands separate. Here's yours.

SADE: Thanks.

RUSH: My turn. I'm discardin' this king.

SADE: I guess we were *mean* to your father. He . . . oh, lands, there I go again: played a diamond for a spade.

RUSH: I don't see how you can get mixed up on diamonds an' spades, mom. One's red an' the other's black.

SADE: I mean hearts an' clubs.

RUSH: [*Chuckles*] Hearts are red, clubs are black.

SADE: [*Giggles*] *You* appreciate what I mean.

RUSH: Straightened out now?

SADE: Yeah. [*Discards*] *There*.

END OF SCRIPT

ANNOUNCER: Which concludes another brief interlude at the small house half-way up in the next block.

1939

VIC EXPLAINS
HOW A
DOOR-BELL RINGS

ANNOUNCER: OPENING AND COMMERCIAL CREDITS
INTRODUCTION: Well sir, it's twelve-thirty o'clock as our scene opens now, and here in the kitchen of the small house half-way up in the next block we discover Mr. Victor Gook and Mrs. Victor Gook and their young son Mr. Rush Gook just about finished with their noon-day meal. And there's table-talk. Listen.

RUSH: I tell you people frankly, I was infuriated.

SADE: You better *stop* gettin' infuriated all the time.

VIC: Yeah . . . weather's too warm.

RUSH: I wasn't the *only* infuriated individual. Smelly *Clark* was infuriated. Blue-tooth Johnson was infuriated. Even Milton Welch that hardly ever gets infuriated was infuriated.

SADE: You kids *pick* on Nicer.

RUSH: No, we don't. He aggravates us. Does it on purpose.

SADE: You two boys are next-door-neighbors, it'd pay ya to get *along* with each other.

RUSH: *I* do *my* best. *I'm* a *peace*-loving fella. Why, gov, *you've* got a good head on your shoulders.

VIC: Thanks.

RUSH: Wouldn't *you* get infuriated listening to Nicer Scott make infuriating remarks?

VIC: Very possibly.

RUSH: He'll look you right in the eye cool as a cucumber an' make the statement he's got eighty-nine pairs of pants in a cold-storage ware-house in Burlington, Iowa.

VIC: Most infuriating.

RUSH: *I'll say.* This morning he made the statement he had no sense of *taste*.

VIC: *Enormously* infuriating.

RUSH: "I got no sense of taste, fellas," he says. "Bananas an' ice-cream an' pork-chops an' watermelon all got the same flavor for me."

VIC: Um.

RUSH: Infuriating?

VIC: Yeah.

RUSH: Blue-tooth Johnson says, "Look here, Nicer, how about jelly an' peanut brittle? *They* don't have the same flavor for ya, do they?" Nicer says, "In *my* mouth jelly an' peanut brittle taste identical." Blue-tooth says, "Holy smoke, they *can't*. Jelly is all soft an' squishy while peanut brittle is tough and chewy." Nicer smiled that oily triumphant smile of his. "*Prove* it," he says, "*prove* jelly an' peanut brittle don't taste the same in my mouth."

VIC: Um.

RUSH: Infuriating?

VIC: Yeah.

RUSH: Infuriating as a *horse*. Why, by George, even Milton Welch that hardly ever gets infuriated was infuriated by Nicer's infuriating remarks. Infuriated fellas can be infuriated by . . .

SADE: [*Wearily*] Hey, let's *forget* this "infuriated" business a minute. [*Changing the subject*] Vic, Mr. Erickson was here again this evening.

VIC: Really?

SADE: [*Giggles*] Brought me a *gift*.

VIC: I'll bet.

SADE: That's the *truth*. New electric bell for the front door.

VIC: Has the *heat* got the old hyena?

SADE: He *has* changed recently. Guess it's because he can't rent his house. His failure has made him kind of gentle an' half-way *thoughtful*, don't ya know.

VIC: Um.

SADE: Rush, in on the bottom pantry shelf go fetch our new electric bell.

RUSH: Okay.

SADE: [*To Vic*] Yeah . . . he's been a different *person* these last few weeks. I like to fell over dead when he give me the door-bell this morning.

VIC: Why didn't he *install* it?

SADE: I told him not to bother. He's so *pokey* when it comes to odd jobs around the house. It'd of took him all day. *You* can slap it on the wall, can't ya?

VIC: Sure.

SADE: Understand *how?*

VIC: I know electric bells like I know the palm of my hand.

SADE: I expect I could do it myself if I tried.

VIC: Probably could.

RUSH: [*Off*] You tell Mr. Erickson about me breakin' the cellar window, mom?

SADE: [*To Rush*] No. [*To Vic*] *Thought* of doin' it, but I didn't quite have the nerve.

VIC: He'll notice it himself one of these days.

SADE: I expect he will.

RUSH: [*Returning*] This looks like a high-class door-bell.

SADE: Uh-huh, so shiny an' nice.

238

RUSH: [*Closer*] Heck of a lot better'n our old one.

SADE: Yes. Did you bring the little envelope with the screws?

RUSH: [*Up*] This is it, ain't it?

SADE: Yeah.

VIC: Give *me* the pretty door-bell, Waste-basket.

SADE: [*To Vic*] Maybe you'll have time to get it workin' this noon, huh?

VIC: Sure. Won't take me five minutes . . .

SADE: Wanta watch out you don't get an electric shock.

VIC: No danger in the world when ya know *how*.

RUSH: A guy *can* get a shock off a door-bell.

VIC: A *smart* guy can't. *Hey,* do either one of you jolly folks know how a dingus like this *works*?

SADE AND RUSH: Electricity.

VIC: Electricity is simply the *power*. What actually makes this little hammer hit the bell?

SADE AND RUSH: Electricity.

VIC: [*Chuckles*] Aw, shucks. Look, if I give you some electricity an' a door-bell, could you make electricity *ring* the door-bell?

SADE AND RUSH: Sure.

VIC: How?

SADE AND RUSH: Connect'em *up*.

VIC: I guess I better *explain* somethin' here.

RUSH: There's no *mystery* to it, gov. Ya press the button, it makes the electricity whip along the wire to the bell, an' the bell *rings*.

VIC: What *is* electricity, by the way?

RUSH: It's the stuff that comes outa the battery.

VIC: A very brilliant answer. I s'pose if I asked you what your *feet* were you'd say they were the stuff that comes outa your *shoes*.

RUSH: Electricity is . . . somethin' like *gas*.

VIC: Oh, my. An' you a lad goin' on fifteen.

RUSH: Well, it *is* somethin' like gas. They both makes things *go*. Run engines an' so on.

VIC: Okay, then. If somebody asked you what electricity was you'd describe it by sayin' it was something like gas, huh?

RUSH: Sure.

VIC: If somebody asked you to describe a penny I bet you'd tell'em it was somethin' like a *dime*.

RUSH. No.

VIC: Do *you* know what electricity is, Sade?

239

SADE: Yes, but I can't *explain* what it is.

VIC: All right, let me *tell* you somethin'. *Nobody* knows what electricity is. *Nobody* can define it.

SADE: Aw.

VIC: I speak truth.

SADE: You better go around an' see Mis' Willett's man. He's an electrician.

VIC: Mis' Willett's man don't know any more about electricity than *I* do.

SADE: He's sure foolin' the public then. I understand he gets seventy cents an *hour* for knowin' about it.

VIC: He gets seventy cents an hour for *workin'* with it. But he don't know what it *is*. *Nobody* knows what it is. Electricity is an unknown quantity. All we know about electricity is that it's a series of impulses that can be made to travel along a wire. Those impulses have the ability to magnetize a piece of metal. *A* piece of metal that's magnetized draws other pieces of metal *towards* it. There we have *action. Work.* See?

SADE AND RUSH: No.

VIC: Very good. I'll show you how this *door*-bell works.

RUSH: We know how it works.

VIC: How's it work?

RUSH: Electricity.

VIC: I'm glad *strangers* ain't present. They'd *jeer* at me for havin' fathered such a half-wit tramp.

RUSH: I s'pose electricity *don't* make it work.

VIC: If you'll pay *attention* five seconds I'll *tell* you what makes it work.

RUSH: [*Stubbornly*] Electricity.

VIC: Sade, I think we better keep this man out of sight till he gets a little brighter. In his present condition, it ain't safe to let him out on the street. He's liable to get run over or somethin'.

SADE: Electricity *does* make the door-bell work, don't it?

VIC: Electricity in the abstract, *yes*. But its *mechanical* application is . . . Well, let me *show* ya here. See these two little round businesses?

SADE: Yes.

VIC: They're called coils. That simply means they're coils of wire. Charged with current they produce a magnetic field.

SADE: Do they?

VIC: Yes. Now watch. I'll make this simple as pie. Suppose you push the door-bell button out front on the front porch.

RUSH: [*Buzzes*] Bzzzzzzzzzzzzz.

VIC: Keep quiet. Sade, you push the door-bell button out on the front porch.

SADE: All right.

VIC: All *right*. When you do that you permit electricity to flow through a fairly heavy wire. It flows along that fairly heavy wire till it gets to this bell. All right. When it gets to this bell it enters these coils. Follow me so far?

SADE: Yeah . . . makes the bell ring. Mis' Applerot was tellin' me her brother made a radio set that . . .

VIC: It *don't* make the door-bell ring.

SADE: Huh?

VIC: It *don't* make the door-bell ring.

SADE: Why not?

VIC: It just *don't*.

SADE: Broke?

VIC: *No*, it ain't broke. *Listen* to me now. You press the button out on the front porch. That permits the electricity to . . .

SADE: Oh, it ain't *connected*.

VIC: [*Getting irritated*] What?

SADE: It ain't *connected*.

VIC: It is *too* connected.

SADE: You got it right there in your hand.

VIC: We're *pretending* it's connected.

SADE: Well, goodness, do we hafta *pretend* somethin' just to understand . . .

VIC: If you'll pay me a nickel's worth of attention I'll make this easy as pie. You're out on the front porch now, you wanta ring the door-bell so you press the button. Here's what happens. In pressing this button you permit current to flow through a fairly heavy wire. So far so good. That current travels along an' finally gets to this bell. What happens? It goes through these coils an' makes a magnetized field. Fine. *Now* . . . you see this little bar?

SADE: Yes.

VIC: See it, Rush?

RUSH: Yeah, but I don't catch on to the reason why . . .

VIC: I'm *tellin'* ya, doggone it. Save your questions until I'm through. Ya both see this little bar?

SADE AND RUSH: Yeah.

VIC: Okay. This little bar is directly over these coils. We've allowed electricity to enter these coils which makes'em, as I've explained, a magnet. So what happens?

SADE AND RUSH: The bell rings.

VIC: *Right.* That's fine. You've hit the nail on the head. The bell rings.

SADE: Well, I guess I'll start in on my dishes an' . . .

VIC: *Wait. Why* does the bell ring?

SADE AND RUSH: Electricity.

VIC: Aw, quit sayin' electricity. *Look* . . . the hammer that hits the bell is attached to this little bar. When the coils become a magnet they pull the little bar *down.* That pulls the hammer up against the bell an' we hear it ring.

RUSH: Sure.

VIC: Don't say "sure" so *quick.* So far we've only got the hammer to hit the bell one time an' one time only. How we gonna release the hammer so that it can hit the bell *again?*

SADE AND RUSH: Electricity.

VIC: [*Tough*] Aw, for gosh sakes.

SADE: [*Giggles*] Well, lands, how ya expect *us* to . . .

VIC: Do you understand what I've told you so far? Do you see that the current makes a magnet: that the magnet pulls the hammer against the bell?

SADE: Sure.

VIC: Do you see somethin's got to be done to get the hammer *loose* from the bell so it can give *another* lick?

SADE: Sure.

VIC: All right. Now here's the cute way that's done. Before the current *reaches* the coils it hasta go up through the hammer *itself.* I'll trace the complete circuit for ya. Watch my finger. The current comes up here along this wire, through the hammer, through the bell an' down to the coils. That clear?

SADE AND RUSH: Yes.

VIC: Very good. *Now* . . . as we've seen, once the current gets to the coils it makes a magnet, pulls down the bar, brings over the hammer, an' the bell rings.

SADE AND RUSH: Uh-huh.

VIC: *But* . . . as soon as the bar is pulled *down,* the circuit is broken. See that?

SADE AND RUSH: Yes.

VIC: Because the hammer has been pulled away from its contact point. Fine. With the circuit broken, the coils are no longer magnetized, the bar swings back, an' the hammer falls away from the bell, the circuit is *complete* again. So the whole business repeats itself again. The hammer rings the bell breaking the circuit, the hammer

242

falls back where it was at first *resurrecting* the circuit. An' so we have the bell ringing just as long as we press the button. Got it?

SADE AND RUSH: No.

VIC: I'll make it plainer. I'll give you an example. Suppose a boy is chasing his uncle with a baseball bat.

SADE AND RUSH: Uh-huh.

VIC: To make it better let's have the boy chasin' his *mother* with a baseball bat.

RUSH: That makes it *worse*.

VIC: Huh?

RUSH: It's worse for a boy to chase his *mother* with a baseball bat than it is for a boy to chase his *uncle* with a . . .

VIC: Oh, pipe down. Sade, this boy is . . . Oh, *here.* Here's an example. You've seen pictures in the funny paper where a guy is sitting in a wagon, haven't ya, an' he's got a piece of meat on a long stick?

SADE: Guess so.

VIC: He's holding this piece of meat out in front of his horse's nose. The horse runs to catch up with the meat but he never catches it because he's pulling the wagon with the guy in it that's *holdin'* the meat out in front of him.

SADE: Oh, uh-huh.

VIC: That same thing is true of this door-bell.

SADE: Yeah.

VIC: *You* get it, Coal-scuttle?

RUSH: Sure.

VIC: Interesting, ain't it?

SADE AND RUSH: Yeah.

VIC: [*Getting up*] Well, I might as well *install* this jigger, I guess. My tools in the basement, kiddo?

SADE: They're in the fruit-room. I pushed the box back up against the wall.

VIC: [*Moving off*] Okay.

SADE: [*After him*] Don't bother my *other* things down there.

VIC: [*Off*] No.

SADE: [*After him*] Maybe you better slip on your overalls.

VIC: [*Off*] Okay.

SADE: [*To Rush*] Wanta help me with my dishes, son?

RUSH: All right.

SADE: Say, I just betcha this is an *expensive* door-bell.

RUSH: Looks like it.

243

The Small House Half-way Up in the Next Block

SADE: So *shiny* an' nice.
RUSH: Uh-huh.
SADE: Know how it works?
RUSH: No. Do you?
SADE: No.
END OF SCRIPT
ANNOUNCER: Which concludes another brief interlude at the small house half-way up in the next block.

Undated

RUSH'S SLUMBER
PARTY ENTERS
BY THE WINDOW

ANNOUNCER: OPENING AND COMMERCIAL CREDITS
INTRODUCTION: Well sir, it's about eight-thirty o'clock in the evening as we join our friends at the small house half-way up in the next block now, and here they are in the living-room. Mr. and Mrs. Victor Gook are seated side by side on the davenport, while their son, Mr. Rush Gook—who has just this moment arrived home from somewhere—stands near the library table uncomfortably enduring a barrage of parental interrogation. Listen.

SADE: What wild crazy stunt is *this* now?

RUSH: Every time I do something, people call it a "wild crazy stunt." Gosh, mom, you don't know anything *about* it yet. You're not familiar with any of the details.

SADE: If you've got a step-ladder propped up against the side of the house an' your bedroom window open so a gang of kids can climb in the . . .

RUSH: Let me *tell,* mom. Let me tell my story an' when I get through you can tear it to pieces. Ain't that fair, gov?

VIC: Sure.

RUSH: Otherwise, mom, you'd be bawling me out in the *dark.*

SADE: I'll say. Is the step-ladder propped up against the side of the house *now?*

RUSH: It is.

SADE: An' your bedroom window's open?

RUSH: It is.

SADE: Are there any kids in the house yet?

RUSH: I don't know whether there are or not.

SADE: [*To Vic, giggling acidly*] *That's* fine, huh? Maybe we got *company* upstairs. Maybe we got company upstairs an' maybe we *haven't* got company upstairs. Anybody walkin' along the street that feels like it is welcome to climb the step-ladder an' come in our residence an' make theirselves at home.

RUSH [*Gently patient*] Mom, if you'd give a guy a chance to *explain.*

SADE: [*Airily*] Explain away.

RUSH: I figured out this plan for you an' gov's special *benefit.*

SADE: Glad to hear it.

RUSH: I didn't want you people to be *disturbed.*

SADE: Uh-huh.

RUSH: Instead of coming through the door an' tracking across the rug an' *bothering* you an' gov, my friends will simply ascend the step-ladder, enter my room an' go to bed.

VIC: How delightfully informal.

RUSH: *Yes.* See, mom, the point is *this:* my friends will be showing up at different *times.* Smelly Clark will arrive about a quarter to nine. Rooster Davis a little later. Willis Roreback is due *now.* So is Blue-tooth Johnson. If they all entered through the *door* you people'd be disturbed every couple *minutes.*

SADE: Hey, how many boys did you *invite* to spend the night here?

VIC: I was about to ask that question myself. You just named *four.*

SADE: *Four* kids can't all crowd in your bed.

RUSH: They don't *expect* to. Various individuals will sleep on the *floor.* I'll get blankets an' quilts out of the hall-way closet an' my friends can just curl up any old place in my room. As a matter of fact I intend to sleep on the floor *myself.*

SADE: [*Sadly*] Rush, it seems to me a great big enormous grown-up high school gentlemen would be about old enough to . . . [*Telephone*]

VIC: [*Mildly*] Telephone is ringing, telephone is ringing.

RUSH: I'll get it. Prob'ly one of the fellas.

VIC: [*To Sade*] Any special reason why we're entertaining all this company, Doctor Sleetch?

SADE: [*Briefly*] Kids are going off on a hike in the morning.

VIC: Oh.

SADE: [*Briefly*] Saturday outing.

RUSH: [*To phone*] Hello? Yes. Oh, yes, Mis' Scott. Ah, Mis' Scott . . . [*He's trying to interrupt Mis' Scott's swift flow of speech*] . . . Ah, Mis' Scott . . . *Wait* a second, Mis' Scott. That's O.*K.,* Mis' Scott. Ah, Mis' Scott . . . no, listen. They're *friends* of mine, Mis' Scott. *Friends* of mine. Yeah. We're going on a hike tomorrow morning an' I told 'em to climb to my room by usin' that step-ladder so my father an' mother wouldn't be disturbed. Yes. Uh-huh, Scared ya, huh? Well, it's perfectly O.K. All right, Mis' Scott. Good-by, Mis' Scott.

[*Hangs up*]

VIC: [*Dryly*] *That* telephone conversation wasn't hard to interpret.

SADE: [*Sharply*] She saw fellas skulking up that step-ladder an' thought it was burglars an' got half scared to death?

RUSH: Ah—she never said she got scared to *death.* She said she just happened to glance out her window an' seen a shadowy figure crawling in my room an' her heart jumped in her mouth an' she . . .

SADE: [*Disgust*] Oh, for mercy sakes.

RUSH: I explained it to her. She's completely at ease now.

VIC: [*With curiosity*] I wonder who's upstairs.

RUSH: Leland Richards an' Milton Welch prob'ly. They both said they wished to retire early.

VIC: You never named them two guys *before.*

RUSH: Didn't I?

VIC: No. You named Smelly Clark, Rooster Davis, Willis Roreback, an' Blue-tooth Johnson.

RUSH: Leland an Milton are *also* going on the hike.

VIC: That makes *six* sharing your sleeping-chamber.

SADE: *Seven altogether.* [*Disgust*] Rush, what a mutton-head you are.

RUSH: [*Indignant*] *Why?* We wanta all start off on our hike in the morning *together.* Why *shouldn't* we all spend the night in the same place? *You* people aren't gonna be disturbed.

SADE: [*Heatedly*] No, an' we better *not* be *either.* If them chums of yours make any noise tonight or start runnin' around loose in the hall I'll bet I settle their hash in quick order.

RUSH: [*Quietly*] I give you my solemn word there won't be a *sound.* You people won't hear a *pin* drop. If there's . . .

[*Dull heavy thud from upstairs*]

VIC: [*Dryly*] A pin just dropped.

SADE: [*Alarmed*] What *was* that?

VIC: Don't you recognize the vibration of a pin dropping? Why, I . . .

SADE: Sounded like a human *body* hittin' the floor.

RUSH: Nothin' to get *excited* about. Prob'ly LeRoy Snow an' Emmett Carlson havin' a friendly scuffle. They both love rassling.

SADE: [*Wearily*] Such stuff as goes on in this house. Sometimes I just don't know.

RUSH: They've *already* quieted *down.* In eight seconds they'll be in bed an' asleep.

SADE: [*Wearily*] Step-ladder propped up against our residence so anybody walkin' along the sidewalk can just climb right in an' hit the hay.

RUSH: I figured you'd *like* that idea, mom.

SADE: [*Airily*] Oh, I *do. Love* it.

RUSH: Saves wear an' tear on the *rugs.* Keeps you an' gov from bein' *bothered.*

SADE: *I'll* say.

VIC: Peanut-brittle, old Inner-sole.

RUSH: Yeah?

VIC: You just mentioned the names of LeRoy Snow an' Emmett Carlson.

RUSH: Uh-huh.

VIC: Brings the grand total of your guests up to *eight.*

RUSH: They'll all sleep O.K. on the floor.

VIC: Let us hope so.

RUSH: [*Confidently*] Sure.

VIC: After I've retired for the night I am apt to be gruff an' short-tempered if suddenly awakened. I might even be violent. It might be wise to tip your pals *off* to that fact.

RUSH: You people won't hear a *sound.*

VIC: Fine.

RUSH: Like I say, I'm gonna get quilts an' blankets an' comforters outa the closet an' put 'em around on the floor an' . . .

[*Telephone rings*]

VIC: [*Mildly*] Telephone is ring . . .

RUSH: [*Quickly*] I'll get that.

SADE: [*To Vic*] More of our neighbors frightened outa their wits.

VIC: Very likely.

RUSH: [*To phone*] Hello? Oh, hello, Mis' Call: don't let that bother ya a bit. No: they're friends of mine. Yeah. Well, a bunch of us are gettin' up early in the morning to go on a hike. We just thought we'd all spend the night here together an' get an early start an' no foolin' around. Yes. I'm sorry if you got scared. Yes. All right, Mis' Call. Certainly. Good-by.

[*Hangs up*]

SADE: [*Meaning it*] Rush, this is disgraceful.

RUSH: Well, heck, *I* thought it'd . . .

SADE: Out and *out* disgraceful.

RUSH: Review the *facts,* mom. You give me permission to get up at six o'clock in the morning an' go on a hike. You also give me permission to invite a few of my friends to spend the night with me. I was grateful to ya for your kindness an' doped out this step-ladder scheme to save you an' gov the annoyance of havin' a bunch of fellas trampin' across your rugs. Surely you appreciate the . . .

[*Dull heavy thud in the distance*]

SADE: [*Affrighted*] Mercy me!

VIC: [*Dryly*] Another pin dropped.

SADE: What on earth they *doin'*?

RUSH: Prob'ly Art Armbruster an' Fat Vogel are . . .

SADE: Vic, go up an' see.

VIC: I'm a little *scared* to venture . . .

250

RUSH: *No,* gov. *Don't* go up.

VIC: Why not?

RUSH: I got an idea it's Art Armbruster an' Fat Vogel. You're not acquainted with them. They'd be *embarrassed* if my father walked in an' looked tough at 'em.

VIC: Who are Art Armbruster an' Fat Vogel?

RUSH: Friends of mine from high school. Art Armbruster resides on North Park street an' Fat Vogel resides 718 West Mill street. They're both very high-class individuals.

VIC: Two *new* names for our roster. How many does *that* make?

RUSH: I don't know . . . but *they'll* be quiet.

VIC: Believe I'll count up. Smelly Clark—Blue-tooth Johnson—Rooster Davis—Le Roy Snow—Milton Welch—Leland Richards—Willis Roreback—Emmett Carlson—Art Armbruster—an' Fat Vogel. *Ten.* [*To Sade*] Kiddo, we're entertaining ten guests tonight.

SADE: [*To Rush, tough*] You think you're awful awful smart pullin' off a stunt like this. *Don't* ya?

RUSH: Mom, I never saw any reason why you'd *care.* Gosh, I bet you'll never realize anybody's in my *room* once the lights are turned off an' everybody's asleep an' . . .

[*Telephone rings*]

VIC: Telephone is ringin' . . .

RUSH: [*Quickly*] I'll get it.

SADE: [*Briefly*] No, ya won't. Sit still. I'll get it myself.

RUSH: Very possibly it's one of my . . .

SADE: Very possibly it is; yes. Sit still. [*To phone*] Hello? Oh, yes, Mis' Elders. [*Giggles*] We *know* about that, Mis' Elders. Yes. They're friends of Rush's. Yes. Oh, just children's foolishness. Yes. No, that's all. I'm sorry if you were frightened. [*Giggles*] Well, thanks for calling anyway, Mis' Elders. All righty. Surely, Mis' Elders. Good-by. [*Hangs up*] [*To Vic*] Yes sir,—no mistake about it—we got a real grown-up educated *high*-school gentleman livin' in this house.

VIC: What's liable to *happen* is the neighbors notifyin' the *police* instead of calling us up.

SADE: Wouldn't *that* be lovely!

RUSH: I hardly think the police would . . .

SADE: Mis' Elders said she saw two fellas crawlin' in one of our bedroom windows. They both had pullover sweaters on.

RUSH: Leo Tuckett an' Walter Greetch.

VIC: Who?

RUSH: Leo Tuckett an' Walter Greetch. *They* wear pullover sweaters. I want you to *meet* Leo Tuckett an' Walter Greetch, gov.

They're just about as high-class individuals as you ever... [*Loud clatter from upstairs*]

SADE: [*Distressed*] Oh, my, my, my.

VIC: Sounded like somebody pushed the *dresser* over.

RUSH: [*Uncomfortably*] I... guess I better go *up* there.

VIC: Might be a *very* good *idea*.

RUSH: [*Moving off*] I'll see that you people aren't disturbed another time.

VIC: Mighty white of ya.

RUSH: [*Moving off*] I'll close my bedroom door an' tell all the guys to go right to sleep. You won't hear a single sound.

VIC: [*Not loud*] Um.

RUSH: [*Moving off*] Ah—good night.

VIC: Night.

RUSH: [*Moving off*] Good night, mom.

SADE: [*Not loud*] *I'll* say.

VIC: [*To Sade*] Leo Tuckett an' Walter Greetch. Two *more* shining names for our roll of honor.

SADE: Um.

VIC: What'd I say the grand total was?

SADE: Don't know.

VIC: Well—Smelly Clark—LeRoy Snow—Blue-tooth Johnson—Leland Richards—Milton Welch—Willis Roreback—Emmett Carlson—Art Armbruster—Fat Vogel—Rooster Davis—Leo Tuckett an' Walter Greetch. *Twelve, I* make.

SADE: Twelve boys climbed up a step-ladder an' crawled in our bedroom window.

VIC: Twelve boys will *sleep* at our house tonight. *Thirteen,* counting our *own* little angel.

SADE: Wonderful thing, huh?

VIC: Yes, indeed. I am delighted to be able to...

[*Dull heavy thud in the distance*]

SADE: [*To Vic*] Listen.

VIC: *I* heard it. [*In the distance another thud followed by a clatter of heavy objects*]

SADE: [*To Vic, distressed*] Oh, my, my, my.

RUSH: [*In the distance, is heard screaming*]

SADE: [*To Vic*] Oh, my, my, my!

VIC: [*Mildly, chuckling*] Hi-de-hi, ho-de-ho.

SADE: [*Completely defeated*] Golly!

VIC: Kiddo.

SADE: [*Sighing*] What?

VIC: Would ya like to stay at a hotel tonight?

END OF SCRIPT

ANNOUNCER: Which concludes another brief interlude at the small house half-way up in the next block.

1940

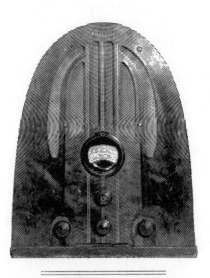

UNCLE FLETCHER
IS SENDING
THREE BULL-DOGS

THEME

INTRODUCTION: Well sir, it's late afternoon as our scene opens now and here in the kitchen of the small house half-way up in the next block we find Mr. Victor Gook and his son, Mr. Rush Gook. The gentlemen have just this moment arrived home from office and from school. Listen.

RUSH: Believe I'll put on my old clothes an' beat it over to Tatman's vacant lot. Blue-tooth Johnson an' Willis Roreback are . . .

SADE: [*In living-room*] That you, Rush?

VIC: [*To Rush*] Mama hollers. [*Calls*] Hi.

SADE: [*Off*] Vic?

VIC: [*Calls*] Both of us.

SADE: [*Off*] Come in here.

VIC: [*Not loud*] Okey-dokey-wokey.

SADE: [*Off*] Quick.

RUSH: [*To Vic, apprehensively*] What's *this* now?

VIC: [*Apprehensively*] One *wonders*.

RUSH: Hope we don't hafta re-arrange the *furniture*. That's the tone of voice mom *uses* when she gets the furniture-movin' fever. By George, I . . .

SADE: [*Closer*] How long's it take a letter to get to Dixon?

VIC: [*Raising voice*] Beg pardon, Sadie.

SADE: [*Closer*] I'm writin' a letter to Uncle Fletcher. When'll he get it if I mail it right away?

VIC: Tomorrow morning.

SADE: [*Almost up*] The bullet that choked Billy Patterson fell in our lap *this* trip.

VIC: What's the trouble, Doctor Sleetch?

SADE: [*Upset*] He's sending us three bull-dogs.

VIC: Uncle Fletcher is?

SADE: [*Tight-lipped*] Three fierce full-grown bull-dogs.

RUSH: [*Enthusiastic*] By *George*.

SADE: [*To Vic, tight-lipped*] We've got to head him off.

RUSH: [*Enthusiastic*] By *George!* If you're not foolin', mom, an' this is actually *true*, I'll be the happiest human being in the Universe. I'll . . .

SADE: What'd I do with the letter? Guess I left it out on the buffet. Go see, Willie. Hurry.

RUSH: I hope you don't . . .

SADE: [*Sharply*] Scoot. [*To Vic*] I'm tryin' to write an answer here.

257

I wanta put the ky-bosh on the bull-dogs without hurtin' his feelings. [*Upset*] *Imagine* it! *Three!*

VIC: [*Chuckles*] This beats the ten barrels of *oysters*. It overshadows every one of Uncle Fletcher's previous efforts. In fact you could lump his previous efforts altogether an' . . .

SADE: I've got to finish my note here, Vic, an' get it in the mail-box.

VIC: Go ahead: I'll keep quiet.

SADE: [*Appalled*] Lands, what if he's already *expressed* the bull-dogs?

VIC: Did he *say* he was . . .

RUSH: [*Coming up*] Mom, you're gonna think this *over* before you turn down a wonderful . . .

SADE: [*Briefly*] Give that to your father. An' don't run off any place. I'll want you to run to the mail-box in a minute. Vic, would it get to Dixon any sooner if he took it direct to the post-office?

VIC: Might.

SADE: He can *take* it direct to the post-office then. Don't run off, Willie.

RUSH: Don't worry. If there's any possibility of me gettin' three bull-dogs I'll stick around till the *cows* . . .

SADE: [*Bitterly*] You'd *like* that, huh? You'd *like* three fierce bull-dogs here in the house.

RUSH: I'd *love* it. By George, mom, if you wanta make me completely happy you'll . . .

SADE: Let's not chat. I wanta write this note an' get it started for Dixon. Vic, it's hard to figure out what to *say*.

VIC: Yeah.

SADE: Person don't wanta hurt his *feelings*.

RUSH: Why don't you let him go ahead an' *send* the bull-dogs? We can keep 'em for a period of say six months an' then . . .

SADE: [*To Vic*] What's *he* say again?

VIC: Uncle Fletcher in his letter?

SADE: Yeah.

VIC: He says . . . (ah) . . . "Dearest Sadie. I hope the beautiful spring days find you an' your family healthy an' happy. I've had a series of minor head-colds but on the whole have been feeling . . ."

SADE: Skip down to where he talks about the dogs.

VIC: Is that on the first page or . . .

SADE: Give it to me.

RUSH: Mom, don't you think you better think this *over* before ya jump in an' make a decision? You wouldn't wanta be hasty an' then have a lotta regrets afterwards. There's considerable to be said in favor of owning three bull-dogs. Why, off-hand I can name you a *dozen* reasons why three bull-dogs would . . .

VIC: Don't talk loony, Pillow-case.

RUSH: I'm talkin, *smart.* I . . .

SADE: [*Briefly*] Here. Listen, Vic.

VIC: Um.

SADE: [*Reads*] "I am sending you three bull-dogs by express."

VIC: Just like that, huh?

SADE: Just like that. "I am sending you three bull-dogs by express."

VIC: Don't he go ahead an' explain . . .

SADE: Yes. Further down.

RUSH: No, gov, but ownin' three bull-dogs is . . .

VIC: Oh, go 'way.

RUSH: Owning three bull-dogs is . . .

SADE: Here.

RUSH: . . . something *any* human being would be proud to . . .

SADE: [*Sharply*] Rush, will you be quiet a minute?

RUSH: [*Excited*] It's difficult for an individual to hold their tongue if there's any possibility of owning three . . .

SADE: [*Briefly*] *There* isn't.

RUSH: [*Excited*] No, but . . .

VIC: [*Rather sharply*] Pipe down, Sam.

SADE: Here's what he says. [*Reads*] "Two weeks ago I attended a Stag Dinner an' made the statement I'd like to own a bull-dog. Several of my friends overheard the remark an' in the last few days I have been presented with *four.*

VIC: [*Aghast*] Holy smoke!

SADE: [*Reads*] "Well, Sadie, I know boys love dogs an' I know Rush is no exception. So I am . . .

RUSH: [*Excited*] They're *mine* then. They're *my* bull-dogs. *I'm* the party that . . .

SADE: *Will* you be still?

RUSH: [*Excited*] You people can't refuse a present intended for *me.* Why, Civilization *couldn't* sink so low . . .

VIC: [*Laughing*] Pipe *down,* George, doggone it.

SADE: [*Reads*] "So I am putting them on the train. They're full-grown an' fierce an' will hafta be kept in chains until you get to know them."

VIC: [*Aghast*] Imagine three fierce full-grown bull-dogs down cellar chained to the furnace.

SADE: I like to *fainted* when I read this.

RUSH: [*Excited*] *Listen*—them bull-dogs are mine. *You* people can't turn down . . .

SADE: Rush, must I ask you to leave the room? [*To Vic*] Hey, can't a person buy Special Delivery stamps?

VIC: Sure.

SADE: He'll get the letter even quicker with Special Delivery stamps, won't he?

VIC: Yeah.

SADE: Buy *two* of 'em at the post-office, Rush. No, buy *three*. An' paste 'em on the front where they'll show up good.

VIC: He says, "I am putting them on the train." Great guns, what if he's already *done* it!

SADE: Heaven forbid! Listen an' see how ya think this sounds.

VIC: Shoot.

RUSH: [*Desperate*] I'll tell ya what I'll do:—I'll take my three bull-dogs some place *else*. You people won't even need to *see* 'em. I'll take my three bull-dogs some place where . . .

VIC: Arthur, are you crazy?

RUSH: [*Desperate*] If Uncle Fletcher wants to make me a present of three bull-dogs I am entitled to . . .

SADE: Listen an' see how ya think this sounds, Vic.

VIC: Go ahead. *Silence* from *you*, Thumb-tack.

SADE: [*Reads*] "Dear Uncle Fletcher. Just received your lovely letter. We are all fine an' well. About the bull-dogs I guess maybe you hadn't better send them." That too blunt?

VIC: It's not blunt *enough*. Why don't ya start right out, "No bull-dogs." "No bull-dogs, no bull-dogs, no *bull*-dogs."

SADE: Uncle Fletcher's *sensitive*, Vic. *We* don't wanta ride rough-shod over his feelings. Bess says he *cries* a lot these days. An old fella like that is kinda *childish* when he thinks he's being . . .

VIC: O.K., suit yourself. But I'd make it as strong as *possible*. Great guns, I get the shivers just *thinkin'* of three fierce full-grown bull-dogs chained down cellar.

RUSH: [*Desperate*] Let me *implore* you people not to be hasty in this . . .

SADE: [*Sharply*] You outa your *head*?

RUSH: [*Desperate*] No I'm not outa my head. I . . .

SADE: Do you think for one single second we'd even have *one* dog around here?

VIC: Let *alone three*. An' *man*-eaters at *that*.

RUSH: [*A groan of real suffering*]

SADE: I go ahead an' I say . . . [*Reads*] . . . "We decided long ago we didn't have room for pets our house being so small. Rush thanks you very much for your thoughtfulness but it really is impossible for him to accept." An' then I tack on a little talky-talk trash an' close.

VIC: Uh-huh.

SADE: [*Briskly*] All right, sonny, put on your hat an' run to the post-office with this. An' don't dawdle.

RUSH: [*Desperate*] Isn't there *anything* I can . . .

SADE: An' don't forget the Special Delivery stamps. Buy *four* of 'em.

VIC: It don't make any difference how *many* ya buy, Sade.

SADE: Don't it?

VIC: No. He'll receive it by special messenger whether ya buy one stamp or sixty.

SADE: [*To Rush*] All right, just buy one. But paste it on the front good.

RUSH: Will ya give me three minutes to attempt to convince you people . . .

SADE: No. Trot.

VIC: [*A thought*] *Hey!*—Why not *telegraph?*

SADE: Telegraph?

VIC: *Sure.* Then he'll hear from us in the next half *hour.* Holy smoke, a letter won't reach him till around noon tomorrow. He might be puttin' his half-wit bull-dogs on the train first thing in the morning. If he does we'll be too late an' . . .

SADE: All right, let's *do* telegraph.

VIC: Should of thought of that before.

SADE: What'll we *say* in the telegram?

VIC: Say the same thing you wrote in your letter.

SADE: [*A fleeting doubt*] Be pretty *expensive* so many words.

VIC: What do *we* care. If it costs us nine *dollars* it'll be better than . . .

SADE: Yeah. All right.

VIC: I'll take my pencil an' fix up a wire sayin' approximately what you say in your . . .

SADE: *Wait* a second though.

VIC: Huh?

SADE: Uncle Fletcher's *scared* of telegrams.

VIC: Is he?

SADE: Scared stiff. We wouldn't want him to fall over in a *heap.*

261

VIC: Better run the *chance.* Imagine three fierce *bull*-dogs under foot.

SADE: [*Reluctant*] All right.

VIC: I'll fix up a wire.

SADE: All right.

RUSH: [*Desperate*] *Listen,* people: if you'll let me have them bull-dogs I promise I'll make straight A in school next semester an' keep the lawn mowed all summer an' . . .

SADE: [*Giggles*] Rush, you're an idiot.

RUSH: I'm *not* an idiot. I'm a flesh-an'-blood human being an' . . .

VIC: Kiddo, I got a *better* idea. Long *Distance.*

SADE: *Telephone* Uncle Fletcher?

VIC: *Sure.* That way you can let him down easy an' he'll . . .

SADE: All right.

VIC: Want me to handle it?

SADE: Go ahead.

RUSH: [*Desperate*] *Mom!* Gov! I realize I haven't been perfect around here an' I realize I . . .

SADE: Oh, *stop* it.

VIC: Yeah. I hafta have quiet.

RUSH: [*Agonized groan*]

SADE: [*With some sympathy*] Rush, use your common sense.

RUSH: [*Groan of suffering*]

VIC: [*To phone*] Operator, I wanta put in a Long Distance call to Dixon, Illinois. Yes. Mister Fletcher Rush. One second. [*To Sade*] What's his number?

SADE: I don't know, but it don't make any difference. The Dixon telephone people know where to get a-hold of him. Didn't have any trouble the other time we called.

VIC: [*To phone*] They know how to reach him in Dixon, Operator. Yes. Fletcher Rush. Yeah. "R" like in "Rover." All right—thank you. [*Hangs up*] She'll ring back when she makes the connection.

SADE: I'll answer.

VIC: Yeah, maybe ya better.

RUSH: [*Heart-brokenly*] I feel like I've lost ten years off'n my life.

VIC: [*Not without sympathy*] Soup-ladle, quit bein' a chump. *Sure* you'd like to have three fierce bull-dogs. *We* know that. But use your *head.*

RUSH: [*Desolate*] Feel like I've lost ten years off'n my life.

SADE: I felt like *I'd* lost ten years off'n my life when I read that letter while ago. Why, I *trembled.*

VIC: Three fierce bull-dogs chained in our basement. [*Aghast at the thought*] Holy smoke!

SADE: [*Sadly*] Uncle Fletcher, Uncle Fletcher.

RUSH: [*Heart-brokenly*] Never in the entire course of my miserable career have I . . . [*Telephone*]

VIC AND SADE: There he is.

SADE: I'll get it.

RUSH: [*Heart-brokenly*] You can tell him for me that I . . .

VIC: Let's have quiet.

SADE: Yeah, everybody be still. [*To phone*] Hello? Hello, Uncle Fletcher? Hello? Uncle Fletcher? *Hello,* Uncle Fletcher this is *Sadie,* Uncle Fletcher. *Yes.* Uncle Fletcher, don't send any bull-dogs. I say don't send *any bull*-dogs. *Bull*-dogs. [*Almost in a panic*] Don't send any *bull*-dogs, Uncle Fletcher.

END OF SCRIPT

ANNOUNCER: Which concludes another brief interlude at the small house half-way up in the next block.

1940

VIC'S WIDE-
BRIMMED HAT

ANNOUNCER: OPENING AND COMMERCIAL CREDITS

INTRODUCTION: Well sir, it's late afternoon as we enter the small house half-way up in the next block now, and here in the living-room we find Mr. and Mrs. Victor Gook and their son Mr. Rush Gook. The two male members of the family are seated side by side on the davenport. They look vaguely conspiratorial. Sade stands near the library table eyeing them suspiciously. And she's saying . . .

SADE: I never *heard* of anything so fishy.

VIC: You are unwontedly incredulous, Doctor Sleetch.

SADE: *I'll* say I am. Why on earth would Kleeberger's make you a *present* of a hat?

VIC: I explained that.

SADE: Ya certainly didn't explain it *satisfactory*.

VIC: On what point are you skeptical?

SADE: I'm skeptical about the whole business. Rush, did your father slip you a quarter to tell that story?

RUSH: [*Chuckles*] *No.*

SADE: Look at ya laugh.

RUSH: [*Chuckles*] Innocent guys *always* laugh guilty when they're accused of something. Regular unwritten *law*.

SADE: You were walking down Center Street, huh, an' right out of a clear sky Kleeberger's clerk button-holed ya?

RUSH: I was walking down Center Street on my way to the jewelry store to get gov's watch.

VIC: It was being repaired, Sade. It needed regulating an' oiling an' . . .

SADE: Yes, I heard you two fellas makin' your arrangements this noon. Go on, Rush: you were walking down Center Street.

RUSH: When I passed Kleeberger's store one of the clerks was standing in the doorway. He says, "You're the Gook boy, aren't ya?" I said I was. "Step inside a minute," he says, "I've got a package for your father." That's the absolute *truth,* mom, Cross my heart an' hope to die, eat a banana an' holler hi.

SADE: [*Emphatic*] Mighty darn funny.

VIC: The clerk say anything else, Ash-tray?

RUSH: He said, "This is a hat. Give it to your father with the compliments of Kleeberger's haberdashery."

SADE: [*Highly skeptical*] Mighty darn funny.

VIC: *I* see nothing strange about it.

SADE: Why should Kleeberger's make you a present of a hat?

VIC: I'm a customer of long standing. Making me a present of a hat was a gesture of *appreciation*. Besides I stopped by yesterday an' paid my bill.

SADE: [*Significantly*] Oh, you were *in* there yesterday, huh?

VIC: *Sure* I was in there yesterday.

SADE: [*Significantly*] Uh-huh.

VIC: [*Coldly*] Something in your tone of voice, Sadie, suggests that my stopping into a furnishings store to pay my bill constitutes a hideous crime.

SADE: How much was your bill?

VIC: Two dollars.

SADE: Kleeberger's were so grateful to ya for payin' 'em their two dollars that they gave you an eight-dollar hat, huh?

VIC: [*Brief chuckle*] I never *seen* such a suspicious person.

SADE: Um.

VIC: Kleeberger's know I like wide-brimmed hats. Also they know my wife has never permitted me to *buy* a wide-brimmed hat. So, doggone it, they *give* me a wide-brimmed hat. Like I say, it was a gesture of appreciation. I've spent a good deal of money in their store during the last seven years.

RUSH: [*After a pause, laughs*] Mom, quit *looking* at me.

SADE: [*Urbanely*] Whatcha *laughin'* so foolish' about? Why is the back of your neck getting all red?

RUSH: [*Chuckles*] *Everybody* acts guilty when they're accused of something. *I'm* not in cahoots with gov. I told the absolute *truth*.

VIC: [*Coldly*] *I* see no reason to doubt the lad.

SADE: [*To Rush*] Your father slip you a quarter?

RUSH: He slipped me a quarter but that was for . . .

SADE: [*Pouncing*] Oh, he *did* slip ya a quarter!

RUSH: That was for going downtown to the jewelry store an' gettin' his *watch*.

SADE: Oh.

VIC: [*Suavely*] The point is, kiddo, Kleeberger's felt that it'd be a smart stroke of policy to . . .

SADE: *I'll* tell ya what the *point* is. In the last couple years you've tried stunt after stunt after *stunt* attemping to get a wide-brimmed hat for yourself. You've had wide-brimmed hats sent out on approval; you've doctored up stories where you won wide-brimmed hats on a *bet;* you've even come home here with wide-brimmed hats an' claimed you took the wrong hat off'n the hook in the restaurant an' some *other* man got yours. I've *forgot a hundred* of the schemes you've tried. Is it any *wonder* I'm suspicious when you plank a wide-brimmed hat on the library table an' say Kleeberger's give it to ya for payin' a little dinky two-dollar debt?

VIC: [*Coldly*] I'm afraid you are determined to . . .

SADE: *I'll* say I'm determined. Vic, you can't *wear* wide-brimmed hats. They make ya look like a peeled onion.

VIC: [*Gently*] Rush, my boy.

RUSH: Uh-huh?

VIC: Hand me that hat.

RUSH: O.K.

VIC: I'll place it on my head an' ask you an' your mother to take the roles of unprejudiced judges an' say whether or not I look like a peeled onion.

RUSH: [*Chuckles*] Mom's *still* looking at me peculiar.

VIC: If you are innocent at heart you needn't quail from the stares of your tormenter.

RUSH: [*Chuckles*] *I'm* not in any conspiracy with gov.

SADE: Aren't ya?

RUSH: [*Chuckles*] *No.*

SADE: Look at ya laugh.

RUSH: [*Chuckles*] *Anybody'd* laugh. Human nature.

SADE: Uh-huh.

VIC: My hat is on my head, Sade. Do I look like a peeled onion?

SADE: [*Simply*] Yes.

VIC: [*Coldly*] You say that automatically. I am convinced that this is a very becoming lid.

SADE: What'd ya pay for it?

VIC: [*Walking into a trap*] Eight dollars. It is worth . . . [*Suddenly frantic*] I didn't *pay anything* for it. *The price* is eight dollars.

SADE: [*Simply*] Your tongue kinda slipped on ya, didn't it?

VIC: [*Tough*] This is ridiculous.

SADE: [*Simply*] It's *more* than ridiculous. It's *childish.*

VIC: [*Tough*] Step to the telephone. *Call* Kleeberger's. *Inquire* if one of their clerks didn't stop Rush an' give him a hat to take home to his father.

RUSH: That's the absolute A-number-one *truth,* mom. Cross my heart an' hope to die, eat a banana an' holler hi.

SADE: [*Simply*] I'm not doubting ya, Willie.

RUSH: No?

SADE: Not any more. I'm satisfied you told exactly what happened. Kleeberger's clerk *did* button-hole ya. You *were* given that funny hat to bring home. *You* were just the *cat's* paw in this scheme.

VIC: [*Outraged virtue*] What's *this* now?

SADE: [*Simply*] I was *wrong* about you an' *Rush* bein' in cahoots. Couple *other* parties were in cahoots.

VIC: [*Coldly*] *Clarify* that statement please.

SADE: [*Simply*] It don't need clarifying.

VIC: [Coldly] You are implying that a plot was hatched . . .

SADE: . . . between you an' Kleeberger's clerk, yes.

VIC: [*Amused but somewhat brittle laughter*]

SADE: [*After listening a while*] Take off that awful hat. Makes ya look like a peeled onion.

VIC: [*Coldly*] Dropping for the moment this infantile controversy about whether or not Kleeberger's give me a free hat, let me read you a piece I clipped out of the paper.

SADE: Um.

VIC: I have it here in my pocket.

SADE: Um.

RUSH: I'm glad you finally decided I was innocent, mom. [*Chuckles*] Heck, I couldn't tell stories to *you* an' get away with it. You appreciate I . . .

VIC: May I have your attention, Sade?

SADE: That thing perched up on your head makes ya look like a cowboy from the Wild West Show.

VIC: [*Coldly*] May I have your attention please:

SADE: Um.

VIC: [*Reads*] Wide-brimmed hats to be popular this summer. Albert Breep, well-known Belvidere, Illinois, man-about-town, announced at a meeting of haberdashers in Galena that there is a distinct trend towards broad brims in men's head-wear. Mr. Breep is a close student of style trends an' his opinions are highly respected throughout the middle west.

SADE: Um.

VIC: So ya see, *everybody's* gonna look like a peeled onion. *Everybody's* gonna wear wide-brimmed hats this summer.

SADE: *You* look like a peeled onion right *now*.

RUSH: Smelly Clark's Uncle Strap loves to reminisce over . . .

VIC: I happen to have *another* clipping on this same *subject*.

SADE: Um.

VIC: Listen to *this*. [*Reads*] Gloria Golden, glamorous star of talking pictures, admires men who wear hats with generous brims. "Broad brims give character to the face," she told reporters recently.

SADE: [*Briefly*] Hi-de-hi.

VIC: Still *another* clipping I'd like to have you hear.

SADE: [*Simply*] *Lots* of clippings.

VIC: [*Reads*] K. Z. Globbers, who resides in the south-western part of eastern North Dakota, announces that the men in his section of the country are adopting wide-brimmed hats almost universally. "Wide-brimmed hats," says Mr. Globbers, "are fashionable as well as useful. They provide fine sun-shades in addition to being smart an' swanky."

SADE: Um.

VIC: [*As though he's conclusively proved something*] So ya *see*?

SADE: When'd you cut all that stuff outa the paper?

VIC: This morning.

SADE: Really? Quite a coincident.

VIC: *What's* quite a coincident?

SADE: Quite a coincident that you cut pieces outa the newspaper about wide-brimmed hats in the morning an' Kleeberger's store makes you a present of a wide-brimmed hat in the afternoon.

VIC: [*Coldly*] Sadie, if I had your suspicious nature I would . . .

SADE: [*Simply*] Never mind my suspicious nature. I've added up two an' two at last an' got four.

VIC: An' what exactly do you mean by *that*, pray?

SADE: You fixed it up with the Kleeberger clerk to stop Rush when he went past the store today.

VIC: Really?

SADE: [*Easily and matter-of-factly*] Yesterday when you paid your bill you bought that crazy hat. You told the fella to stand in the door-way at three o'clock this afternoon an' your son would come by. You told him to buttonhole your son an' give him the hat. You told him to tell your son to tell his mother the hat was a gift from Kleeberger's.

VIC: [*Vastly amused*] That's rich, Sade. That *is* rich.

SADE: I heard you making arrangements with Willie at noon. What *were* those arrangements again, Rush?

RUSH: Gov told me to go to the jewelry store an' pick up his watch.

SADE: The jewelry store is on Center Street. He knew you'd hafta pass Kleeberger's.

VIC: [*Laughing*] By George, talk about your far-fetched *yarns*.

SADE: [*To Rush, composedly*] Wasn't something said about the *time*?

RUSH: Gov told me to show up at the jewelry store at three o'clock on the dot.

SADE: Why did he insist it had to be three o'clock on the *dot*?

RUSH: [*Chuckles*] Darned if *I* know.

VIC: [*Blustering*] I like stuff done *systematic*, Sade.

271

SADE: [*Ignoring this*] You simply told Kleeberger's clerk to be standing in his door-way at three o'clock. Your son would come past.

VIC: [*After a pause*] Do you think you'll ever get me to *admit* any such a feeble-minded scheme?

SADE: Feeble-minded is right. [*Little giggle*] I never *heard* of anything so transparent. After the bushels an' bushels an' bushels of stunts you've pulled off tryin' to get yourself a wide-brimmed hat, did you think I'd be fooled by *this* one? Kleeberger's give you an eight-dollar hat because they're grateful to ya for payin' a two-dollar debt. An' then flashin' them *newspaper* clippings on me. [*Giggles*] [*After a pause*] I guess it was a pretty good trick where you had the fella button-hole *Rush* an' all, but it just wasn't good *enough*.

VIC: [*Cold and dignified*] I have nothing to say.

SADE: [*Briefly*] The hat'll hafta go back.

VIC: [*Cold and dignified*] Will it?

SADE: Yes—the hat'll hafta go back. [*After a pause, somewhat sharply*] Wish you'd take it *off*. Makes ya look like a peeled onion.

END OF SCRIPT

ANNOUNCER: Which concludes another brief interlude at the small house halfway up in the next block.

1940

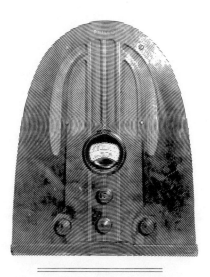

**LODGE BROTHERS
ASK TO MAKE
A STOPOVER**

THEME
ANNOUNCER: OPENING AND COMMERCIAL CREDITS
INTRODUCTION: Well sir, it's late afternoon as we approach the small house half-way up in the next block now, and Mr. and Mrs. Victor Gook and young Mr. Rush Gook are assembled on the front porch. Vic has just this moment introduced a subject which his wife finds upsetting. Listen.

SADE: [*Tough*] We'd hafta shuffle ourselves all *around*.

VIC: Naw.

SADE: How about *beds*?

VIC: They're bringing their *own* beds. Go get the letter, Rush.

RUSH: Where is it?

SADE: [*Snappishly*] How ya *mean* they're bringin' their own beds?

VIC: They've got a folding double-decker.

SADE: [*More angry than curious*] What's that?

VIC: You never heard of a double-decker bed?

SADE: No.

RUSH: *I* have. Smelly Clark's Uncle *Strap* . . .

SADE: [*To Vic, tough*] Why do we have stuff like this all the time? [*Scornfully*] Robert an' Slobert Hink. *I* never met Robert an' Slobert Hink. Far as *that* goes, *you* haven't *either*. An' still we're s'posed to throw open our *house* to 'em.

VIC: [*Quietly*] Not at all, Sade. All you've got to do is say you'd rather not have 'em an' that's the end of it. Robert an' Slobert Hink, I assure you, are not the kind of fellas that'd intrude where they're not wanted.

SADE: [*Disliking the names*] Robert an' Slobert Hink.

VIC: [*Quietly*] The weather is too warm for controversy an' heated argument. I suggest we change the subject. What'd you do today, Rush?

RUSH: Played ball.

VIC: [*Pleasantly*] Uh-huh. I hope your team gave a good account of itself an' won a glorious . . .

SADE: [*Tough*] Did they just write an' *invite* themselves?

VIC: [*Pleasantly*] Robert an' Slobert Hink?

SADE: [*Disliking the names*] Oh, Robert an' Slobert Hink. *Names* ain't even civilized.

VIC: [*Pleasantly*] People cannot help their names, Sade. We must go through life with the names our parents . . .

SADE: Did they just write an' *invite* themselves?

VIC: Go get the letter, Rush.

275

RUSH: Where is it?

SADE: [*Exasperated*] Ruthie an' I half-way got it fixed for all of us to play Five *Hundred* Saturday evening.

VIC: [*Pleasantly*] Very well:—in the morning I will *notify* Robert an' Slobert. I will advise them that a visit at this particular time would not be convenient. So you played baseball today, did you, Rush?

RUSH: Yeah.

VIC: Extremely *torrid* for outdoor sports. You boys must be careful these scorching days that you don't . . .

SADE: [*Snappish*] Hey, you don't need to sit there an' act like *I'm* being mean. If you want to entertain these fellas over Saturday you know good an' well you *can*. What exasperates *me* is there's *always* some wild business like this falls in our lap.

VIC: [*Pleasantly*] Wild business?

SADE: Complete strangers invite themselves to come an' enjoy our hospitality.

VIC: [*Gently*] *I* don't look upon Robert an' Slobert Hink as complete strangers. They are both active workers in the lodge. Chicago Headquarter of the Sacred Stars of the Milky Way are always singing their praises. In addition to that, Robert an' Slobert like myself are enthusiastic students of parade procedure. If the three of us got together we'd have a *glorious* time discussing parades.

SADE: [*Unhappily*] You *want* 'em then, huh?

VIC: [*Pleasantly*] Not if *you* don't, kiddo.

SADE: [*Exasperated*] Oh, lands.

RUSH: You people talkin' about . . .

SADE: [*To Vic*] Is the idea of their *visit* to discuss parades?

VIC: [*Gently*] No. You didn't give me a chance to *divulge* the idea of their visit. As soon as I said Robert an' Slobert Hink wanted to spend Saturday an' Sunday night with us you jumped down my collar.

SADE: [*Has no answer for that so says sulkily* . . .] Um.

VIC: They are on their way to Peoria. They merely wish to stop over with us in order to break the hardship of the long journey. Go get the letter, Rush.

RUSH: Where is it?

SADE: [*Tough*] Hardship of the long *journey?*

VIC: Yes.

SADE: They live in Hoopeston, don't they?

VIC: Yes.

SADE: How far *is* Hoopeston from here?

VIC: Twenty-five miles, I guess. Maybe thirty.

SADE: An' how far is Peoria from here?

VIC: Forty miles.

SADE: Seventy miles from Hoopeston to Peoria?

VIC: Approximately.

SADE: Are they making the trip on *foot?*

VIC: [*Stiffly*] Your question is bizarre, Sade. What would lead you to such an assumption? I am entirely persuaded Robert an' Slobert are not walking from Hoopeston to Peoria. I am quite satisfied they are driving their automobile.

SADE: [*Acid*] I'm talking about that "breaking up the hardship of the long journey" business. Since when did seventy miles get to be a long journey if a person's got a car? They oughta be able to whiz over to Peoria in two hours. Why, Fred *Stembottom* in that old rattle-de-trap of *his* drove to *Chicago* in five hours—an' Chicago's a hundred an' *forty* miles.

VIC: [*Gently*] I see no point in continuing to debate the matter. So you played baseball today, did you, Rush?

RUSH: Yeah.

VIC: I met your friend Blue-tooth Johnson on the street an' he said . . .

SADE: What was all that about a *bed?*

VIC: They are bringing their *own* bed.

SADE: Carrying it in their automobile?

VIC: Yes. It is a double-decker.

SADE: [*Disliking any part of it*] An' what's that?

RUSH: *You* know, mom. Kinda like the berths in a sleeping car on the train. One individual sleeps up above an' the other individual sleeps down below.

SADE: [*To Vic*] Where would we *put* such a contraption?

VIC: A double-decker bed will fit in any place. Kitchen, living-room or hall. Go get the letter, Rush?

RUSH: Where is it?

VIC: [*Somewhat sharply*] I *told* ya nine *times.*

RUSH: [*Little chuckle*] No, ya never. I *inquired* nine times but you always . . .

VIC: In the inside pocket of my coat.

RUSH: Where's your coat?

VIC: Layin' over the bannister in the hall.

RUSH: O.K.

SADE: [*To Vic*] Let's say seventy miles *is* a horrible long journey. Let's say going from Hoopeston to Peoria *is* a monstrous back-

breaking trip. All right, why do they hafta break up the awful hardship of it by stayin' over at a person's house *two* nights. *Saturday*
night an' *Sunday* night, you say. Hoopeston is thirty miles from here.
Are they gonna drive that little measly thirty miles in their automobile an' then be so worn out an' done in they hafta rest several *days?*

VIC: [*Gently*] They wish to spend a little time with their friend Vic
Gook.

SADE: [*Tough*] You're *not* friends though. Haven't even *met* each
other.

VIC: [*Gently*] Considerable correspondence has passed back an'
forth between us. [*Sweet and kind*] Kiddo, let's not go ahead any
further with this. *Forget* it.

SADE: Um.

VIC: [*Gently*] What do I smell? Flowers? They are very aromatic.
Mis' *Donahue's* flowers, ain't they?

SADE: [*Back to the other*] No, but you're making me out mean an'
selfish. *I'll* entertain whoever you invite here. *You* know that. But
complete strangers comin' to spend Saturday, Saturday night,
Sunday, an' *Sunday* night. [*Unhappy giggle*] Complete strangers
named Robert an' Slobert Hink that are bringing a berth out of a
sleeping car with 'em.

VIC: [*Gently*] They are not bringing a berth out of a sleeping-car
with 'em. They are bringing a double-decker bed. [*Sweetly*] Sade,
there is absolutely no reason for you to work yourself up. If I'd
known you'd re-act in this manner I'd never of mentioned the thing.

SADE: [*Sulkily*] Saturday evening Ruthie an' I had it all fixed for
the four of us to play Five Hundred.

VIC: [*Gently*] We play Five Hundred several nights outa the week.

SADE: Not any "several" nights outa the week we don't.

VIC: [*Gently*] *Always* at least *once;* more often than not *twice.* It
seemed to me that missing one game of Five Hundred wouldn't be
any great privation inasmuch as we can . . .

RUSH: [*Up*] Here y'are, gov.

VIC: [*A gentle rebuke*] You took a long time about it, my boy.

RUSH: Never realized you were in a hurry. I went out in the kitchen
an' got a drink of water. Had to let the faucet run quite a while
before it got cold.

VIC: Um.

SADE: [*Little giggle*] Wish you'd quit usin' that lah-de-dah sweety-
sweet tone of voice.

VIC: [*Gentle surprise*] Me?

SADE: Yeah.

VIC: [*Pleasant chuckle*] I wasn't aware I was . . .

SADE: *Oh,* no. *You're* not aware. Just *doin'* it to make *me* out an old vinegar-face.

VIC: [*Gently*] I *assure* you I . . .

SADE: [*Little giggle*] Never mind. Go ahead an' read your letter.

VIC: [*Gently*] Very well.

RUSH: [*To Sade, chuckling*] Gov's all of a sudden turned to axle-grease an' peach-butter.

SADE: Hasn't he though? [*Giggles*] An' your *mother's* a regular *brute!*

VIC: [*Gently, after a brief pause*] Do I have your attention?

RUSH: [*Cheerfully*] Sure.

VIC: [*Ignores this and says gently to Sade*] Do I have your attention, kiddo?

SADE: Go ahead.

VIC: [*Reads*] Dearest Skybrother Gook. In hoc agricola spittle ad semper adsit puellorum hunc. Dim-wit non-disputandum cabbage et cetera. Cornucopia est divisa ob cabbage bop. Sinus trubble sint huious dum cluck . . .

SADE: [*In impatient low tones*] Oh, lands.

VIC: [*After a brief pause, gently*] Shall I skip the Latin?

SADE: Suit yourself.

VIC: [*Reads*] Robert an' Slobert Hink are the writers of this letter, old man. We have business in Peoria next Tuesday an' as we are leaving Hoopeston at six o'clock Saturday morning we wondered if you wouldn't like to have us stop by an' visit you when we arrive in your city to break up the cruel hardship of the long journey. We thought we could spend Saturday an' Sunday with you an' your family an' leave for Peoria early Monday morning. We have a brand-new automobile and we're bringing our double-decker bed so you people won't be inconvenienced by . . .

SADE: They've got a brand-new automobile an' they're leaving Hoopeston at six o'clock Saturday morning, huh?

VIC: Yes.

SADE: They'll be here before we're even *up.*

RUSH: [*Chuckles*] Won't take any time at *all* to drive thirty miles in a brand-new *car.*

SADE: They're gonna drive thirty miles in their brand-new car an' then stay in our house all day Saturday, Saturday night, all day Sunday an' Sunday night to break up the cruel hardship of their long journey.

RUSH: [*Laughs*]

VIC: [*After a pause, gently*] Shall I resume the letter?

SADE: [*Go ahead*] Um.

VIC: [*Reads*] We are both looking forward to seeing you and to parading around your home.

SADE: [*Sharply*] How's that?

VIC: Robert an' Slobert, like myself, are parade *enthusiasts.*

SADE: They wanta *march?*

VIC: As their letter indicates they are hoping to put certain stratagems, maneuvers, tactics, and formations into actual practice.

SADE: It says "parading around your home." Do they mean parading around *inside* our home or parading around *outside* our home?

VIC: Outside, of course.

SADE: I see.

VIC: It is their wish that the three of us march back an' forth across the lawn.

SADE: What'll the neighbors think of that?

VIC: [*Gently*] It is a matter that hardly *concerns* the neighbors.

SADE: It's a matter that'll concern Mr. *Donahue.* He'll be trying to *sleep.* Probably telephone the *police* if a bunch of fellas tramp along outside his window shouting orders an' commands.

RUSH: [*Imitates a parade marshal*] Forward! *March!* Eyes *front!* At *ease!* Parade *dress!* Forward double-quick—*March!*

VIC: [*Gently*] When you are quite finished, Arthur, I will resume reading this letter.

RUSH: Um.

VIC: [*Reads*] If for any reason you are unprepared to receive us, old man, kindly drop us a line. In sunt bello nomenclature itch. Oppo dingy dum hobo hunc. Adsit amor skittle blot. Yours affectionately. Robert and Slobert Hink.

SADE: [*After a long pause*] Well—ya want 'em?

VIC: [*Sweetly gentle*] Not if *you* don't.

SADE: [*Unhappy giggle*] Vic, quit makin' me feel so selfish an' mean. Of *course* I don't want 'em. Who *would* want fellas named Robert an' Slobert to come an' stay two whole days an' two whole nights an' march around your front yard an' sleep in the kitchen in a sleeping-car berth?

VIC: [*Sweetly gentle*] Very well. What you've said is entirely sufficient. Just forget it. I suggest we talk of *other* matters. Rush.

RUSH: Yeah?

VIC: [*Pleasantly*] How did you spend the afternoon?

RUSH: Playin' baseball.

VIC: [*Pleasantly and in mild surprise*] Really?

RUSH: [*Chuckles*] I *told* ya so half a dozen *times.*

VIC: [*Sweetly gentle*] Baseball is a fine sport. It toughens young muscles an' teaches a boy the spirit of honorable competition.

RUSH: [*Chuckles*] Uh-huh.

SADE: [*Unhappy giggle*] Vic.

VIC: [*Sweetly*] Yes?

SADE: [*Unhappy giggle*] You stop.

VIC: [*Sweet and gentle surprise*] Stop what?

SADE: [*Unhappy giggle*] Makin' me feel so selfish an' mean.

END OF SCRIPT

ANNOUNCER: Which concludes another brief interlude at the small house half-way up in the next block.

1940

**SADE'S HOUSE
IS NOT THE WAY
SHE LEFT IT**

THEME

ANNOUNCER: OPENING AND COMMERCIAL CREDITS

INTRODUCTION: Well, sir, it's about seven o'clock as we enter the small house half-way up in the next block now, and here in the living-room we find our friends spending a quiet evening at home. Vic and young Rush are seated side by side on the davenport leafing idly through sections of the newspaper. Sade is established in her husband's easy-chair darning socks. And, at length, she's moved to remark . . .

SADE: It's sure taken me a long time to feel back at home.

VIC: Do you feel back at home *now?*

SADE: [*Little giggles*] Yeah. But it's required three days. *Always* that way when a person returns from a visit. Stuff seems so *queer* somehow. Ya hafta get used to your house all *over* again.

RUSH: That's the way it is when you've been to the *hospital* an' come home.

SADE: Exactly.

RUSH: Smelly Clark's Uncle Strap once come home from the hospital an' didn't recognize his own landlady.

VIC: Possibly a complete *cure* had not been effected.

RUSH: Oh, he *felt* good enough. But he was *weak.* An' his mind was slow. No, *he* didn't recognize his landlady. She come up to his room an' says, "Hand over the rent," an' he said, "Who are *you,* Madame?"

VIC: Um.

RUSH: You talk about your *weak.* Smelly Clark's Uncle Strap was so weak he din't have the strength to keep his *tongue* from lolling out.

VIC: That's bein' pretty weak.

RUSH: World's record. He went around . . .

    [*Producing sounds with his tongue lolling out, after the manner of a very ill person*]

SADE: Oh, ish.

RUSH: [*Chuckles*] He was *plenty* weak.

SADE: [*To Vic*] No, but that's a fact. Taken three whole days for me to feel natural. Just one skimpy week in Carberry an' I come home an' almost feel like I'm in somebody *else's* house.

VIC: Oh well, *Bess* being here over Saturday an' Sunday prob'ly made a difference.

SADE: Yes, of course.

RUSH: *Another* side-splitting feature in connection with Smelly Clark's Uncle Strap is the time he . . .

285

VIC: One gets slightly *weary* of Smelly Clark's Uncle Strap, Corn-crib.

SADE: [*Distaste*] *Yeah.*

RUSH: Um.

VIC: Let us consign Smelly Clark's Uncle Strap to limbo.

RUSH: What's that?

VIC: I haven't the slightest idea.

RUSH: Um.

SADE: [*After a brief pause, giggle*] Tell the actual *truth* this house *isn't* exactly the way I *left* it.

VIC: Do I sense a reflection on me an' Pete's house-cleaning efforts?

SADE: [*Earnestly*] No, not at all. You boys done just *grand.*

VIC: Almost broke our *backs* scrubbing porches an' trash.

SADE: [*Earnestly*] You boys done just *grand.* Like I told ya when Bess was here, I was *astonished* how nice the place looked. I'd never of *believed* it. Why, I thought Mis' *Donahue* or somebody must of come over.

RUSH: We done every bit of it ourselves.

SADE: Done just *grand.*

VIC: What'd ya mean when ya said the house wasn't exactly the way ya left it?

SADE: Well, don't take this wrong, but . . . how'd everything get so sklee-geed *around?*

VIC: Do you know what your mother refers to, Egg-plant?

RUSH: [*Neg.*] Uh-huh.

VIC: What do you refer to, Sade?

SADE: [*Giggles*] A *million* little items. [*Quickly*] Don't think I'm finding *fault* now. You boys done perfectly *wonderful* while I was gone. House neat as a pin. I'd never of imagined in my wildest dreams I could be away in Carberry a whole week an' come back to find things so nice.

VIC: What are the million little items you mention so glibly?

RUSH: Mom's prob'ly got reference to the olive-and-pickle plate you busted.

SADE: [*Quickly*] No, I haven't either. It's all *right* about that olive-and-pickle plate. Accidents will happen. Anyway, I'm so pleased with you boys' performance while I was gone I wouldn't mention it if you had broken *six* olive-and-pickle plates.

VIC: The lady loves us. Cow-pasture.

RUSH: [*Little chuckle*] Yeah.

SADE: [*Giggles*] What I meant by stuff bein' sklee-geed around . . .

[*Halts*] . . . Well, how'd our picture of the Snow-clad Rocky Mountains get over on *that* wall?

VIC: I haven't the slightest notion.

SADE: Have you, Willie?

RUSH: Yes.

SADE: [*Giggles*] Did you think it'd look *better* on that wall?

RUSH: Blue-tooth Johnson was here one evening last week. He was eatin' licorice buttons. The front door-screen was a-jar an' he attempted to blow a licorice button through the crack. The licorice button, of course, was sticky. Blue-tooth missed the crack in the door an' the licorice button hit the wall an' stuck. It . . . a . . . left a black stain on the wall-paper so I covered it up with the picture of the Snow-clad Rocky Mountains.

SADE: [*Without rancor*] Oh . . . that's the way of it, huh?

RUSH: Yes.

VIC: I'm glad *I* don't have any feeble-minded friends that spit sticky hunks of candy around the living-room.

SADE: [*Giggles*] *Never* mind, Willie, I don't care.

RUSH: Um.

VIC: I *repeat,* I'm glad *I* don't have feeble-minded friends that spit sticky hunks of candy around the living-room.

RUSH: It was your friend that broke the cold-water faucet in the kitchen. Hank Gutstop.

VIC: [*Coldly*] "Mister" Gutstop to *you,* chum.

RUSH: All right, "Mister" Gutstop then.

VIC: It is *unseemly* for an urchin like you to refer familiarly to adults.

RUSH: *He* sure broke our cold-water *faucet.*

VIC: By *accident,* Sade. He exerted too much pressure an' . . .

SADE: *That's* all right. It was about ready to break before I went to Carberry. Loose as my shoe.

VIC: Um.

SADE: [*Curiously*] When Bess an' I walked in this room last Friday afternoon first thing I noticed was the easy-chair in *that* corner. Who moved it an' for what?

VIC: Ask *Inner*-sole here.

SADE: [*Giggles*] I'm not *complaining,* Rush. I'm just *wonderin'.*

RUSH: Blue-tooth *Johnson* moved the easy-chair.

VIC: [*To Sade, dryly*] You are able to gather, I presume, that Blue-tooth Johnson was a frequent visitor during your absence.

SADE: [*Generously*] *Blue*-tooth's welcome. *Blue*-tooth's a nice boy.

[*To Rush*] Why was he rasslin' the easy-chair around?

RUSH: He was desirous of swatting a fly. Needed something to stand on. He used the easy-chair for the purpose an' just neglected to put it back where it belonged.

SADE: Why didn't he select a *straight* chair? Goodness, darn *easy*-chair is *heavy*. Musta been a job luggin' it clear across the whole room. He could have taken a chair outa the *kitchen*. Kitchen chairs don't weigh beans.

RUSH: Blue-tooth's a peculiar fella. Hard to follow his line of reasoning sometimes. Very *deep* individual.

VIC: [*Maliciously*] It was that deep Blue-tooth *also,* wasn't it, who broke the slat in our porch-swing?

SADE: [*Covering up for Rush's friend*] That slat is all right now. I fixed it myself with a tack hammer. [*Back to the other*] Another thing puzzled me was the *throw*-rugs. They *look* nice where ya had 'em an' all but the down-stairs ones were upstairs an' the upstairs ones were down-stairs.

RUSH: We took 'em all out on the porch at a clatter when we were cleaning up. Took 'em out to *shake* 'em, see?

SADE: [*Interested*] Uh-huh.

RUSH: Well, I was the party that arranged 'em on the floor again an' I couldn't remember which was which.

SADE: [*Mildly surprised*] Ya couldn't?

RUSH: Well, I wasn't *sure*.

SADE: You got 'em *completely* backwards. You didn't have *some* of the upstairs throw-rugs down-stairs an' *some* of the down-stairs throw-rugs upstairs. You had every single one of the upstairs throw-rugs down-stairs an' every single one of the down-stairs throw-rugs upstairs.

RUSH: Um.

SADE: [*Giggles*] I'm not bawlin' ya *out,* Willie.

RUSH: [*Chuckles*] O.K.

SADE: [*Brief pause*] The hot-water hydrant in the bath-tub was on the cold-water side an' the cold-water hydrant was on the hot-water side.

VIC: Blue-tooth Johnson.

RUSH: No, it *wasn't* Blue-tooth Johnson. *I* done that, mom.

SADE: [*Curiously*] Why?

RUSH: I was takin' a bath an' reading a Third Lieutenant Stanley book an' I unscrewed the hydrants with my toes. They unscrew easy, ya know.

SADE: Yeah, I know.

RUSH: Well, when I got through with my bath I screwed both faucets back again but didn't notice I had 'em mixed up.

SADE: [*Curiously*] [*After a pause*] Son, the pillows off'n your bed were on *our* bed. *Our* pillows were on *your* bed. How come?

RUSH: I *aired* all the pillows an' sheets an' blankets an' stuff. Hung 'em out the window the morning of the day you come home.

SADE: An' got 'em mixed up when ya put 'em back, huh?

RUSH: I imagine.

SADE: [*Brief pause*] The books in the book case: what happened to them?

RUSH: Speak to *gov* on *that* subject.

VIC: Blue-tooth Johnson.

RUSH: [*Hotly*] *No* sir, *not* Blue-tooth Johnson.

VIC: [*Imperturbably*] Blue-tooth Johnson.

RUSH: Ya can't blame *everything* on Blue-tooth Johnson.

VIC: [*Imperturbably*] Blue-tooth Johnson, Sade.

RUSH: [*Hotly*] Mom, gov sklee-geed the books in the book-case around *himself*.

SADE: [*Placating*] I'm *sure* he did.

VIC: [*Low tones*] Blue-tooth Johnson.

RUSH: [*To Sade*] One afternoon he pulled the whole lodge library out on the living-room floor. He pushed the books back in the bookcase just *any* old way.

SADE: [*Mildly*] Uh-huh. Well, they're all right now. I arranged 'em back where they belong.

VIC: [*Very low tones*] Blue-tooth Johnson.

RUSH: [*To Sade*] You might *also* ask gov who put the floor-lamp on the blink.

SADE: [*To Vic, giggling*] Who put the floor-lamp on the blink?

VIC: [*Loudly*] Blue-tooth *Johnson*.

RUSH: [*Ironical laugh*] Yeah—"Blue-tooth Johnson."

VIC: [*Like a stubborn little girl*] Blue-tooth *Johnson* put the floor-lamp on the blink.

SADE: Wasn't anything really *wrong* with the floor-lamp. I jiggled it a little an' now it works fine. Prob'ly a loose connection some place is all.

RUSH: [*After a pause*] You fellas pop any popcorn while I was in Carberry?

RUSH: I never.

SADE: You, Vic?

VIC: No.

SADE: I found the popcorn popper in my upper right-hand dresser drawer.

VIC: There's a clever band of popcorn popper *thieves* operating in this vicinity. I'm surprised they didn't *flee* with their booty. Prob'ly they heard a noise while they were ramsacking the house an' ran away in terror.

SADE: [*Seriously*] No, but it's *funny* though. I never put any popcorn popper in my dresser.

RUSH: [*Slowly*] I can explain it, mom.

SADE: Oh, can ya?

RUSH: Just remembered. A friend of mine an' I were up in the attic foolin' around an' he saw the popcorn popper an' took it down-stairs with him figurin' it'd be a good thing to catch butterflies an' *insects* in.

SADE: Uh-huh.

RUSH: Well, other interesting diversions took his mind off the butterfly plan an' he left the popcorn popper out on the front porch. I guess when I was picking up around to get the house ready for you and Aunt Bess I must of slipped it in your dresser drawer just to get it outa sight.

SADE: Uh-huh. Who was the friend?

RUSH: [*After a pause*] Blue-tooth Johnson.

VIC: [*Elated and noisy*] *Ha!* Blue-tooth *Johnson!* Didn't I *tell* ya Blue-tooth Johnson, Sade? *Sure,* Blue-tooth Johnson!

SADE: [*Little giggle*] *Blue*-tooth's all right.

VIC: He is a fiend in human form.

SADE: Rush, what become of the calendar that was hanging over the gas-stove when I left for Aunt Bess's?

RUSH: I give it to Eunice Raypole.

SADE: What become of the red-white-and-blue salt-cellar?

RUSH: I dropped it.

SADE: Break?

RUSH: Yeah.

SADE: I noticed somebody filled the starch-box up with sugar an' the cookie-jar with . . .

RUSH: [*Unhappily*] Oh *heck,* mom.

SADE: [*Hastily*] *I'm* not scolding you, son. Not a bit of it. You done *grand* while I was away.

RUSH: [*Unhappy chuckle*] No, but ya keep bringin' up stuff . . .

SADE: [*Hastily*] *I* won't do it any more. I won't mention another *thing.* I just . . . [*Giggles*] couldn't keep from wondering how trash got so sklee-geed *around.*

RUSH: Um.

SADE: But I'll not say another word.

RUSH: Um.

SADE: [*After a pause*] Who wants ice-cream?

RUSH: Ice-cream?

SADE: I'll buy ice-cream for the crowd. It's my treat. You fellas deserve a reward.

END OF SCRIPT

ANNOUNCER: Which concludes another brief interlude at the small house half-way up in the next block.

1940

UNCLE FLETCHER'S
MEALS

ANNOUNCER: Well sir, it's about the middle of the afternoon as our scene opens now, and here in the living-room of the small house half-way up in the next block we find Mr. Victor Gook and his son Mr. Rush Gook. The former is established at the library table with some paper-work he's brought home from the office, while the latter, gelatinously athwart the davenport, somewhat sluggishly glances through a volume of vigorous fiction. We hear . . .

VIC: [*To Rush, sharply*] *Listen.* Somebody's in the kitchen.

FLETCHER: [*In kitchen*] *Oh,* Sadie.

RUSH: [*To Vic*] Uncle Fletcher.

VIC: [*Unhappily*] Oh my.

FLETCHER: [*Approaching*] Hello, Sadie?

RUSH: [*To Vic*] He's coming in . . . you might as well answer.

VIC: [*Calls without much enthusiasm*] Hello, Uncle Fletcher.

FLETCHER: [*Approaching, calls genially*] Well, *Vic* honey, old boy.

VIC: [*To Rush*] I bring work home from the office because I figure it'll be quiet and I can concentrate.

FLETCHER: [*Coming up*] And *Rush* honey on deck *too,* are they? *Afternoon,* Rush honey, old boy. Vic, I bet you brought work home from the office. Am I right? If I'm right, let it go. If I'm wrong, don't say a word. Rush, there's a morsel of something on your cheek.

RUSH: Apple.

FLETCHER: [*With deep satisfaction*] *Fine.*

VIC: [*Briefly*] Are you going someplace, Uncle Fletcher?

FLETCHER: No.

VIC: I asked because I notice you're carrying your valise.

FLETCHER: [*In some surprise*] Why, yes . . . I *forgot.*

VIC: [*Briefly*] Uh-huh.

FLETCHER: The numb-skull fat-head valise completely slipped my mind.

VIC: Um.

FLETCHER: I *am* going someplace.

VIC: Where are you going?

FLETCHER: *Here!*

VIC: [*Briefly*] *I* see.

FLETCHER: [*Rather sharply*] I'm going *here!*

RUSH: You *are* here.

FLETCHER: [*Sharply*] *Who* is here?

RUSH: [*Rather sharply*] *You* are.

FLETCHER: [*Sharply*] *I* am here?

RUSH: [*Sharply*] *Sure* you're here.

FLETCHER: [*Sharply*] This is no place for tiny tots, Rush, honey . . . go down cellar.

VIC: [*Dismally to himself*] I brought work home from the office so I could have it quiet and concentrate.

FLETCHER: [*Tough*] Seeing this valise in my hand, Vic, reminds me that I am in a towering fury. I have come over here to stay with you a few days.

VIC: [*Feebly*] Oh, is that so?

FLETCHER: [*Tough*] You may recall or you may not recall, Vic, that Sadie has frequently invited me to occupy the bedroom at the head of the stairs. Well sir, I am availing myself of that invitation. Conditions at the establishment where I have accommodations has become intolerable and driven me to open rebellion.

VIC: You're in open rebellion against your landlady?

FLETCHER: [*Dramatically*] I am in open rebellion against my land-lady.

RUSH: Has Mrs. Keller laid down the law about . . .

FLETCHER: [*Dramatically*] Mrs. Keller has overstepped the *mark!* Mrs. Keller has piled on the straw that broke the camel's back! Mrs. Keller like the needle's eye has torn the serpent's tooth from the ungrateful child!

RUSH: I expect she insisted on you . . .

FLETCHER: [*Sharply*] Go down cellar, Rush. This conversation is not for the tiny tots. This conversation is strictly for the grown-ups. Go down cellar, sir, I say. Vic, you go down cellar too.

VIC: [*Startled*] Huh?

FLETCHER: I mean you stay *here!*

VIC: [*Rather dryly*] O.K., I believe I will.

FLETCHER: [*Sharply*] Rush, you stay here also.

RUSH: O.K.

FLETCHER: [*Sharply*] Because there's nothing about this conversation which is not suitable for a child to hear.

RUSH: Well, fine.

FLETCHER: [*Sharply*] Vic, go down cellar.

VIC: [*Sharply*] Hey, Uncle Fletcher, aren't you a little off your noggin?

FLETCHER: [*Tough*] Any man would be off their noggin!

VIC: What'd your landlady do?

FLETCHER: [*Bitter laughter*] What'd my landlady do! That's rich!

SADE: [*Off, in kitchen, calls brightly*] Vic, you still working? Can I interrupt you half a minute?

FLETCHER: [*Bitter laughter*] What'd my landlady do! That's rich.

RUSH: [*Pleasantly*] Here's mom home.

FLETCHER: [*A bitter inquiry*] What'd my landlady do, you say?

RUSH: No, I say "here's mom home."

FLETCHER: [*Bitter laughter*] That's rich!

VIC: [*Little tired chuckle*] Oh for Pete's sake, Uncle Fletcher.

SADE: [*Approaching*] I won't disturb you but half a minute, Vic.

VIC: [*Unhappily*] Disturb me a whole minute, disturb me a minute and forty seconds.

SADE: [*Approaching*] Who's that in there with you? Uncle Fletcher?

VIC: [*Briefly*] Yeah.

RUSH: And me, mom.

SADE: [*Coming up, says uneasily . . .*] Ah . . . are you being distracted from your work, Vic?

VIC: [*Bluntly*] Yeah.

SADE: [*Courteously*] Good afternoon, Uncle Fletcher.

FLETCHER: [*Rather dramatically*] Good afternoon, Sadie honey. I have here my valise and I am going to avail myself of your kind invitation to occupy the upstairs bedroom which you said was at my disposal.

SADE: Of course. Is anything wrong? [*Rather sharply, to Rush*] What are you doing bothering your father?

RUSH: It's a long story, mom. But I think I can make the whole thing clear in ten minutes of rapid explanation. In the first place . . .

SADE: [*Briefly*] I'll say what I came in to say, Vic, and then I'll see if I can't shoo this crowd out of here.

VIC: O.K.

SADE: [*Briefly*] I just met Mr. Erickson out in the alley. He's at last managed to get a-hold of lumber for a new railing for our front porch and the carpenters'll be here in the morning.

VIC: Swell.

SADE: He says it'd be a great help if we knocked the old railing loose and tore it off. Then the carpenters could start right in with the construction work without any fooling around. They're awful busy this summer and Mr. Erickson could only hire 'em for five hours. He thinks they can put us up a new porch railing in five hours, but it'd be dandy if we had the old one ripped out so they wouldn't have to bother with trash we could take care of.

VIC: Rush and I will look into the matter after supper.

RUSH: I can rip out that old porch railing myself. The wood is so rotten it crumbles like pie-crust.

SADE: All right, fine—now that's settled. Shall we leave now, Uncle Fletcher? You and I and Rush? Vic's busy with work he brought home from the office. What ya say we three go out on the back steps and sit in the shade?

RUSH: Suits me.

FLETCHER: [*Dramatically*] Sadie honey, conditions at the establishment where I maintain accommodations has become *intolerable.*

SADE: [*Briefly*] You've had another run-in with your landlady, huh?

FLETCHER: I have had a *terrible* run-in with my landlady.

SADE: [*Briefly*] And you want to stay *here* a few days?

FLETCHER: [*Fiercely*] I may want to stay here a *week!*

SADE: [*Briefly*] You know that won't work, Uncle Fletcher. You know Mrs. Keller always comes and gets you and makes you go back home.

FLETCHER: Do you know what Mrs. Keller has *done* this trip, Sadie?

SADE: No. But let's go out in the back yard and discuss it.

FLETCHER: [*Ignores this, speaks fiercely*] My landlady Mis' Keller is leaving tonight for a visit with her brother Charlie!

SADE: In Sweet Esther, Wisconsin?

FLETCHER: No, in Dismal Seepage, Ohio.

SADE: I thought he lived in Sweet Esther, Wisconsin, and was an armed guard in the Wisconsin State Home for the Obstinate.

FLETCHER: Not any more. He *quit* that job. He is now residing in Dismal Seepage, Ohio, where he is employed as an armed guard at the Ohio State Home for the *Agreeable.*

SADE: [*Urgingly*] Let's go outdoors in the shade and sit in the nice breeze and talk. Then Vic can go ahead with his work.

FLETCHER: [*Ignores this, says fiercely*] My landlady Mis' Keller plans to be gone until next Tuesday afternoon. *Five days she plans to be gone!* And you want to know what she's *done!*

SADE: [*Rather sharply*] Not until you and I and Rush are out-doors sitting on the back steps and . . .

FLETCHER: [*Fiercely*] She's laid out my meals for me!

SADE: [*Apologetically*] *I'm* sorry, Vic.

VIC: [*Little unhappy chuckle*] Not at *all!*

FLETCHER: She's laid out my meals for me, Sadie, Vic and Rush honey!

RUSH: I don't believe I quite understand just what you *mean* by that, Uncle Fletcher. I don't . . .

FLETCHER: [*Fiercely*] My *meals, meals!* She'd laid 'em all *out.* For me to *eat!* My suppers I'll eat downtown at the restaurant because in the evenings I require hot food.

SADE: You mean while Mis' Keller is away visiting?

FLETCHER: [*Loudly*] Of course I mean while Mis' Keller is away visiting.

SADE: [*Sharply*] Well, you needn't jump down my throat! I only . . .

FLETCHER: [*Fiercely*] While my landlady is away in Ohio visiting her halfwit brother, I will take my suppers downtown because my system requires hot food. But the rest of my meals—my breakfasts and my dinners—my landlady has got distributed all over the numbskull house. It adds up to ten meals all told. See, there's breakfast and dinner tomorrow, Saturday, Sunday, and Monday. That's eight . . . And breakfast and dinner on Tuesday is two more. She gets back home Tuesday afternoon. Ten meals in all. And them meals is distributed all over the fat-head house!

VIC: [*Rather sharply*] What in thunder you talking about, Uncle Fletcher?

FLETCHER: [*Tough*] My *meals, my meals!* I expect you know what meals is.

VIC: [*Tough*] I have a rough idea, but I . . .

SADE: I know what he means. He means . . .

FLETCHER: [*Exasperated*] Go down cellar.

SADE: [*Sharply*] Who you talking to?

FLETCHER: [*Sharply*] Rush, go down cellar.

RUSH: [*Politely but firmly*] No.

FLETCHER: Listen, I'm trying to *tell* you people something!

SADE: [*Sharply*] Well, you better try to tell it without yelling and . . .

FLETCHER: My tomorrow morning's breakfast Mis' Keller has got laid out all neat and appetizing for me at home on the kitchen table.

VIC: What's the matter with *that?*

FLETCHER: [*Tough*] Will you *listen?*

VIC: [*Shoulder shrug*] Sure.

FLETCHER: My tomorrow's dinner she's got laid out on the dining-room table. Covered with a napkin and looking mighty tasty.

RUSH: I don't see what you object to in *that.* I don't see what . . .

SADE: [*Briefly*] Keep out of it, Willie.

RUSH: Um.

FLETCHER: Saturday's breakfast sits on the library table in the living-room. Saturday's dinner is on the numbskull sideboard. Sunday's breakfast is laid out on the top of the buffet. And Sunday's dinner is on a tray in the lame-brain nit-wit *pantry!* Monday's breakfast sits on my dresser up in my bedroom. And Monday's dinner is perched like a numbskull parrot on the doggone fat-head *piano* stool! Tuesday's breakfast is . . .

VIC: Are you complaining because . . .

FLETCHER: [*Tough*] *What,* Vic?

VIC: Pay *attention* a minute. Are you complaining because . . .

FLETCHER: I'm complaining because my landlady Mis' Keller treats me like a *child! I* can fix my own meals; *I* don't have to have my meals scattered all over the premises like anthracite coal!

SADE: [*Gently*] Mis' Keller arranged your meals like that because she was apprehensive you might get into *trouble* if you fixed 'em for yourself.

FLETCHER: [*Sharply*] Why would I get into trouble?

SADE: [*Somewhat vaguely*] Oh—sharp bread-knives—electricity —gas escaping from the gas-stove—forget and leave the ice-box open and the ice all melt and the food spoil—there's millions of things could happen to a gentleman at home five days preparing his own meals.

FLETCHER: [*Tough*] Am I a half-witted *numbskull?*

SADE: I'm not insinuating *that.* I'm only . . .

FLETCHER: [*Tough*] Suppose Mis' Keller went on a visit and stayed a *year!* Would she leave a year's *meals* strewed about the house? How many days in a year, Rush?

RUSH: Three hundred and sixty-five.

FLETCHER: What's twice three hundred and sixty-five?

RUSH: [*Promptly and honestly*] I don't know.

FLETCHER: [*Tough*] Around seven hundred?

RUSH: Yeah.

FLETCHER: [*Tough*] How'd you like to have seven hundred meals cluttering up every available chair, table, piano-stool, window-sill, side-board, buffet, dresser . . .

SADE: Oh ish, Uncle Fletcher.

FLETCHER: [*Tough*] *Yeah,* "oh ish." I'm the fat-head that pays the rent, ain't I?

SADE: [*Sharply*] Yes. And Mrs. Keller is the fat-head that owns the *house.*

FLETCHER: I will show Mrs. Keller that I have been imposed upon *enough.* I will show Mrs. Keller that I . . .

SADE: [*Briefly*] I bet you don't show Mrs. Keller *nothing.* And I bet Mrs. Keller will be over here directly and shoo you on home.

FLETCHER: Sure she'll be here directly. I'm surprised she's not here *now.* [*Significantly*] Sadie honey, when she arrives . . . I'm going to show her I'm a violent man.

SADE: [*Ironically*] Yeah?

FLETCHER: [*Dramatically*] I'm going to kick your front porch railing to smithereens.

SADE: [*Alertly*] Yeah?

FLETCHER: *I* heard what you told Vic about that front porch railing.

SADE: Mister Erickson wants it ripped loose and torn off.

FLETCHER: Exactly. So the carpenters can start right out in the morning building a new one.

SADE: Uh-huh.

FLETCHER: I will kick that rotten old front-porch railing to smithereens! I will show Mrs. Keller that I am a violent man!

VIC: [*Interested*] You're going to have a terrible fit of *temper* and do that?

FLETCHER: Yes. [*Gently*] Have you any objection, Vic honey?

VIC: None in the world. In fact, I'm *interested*.

RUSH: So am I.

FLETCHER: [*Gently*] Let us all step out on the front porch. Mis' Keller should arrive any moment.

SADE: Are *you* coming, Vic?

VIC: Bet your life.

SADE: What about the *work* you brought home from the office?

VIC: [*With boyish anticipation of pleasure*] This is better. After *you*, Rush.

END OF SCRIPT

ANNOUNCER: And so, backing off to a safe distance, we end our visit, half-way up in the next block, with radio's home-folks, Vic and Sade.